GLANCING VISIONS

GLANCING VISIONS

Surface and Depth in Nineteenth-Century American Literature

Zachary Tavlin

THE UNIVERSITY OF ALABAMA PRESS | TUSCALOOSA

The University of Alabama Press
Tuscaloosa, Alabama 35487-0380
uapress.ua.edu

Typeface: Adobe Jenson Pro

Cover image: Eadweard Muybridge, *Animal Locomotion,* vol. 11, *Wild Animals and Birds,* plate 759, 1887, collotype, Pennsylvania Academy of the Fine Arts, Philadelphia
Cover design: Lori Lynch

Cataloging-in-Publication data is available from the Library of Congress.
ISBN: 978-0-8173-2156-7 (cloth)
ISBN: 978-0-8173-6089-4 (paper)
E-ISBN: 978-0-8173-9450-9

FOR KAREN, PETER, AND SAM

CONTENTS

FIGURES

ACKNOWLEDGMENTS

I am lucky to have many excellent friends, interlocutors, and teachers. Collectively, they deserve at least half of the credit for everything smart about this book (the rest can be blamed on me alone). Leroy Searle is the one at the center of everything. A sager influence would be unimaginable. Bob Abrams, Mikkel Borch-Jacobsen, Raimonda Modiano, and Michael Rosenthal were also there when first ideas were tossed around. I thank them too. Elsewhere, Carl Freedman, David McAleavey, Elsie Michie, and Gregory Schufreider were prime movers. And Marshall Brown's generosity knows no bounds; I hope he knows I know it.

Carolyn Callaghan, Bob Hodges, Sam Hushagen, and Alex McCauley were original sounding boards. Matthew Mersky was the original original. Liz Janssen falls into her own strange, unnamable category. Other notable voices from those early, heady days: Emily Bald, Daniel Bentson, Greg Damico, Navid Ebrahimzadeh, Denise Grollmus, Stephanie Hankinson, Darren Hutchinson, Matthew Hitchman, Anthony Manganaro, John Milligan, Joel Musser, Nicole Peters, Justin Shanitkvich, Alex Streim, Jenny Van Houdt, Zach Torp, and someone else I'm saving for later. And to other friends, here unnamed: I miss you too, dearly.

Anna Kornbluh is the best of all possible comrades. David Greven, Paul Jaussen, Elisabeth Joyce, and Jesse Oak Taylor all extended guidance; I have not forgotten. Many others have offered precious glancing insights in conversation along the way, whether they know it or not: Lucy Alford, Charles Altieri, Jonathan Arac, Steven Axelrod, Ian Balfour, Lauren Berlant, Stephanie Burt, Christopher Breu, Nan Z. Da, Dalia Davoudi, James Elkins, Anne-Lise Francois, Natalie Gerber, Langdon Hammer, Gordon Hutner, Virginia Jackson, Jonathan Kramnick, Charles LaPorte, Marjorie Levinson, Nathaniel Mackey, Sandra Macpherson, Keith Mikos, Moacir P. de Sá Pereira, John

Plotz, Rebecca Ariel Porte, James Searle, Henry Staten, Paul Saint-Amour, Russell Sbriglia, Martha Nell Smith, Shawn Michelle Smith, Michael Warner, and Henry Weinfield. Apologies to any I have missed; I forget you only in this paragraph.

Special thanks to Leonardo Buonomo, Cristanne Miller, Marta Werner, the Emily Dickinson International Society, the Henry James Society, and the Nathaniel Hawthorne Society for helping give parts of this work a public forum. Marta gets an extra laurel wreath for all that she's done and still does. More special thanks to those who have helped support this project financially: Prentiss Clark and the Ralph Waldo Emerson Society, Samuel Coale and the Nathaniel Hawthorne Society, EDIS (again, bless them), Christina Gómez and the School of the Art Institute of Chicago's Liberal Arts Department, *Modern Language Quarterly*, and Allan and Mary Kollar.

Small parts of work previously published have been included in this book and referenced accordingly, in the notes and bibliography. A bit from chapter 1 appeared as part of a cowritten piece, with Alex McCauley, titled "The Art of Extraction and Preservation: Hawthorne's 'Dirty Nature,'" in *Nathaniel Hawthorne Review* 43, no. 2 (Fall 2017): 19–34. Another bit from chapter 2 appeared in my article "On the Road: Reevaluating an American Cultural Ideal," *ESQ* 64, no. 1 (2018): 1–30. And a third bit from chapter 4 appeared as part of a cowritten chapter, with Bob Hodges, titled "Portable Vision, Form, and Objects in Henry James," in *Portable Prose: The Novel and the Everyday*, edited by Jarrad Cogle, N. Cyril Fischer, Lydia Saleh Rofail, and Vannessa Smith (Lanham, MD: Lexington Books, 2019), 1–23 (nonexclusive permissions granted by Rowman & Littlefield). I thank all three for their permission to reprint those words here.

Dan Waterman's editorial guidance and support provided everything I needed at every moment I needed it. *Glancing Visions* may never have existed without him. Kelly Finefrock was a great help in the bottom of the ninth inning. My readers, Michelle Kohler and Shelly Jarenski, made this book better, and I so appreciate their munificence, patience, intelligence, and time. Gail Schermer is one of the spirits in the background, orbiting.

Obliquely, there are a happy few who collaborate on life's important side projects. Greatness abounds in Jeremiah Begley, Allison Greene, Caitlin Kearney, Rohit Kohli, Corey Lasko, Colin Montgomery, Tyler Nash, Michael Robideau, Patrick Tyler, Jason Weischedel, and—of course—Stuart Whitehead.

To the Tavlins: this book is for you. Now you can't say I never show my gratitude! Also, to the memory of Roz and Gus, spread among the rest of the tribe. And to Kirin Wachter-Grene, whose endless conversation and daily labors of love make all the difference, I offer an uncountable heap of thanks. A few of those, surely, can go to our sweet boy Von (but the rest are deservedly yours). Without each of you, all would be lost.

One final dedication: I wrote this book without any time off teaching. I note this difficult fact to shine a flash of light on all who scribble away with less reward and recognition than they deserve.

Introduction

The Art of the Glance

> Precisely the least, the softest, lightest, a lizard's rustling, a breath, a breeze, a moment's glance [*Augen-Blick*]—it is little that makes the best happiness.
>
> FRIEDRICH NIETZSCHE, *Thus Spoke Zarathustra*

The next time you find yourself in a new place, see if you can reflect on how you go about learning your way around. Do you stare at individual signs, landmarks, corners, or parts of the sky? Or do your eyes scan, flit, and jump around your surroundings? When you lose your way, do you stop moving until you find your direction, or do you keep going, trying this path or that by trial and error?

What do you do when you first open a new book? Or, perish the thought, when you start to write one?

Or: what does Walt Whitman do when he walks into a bar? That's not the opening to a joke, but a question about a poem. Whitman is otherwise marginal to the rest of this book, in part because he is so central to everything we think about American literature. Of course, critics have long acknowledged his self-described multitudes, his elegies as much as his ecstasies. His rolling democratic lists, always connecting beings through dilating, tumescent lines, join us all together in death and life, individual instances of a great ball of pulsing material bodies. So what to make of this short lyric, "A Glimpse":

A glimpse through an interstice caught,
Of a crowd of workmen and drivers in a bar-room around the
    stove late of a winter night, and I unremark'd seated in a
    corner,
Of a youth who loves me and whom I love, silently approaching
    and seating himself near, that he may hold me by the hand,
A long while amid the noises of coming and going, of drinking
    and oath and smutty jest,
There we two, content, happy in being together, speaking little,
    perhaps not a word.[1]

It is not that this Whitman has been ignored. Poems like "A Glimpse," and more well-trodden lyrics from the "Calamus" cluster, provide some of the most apposite material for the now-commonplace articulation of a queer Whitman. The crowd he "glimpse[s] through an interstice" is not the multitude of "Song of Myself," which Whitman disappears into even as he grafts their differences onto his own sense of self: "I acknowledge the duplicates of myself . . . // The weakest and shallowest is deathless with me, / What I do and say the same waits for them, / Every thought that flounders in me the same flounders in them."[2] No, here Whitman acknowledges that he goes "unremark'd" from the corner of the barroom. And his fragmentary, occluded vision ends in silence, in loving and perhaps gay contentment, not in the absorptive apostrophe so conspicuous in his verse.

Of course, the poem is not silent. But it presents a model of what Whitman calls "adhesiveness," sticky male-male relations as ideals for connective social bodies, in an uncharacteristically minor key.[3] His speaker catches the scene with a glance, a form of nominally unattached witnessing—the glimpse small enough to go unremarked by the crowd—that nevertheless calls to the youth, beckons him over with a cruiser's sneaky semaphore. The glance reaches out lightly like a hand seeking a mate, coy and childish in the loveliest of ways. The glance is the visual corollary of adhesive touch, bringing bodies together without eating them alive in an engorgement of the celebrated "Me." The glance does not necessarily seek to merge with the object it alights on; often it is content with much less.

But I would not have written this book had I thought glancing's "less" meant less effective than other modes of seeing, or less important, or less interesting.

So what elements characterize the glance? What are glances particularly good for? Here is a preliminary list:

1. *Glances connect the eye to the rest of the body.* Glances coordinate kinesthetic activity, as in the plein air Impressionist's athletic painting where rapid eye oscillation between scene and canvas depends on the hand's dutiful partnership. The eye cannot check up on the hand until after the gestural pattern is complete, which is why the glance must already put the hand in coordinated motion.

2. *Glances reveal our perceptual finitude.* Glances contain an ingrained understanding of the perceiver's physiological constraints. Consider: when my eyes move rapidly along with my body's posture to locate someone in a dense crowd, I am using unreflective habits developed in response to my sensorium's boundaries. I cannot simply see through objects and obstacles in front of me (I do not have x-ray vision), so I glance as a way of working around my perceptual limits. But I have to acknowledge those limits to do so, at least unconsciously.

3. *Glances dissolve hard boundaries between mind and world.* Glancing is a visual means for mind to distribute itself throughout its worldly surround. If we want to alter our own environment to embed our cognition in it—like placing a note to ourselves in just the right spot, where we are sure to notice it later—we must first check out that environment, scan it for its affordances, which we can use as levers to accomplish a task.

4. *Glances probe the forward edge of the present.* Glances are always on the move, and in moving they spill over the cup's edge of the present moment. In this way glances lean, putting one foot on the boundary separating present and future, like a sprinter anticipating the starter's gun. Glances are particularly good at expecting what should or could come next, and are flexible in response to surprise, quickly regrouping and reconsidering. One might explain this feature in evolutionary, adaptive terms, but instead just think about reading a poem, scanning a line up to its enjambment, anticipating the completion of the phrase just before you return to the left margin.

5. *Glances work according to a metric rhythm.* Glances are always cast out and pulled back in, like an expert angler's fishing line. They loop according to a regular(ized) beat but can undergo metric modulation as the speed of the world changes. When we catch something through our glance, we take it in briefly only to shoot our glance back out to pull yet another object into its orbit. The previous example of reading a poem works here too, with attention to its meter rather than its line breaks.

6. *Glances recycle visual garbage.* The eye's saccades, its rapid movements

between points of ocular fixation, allow us to effortlessly change the range of our focus as we gather information about our visual field. But that means most of what enters the eye is useless. Glances are thus hyperefficient sorting mechanisms, like an automatic filter that separates good and bad material in a recycling plant. Glances take in an overflowing mass of visual data and skip over redundancy to grasp those object-features that stand out in the field of light. And out of those selected materials a scene is sufficiently constructed, like a theatrical set built out of a small number of visual details and props.

7. *Glances conceal vision's imprint on the world.* Because glances glide along surfaces, they glean information through the lightest of incisions. To borrow a term from Emily Dickinson, glances are relatively "plashless," like an oar that cuts the surface of the water without making a deep mark, water immediately backfilling the crease. They rarely leave scars. Think about how people "check each other out" in public. If their glances turn into gazes, they risk provoking a reaction, for good or ill. If their glances are quick and subtle enough, the target might not realize anything is up. The world might not even register the look. That's why we call it "stealing a glance."

8. *Glances achieve an active receptiveness.* Even though they conceal and partially negate their own imprint or agency, glances do work. Although they graze objects and seem to move on from them without retaining their imprint on the sensorium, simply dropping objects back into their places, at the end of a series of glances some cluster of visual phenomena has been gathered. Although this is the most ordinary of visual processes, humming in the background of our everyday tasks, it is extraordinarily poetic at the same time. When we glance, we perform the very thing poets like Wordsworth and Keats tried to articulate: a receptivity that is not mere passivity or negation, but an active making.

9. *Glances seek the formal edges of objects.* Glances tend to move to the edges and borders of things—both external and internal—rather than their empty middles. They seek relief, line, shade, and joint. In this way glances go right to boundaries and interstices, all the better to determine where things begin and end, how things were made, and how we might reconstitute an object as something new. And glances seek the new through the adjacent. This is the spatial dimension of the temporal structure described in point 3.

10. *Glances tie our worlds together.* Think back to my initial question: how do we orient ourselves in unfamiliar territory? If at first a few looks here and there confuse, eventually our glance stitches the place together, putting all available signs in immediate contact and quilting our environment through them. Glances establish metonymic chains; in that way, they are

always already literary, world-building and poetic at the same time. They reveal that, in perceiving our world, some assembly is required.

In a move characteristic of my method in the rest of the book, and as a way of stitching the first thread of the cultural world-fabric I hope to lace as we go, I urge us now to glance briefly at a painting. If Whitman's nonpossessive glance sets the tone for a formal theme often downplayed in canonical American literature, there is a more widely understood perceptual attunement that wants to get more out of seeing. In 1836 the English-born American landscape painter Thomas Cole completed both his grand allegorical series *The Course of Empire* and his equally famous *View from Mount Holyoke, Northampton, Massachusetts, after a Thunderstorm*, also known as *The Oxbow*. Both works contain a temporal developmental logic, but in *The Oxbow* it is compressed into a single picture. From left to right, barely off horizontal in diagonal recession, lie three formations: a stormy, craggy foreground with

FIGURE 1. Thomas Cole, *View from Mount Holyoke, Northampton, Massachusetts, after a Thunderstorm* (*The Oxbow*), 1836, oil on canvas, 130.8 cm × 193 cm, Metropolitan Museum of Art, New York

blasted trees and uncultivated vegetation; an abyssal middle hidden by the drop of a clifftop *repoussoir*; and a tranquil, pastoral distance where the Connecticut River Oxbow meanders along picturesquely cultivated and sunlit farmland.

Nearly lost at the top of Cole's sublime overlook is the artist's figure, either gazing or glancing backward (one cannot tell which in a single isolated image) toward the imaginary picture plane. If there is a narrative embedded in the picture, Cole is perched there, no doubt, to paint the pastoral, not his immediate surroundings. But the painting Cole actually produced, the one we look at, needs the juxtaposition in elements arranged diagonally: as in many Hudson River School landscapes, we are privy to an embedded meta-aesthetic process with social ramifications, the cultivation of an optative mood alongside the cultivation of a wild landscape. Industry seems to recruit the eye, perch it up on its prospect. And the prospective vantage of the beholder and the artist—the real one, not the one in the frame—is ideal, because both see the progress of American society in all its stages, excepting the void in the middle where the landscape's mysterious transformation occurs, its secret kept. Avoid the crevasse, and you can take the rest in at once, the whole story fit perfectly into a single frame.

When you take a panoramic view—of a landscape, a geographical area, a field of knowledge—are you gazing or glancing? Or, to simplify the question while begging an answer no less complicated, what do we tend to think we are doing when we look prospectively over a wide expanse? Terminology can easily get in the way here. Lorraine Daston relates "surveyable" perceptions and forms of understanding to the term *coup d'oeil*, associated with the profession of military engineer geographers educated between 1750 and 1850 in Europe. She then translates *coup d'oeil* as "glance," which gives the latter a militant cast, as French officer Jean-Charles Folard describes its jurisdiction: "The military *coup d'oeil* is nothing other than the art of knowing the nature and different sites [situations] of the country in which one is at war or wants to prosecute a war, the advantages and disadvantages of the camps and posts one wants to occupy, as well as those that could be favorable or unfavorable to the enemy."[4] Daston traces the general's "glance" to scholastic (angelic) intuition and Platonic eidos, as each grasps whole forms immediately, all at once as in a flash, from the stable center of a visual field. This is not what I mean by glancing, because it takes a glance to be a single fluorescence instead of a fragmentary piece of a larger ensemble. The coup d'oeil is a form of seeing that is not sensing, hence its relation to Platonic "seeing" that grasps the Form of a thing as Idea. It is cognition divorced, angelically, from the corrupted flesh of body and world. It is the way we use "seeing" to mean nonvisual understanding. Surely you "see" what I mean.

This is a book about glancing, though, a perceptual activity that stays close to the body doing the looking even as it engages the worldly surround and tests its affordances and limitations. Glances have the astonishing capacity to promote both affirmation and critique of reality as it is, as it happens to be structured. This introduction aims to justify two main reasons why thinking through the glance matters. First, we have become so theoretically enthralled by the gaze that we need to refresh our account of visuality and remind ourselves of looking's varieties, what our eyes open for us, rather than continue to rehearse what they foreclose. This is a problem worth addressing all over the humanities and in many disciplines beyond the scope of this book. Second, the glance gives us a promising lever to pry open more specific histories of American literature and its connection to other arts, especially because there are perfectly good reasons why Americanists have been, as I just said about many scholars and critics, "enthralled by the gaze."

Since the field this book explores is one hundred years or so of United States literature from about 1830 to 1930—surveyed more like a lowly scout doing reconnaissance on the ground than a general perched on a bluff—there is a temptation to lead you like a tour guide through the greatest hits of visually oriented Americanist literary scholarship, to deliver a scrapbook (flipped through glancingly) as an entry brochure to my subsequent argument. The problem is that the tour itself is already ingrained conceptually in that field of inquiry. We might say that Cole, in *The Oxbow*, tropes upon the conceptual "origin of the American picturesque," Dennis Berthold's term for the aesthetic cultivated as much in tourism guidebooks as in landscape painting and novelistic description, and which makes viewers and readers of American art gaping sightseers along the path toward millennium.[5] Jennifer Baker knots the Hudson River School's strategic gaze, "aimed to alleviate Americans' fears of a dangerous and savage frontier by positing touristic viewing as a means by which the eye could subdue the landscape and attain safe and pleasurable perspectives on alien, chaotic scenes in the forests and mountains," to the idiom of James Fenimore Cooper's Leatherstocking novels and William Cullen Bryant's nature poetry.[6] Distinct from an English picturesque nostalgic for preindustrial scenes, American visual charms are taken to be forward looking, reaching out for something in the national future, seeing through landscapes and scenes into a noumenal domain as yet disclosed by the artist's, tourist's, and reader-beholder's lifeworlds.[7]

Another way of putting the desire, fulfillable if at all by readers and viewers in an imaginary proleptic headspace: to swallow both the present and future, collapsing temporal difference by tricking the inner eye to disregard anyone and anything not figuring in the national plan. Angela Miller and Albert Boime both argue that the ascendant tradition of nineteenth-century American landscape painting constructed repeatable visual associations to "discipline the random motions of the eye in conformity with a culturally meaningful sequence," so that contingent periods of national crisis and sectional conflict could be assimilated in landscape paintings where nature—and metonymically, nation—appears to bear God's witness, if not always His approval.[8] Boime posits that midcentury American landscapes were "almost invariably" organized like *The Oxbow*, where the view from an elevated patch of wild land looked out over a partially domesticated middle ground to a background containing evidence of industry, proposing a ubiquitous "magisterial gaze" characteristic of the most important American paintings.[9] Miller is one of several scholars who have looked to the panorama as a popular imperial form, with Anne Baker suggesting, about the immense panoramas of the Mississippi River and the overland trails to California, that they told a (literally) unfolding story where "U.S. annexation of Western territory was the culminating moment in a narrative of progress," their paratextual materials further establishing "the panorama artist as a national hero and the representation of western territory as a form of mastery."[10] Of course, alternative accounts of American iconography abound, as in David Miller's *Dark Eden*, which examines the rise of dingier representations of swamps, marshes, and uninhabited beaches around 1850. But while Miller takes these scenes of dank and disorderly materiality to be symptomatic of American consciousness's hidden layers, a dark return of the repressed in an increasingly urban and technological society, his project—true to critical form—still posits a primal visual scene that contains the truth of American culture in its semiosis, its symbolic codes.[11]

By establishing primal visual scenes, Americanists have been free to construct elegant historicist arguments that comprehensively draw comparative arts into wide synchronic orbits. Various American strains of painting, photography, and eventually film are shown to operate ideologically in concert with literary genres like the romance to reproduce the Puritan rhetoric of compact and settlement. Regimes of seeing are then reified as much in our critical narratives as they were in the cultural narratives we work to demystify. The critical tradition of American studies, and the dominant historical understanding of American literature we inherit from it, attends to the gaze of the American "I/eye" over every other form of seeing, and commonly claims that seeing itself—no less than in the landscape tradition running through the Hudson River School—is inherently imperialistic.[12] To complete the syllogism: to the extent that American culture is ocularcentric, it will always remain imperial. Dominant critical paradigms focusing on vision and nation-building hold that the eye of the central American literary form, the romance, is a devourer, reducing the alterity of wide swaths of the American continent (and its inhabitants) into useful, edible forms. That is the eye's Manifest Destiny: to be a different organ altogether, to be a mouth. Elisa New acknowledges the contradiction in a different form, that the "idea of a polity compacted by vision alone, of nation secured in the self's incarnation, of Being achieved in immaculate seeing" corresponds to critical practices "symbiotically bound"—in their "will to comprehensive explanation" and "totalistic romantic rhetoric"—to "the endemic self-enlargements of the literary objects" deemed most representative.[13]

New refers to a critical tradition that thinks big when it thinks American—what could be more American, after all, than to think big? For Myra Jehlen, "the decisive factor shaping the founding conceptions of 'America' and of 'the American'" in literature was "the physical fact of the continent," its dimensions calling for a sweeping vantage.[14] For Donald Pease, American Renaissance writers promoted "visionary compacts" through which Americans could restore or realize a principled, caring cultural community writ large.[15] Sacvan Bercovitch defines the American rhetorical difference as a historically unprecedented merging of national and spiritual aspirations. This union "yokes together the internal and external Kingdom of God by asserting the simultaneity of a geographic locale, America, and a mode of vision": for the Puritan, New England events were types of action that had occurred already in scripture (or, more accurately, antitypes to scriptural types).[16] But as such they were also seen as fulfillments of scriptural promises that would lead in turn to the ultimate fulfillment of the millennium. And Puritan typology did not only include major historical crises: the Puritan must "ratify his every experience, all his thoughts and feelings, by the infallible standard of holy scripture."[17] Thus Bercovitch claims that typology was not an intellectually abstruse system to the Puritan, but came to be his way of seeing and his attitude, automatically so in the lay settler and self-reflectively in the American writer (and, by extension, the American reader).[18]

Many contemporary critics who reject Bercovitch's assumptions about America's Puritan selfhood, whether by developing a transatlantic theory of literary provincialism (following Susan Manning), by attempting to think of Puritanisms in the plural, or by critiquing the very notion of the nation form in an encounter with postcolonial theory, maintain his obsession with large-scale formulations of subjective economies.[19] Because they take the history of Western thought and culture to have been largely ocularcentric, the unwieldy subjective economy of the colonist is constantly theorized as a "way of seeing," even if not primarily organized according to a conceptual system of scriptural antitypes.[20] The work of the critic becomes identifying sight's natural geometry—the discipline of the eye into a meaningful gaze, as a colonizing organ at a time when making colonization palatable was the ideological enterprise of dominant American culture—and then denaturalizing that geometry through analysis.[21]

The idea that vision happens when we translate the world through a "natural geometry" comes from Descartes's optics. The fact that, for Descartes, the geometry behind our visual apprehension of reality is truly natural and not sedimented by social ideology does not make his influence on our assumptions about visual culture any less secure. The claim is when light reflected off objects in the world enters our eyes, the mind makes a fast geometrical calculation based on its angles of incidence. Using that data the mind projects an image of the external world on an interior screen, the mind's eye. From two mortal, finite, often erring material eyes the immaterial mind develops a single image. In a sense, we see blindly, in the dark, with all the light we truly experience coming from inside, from the mind or soul. It is no wonder then that Descartes proposes an analogy between ordinary vision and blindness:

> No doubt you have had the experience of walking at night over rough ground without a light, and finding it necessary to use a stick in order to guide yourself. You may then have been able to notice that by means of this stick you could feel the various objects situated around you. . . . It is true that this kind of sensation is somewhat confused and obscure in those who do not have long practice with it. But consider it in those born blind, who have made use of it all their lives: with them, you will find, it is

> so perfect and so exact that one might almost say that they see with their hands, or that their stick is the organ of some sixth sense given to them in place of sight. In order to draw a comparison from this, I would have you consider the light in bodies we call "luminous" to be nothing other than a certain movement, or very rapid and lively action, which passes to our eyes through the medium of the air and other transparent bodies, just as the movement or resistance of the bodies encountered by a blind man passes to his hand by means of his stick.[22]

The blind man's walking stick is the seeing man's lens and retinal system. Both are very fine sieves. We think we see the world directly and transparently, but in fact we are locked in a camera obscura with a small pinhole. The world is like a movie and we are like homunculi in a dark, empty theater (so dark that we cannot see anything but the projection). The fact that we forget this condition is, in the afterlife of Cartesian optics, the basis for vision's role in ideological formation. We forget that the projector is behind us rather than *of* us, and we forget that the background geometry that goes into our immediate apprehension of the world has been learned and, in many cases, staged. It is no surprise that the most influential theorist of the gaze should be a scholar of cinema.

There might not be something called "gaze theory" were it not for Laura Mulvey's 1975 "Visual Pleasure and Narrative Cinema." Conceptual fountainhead for the term "male gaze," Mulvey's essay uses the cinematic apparatus to explain how male desire and its perceptual extension as voyeurism actively and perniciously defines an entire art form. We read Mulvey, of course, in the wake of a long cultural history of Petrarchism. For in narrative film, as in the conceits of many famous love sonnets, the "function of woman" as viewed object stands "in patriarchal culture as signifier for the male other, bound by the symbolic order in which man can live out his fantasies and obsessions through linguistic command, by imposing them on the silent image of woman still tied to her place as a bearer of meaning, not maker of meaning." Echoing John Berger's art historical analysis of the female form, Mulvey describes a libidinal economy wherein "pleasure in looking has been split between active/male and passive/female," so that women in film become particular kinds of objects whose significance is their "*to-be-looked-at-ness*."[23] Generalizing from individual works to photographic cinema generally, Mulvey bases her claims on a psychoanalytic interpretation of scopophilia, where male and female subjects differ in their sexualized relationship to a charged visual field. The camera cannot *not* be an instrument of the male gaze, which subjects the female form as a preemptive strike against castration anxiety. Visual art, its apotheosis in cinema, is an endless footnote to Salome's dance for a lecherous Herod.

Relying on Jacques Lacan's scenario of the mirror stage, as had apparatus theorists Christian Metz and Jean-Louis Baudry before her, Mulvey finds an echo of the ego's specular development in "the extreme contrast between the darkness in the auditorium (which also isolates the spectators from one another) and the brilliance of the shifting patterns of light and shade on the screen [that] helps to promote the illusion of voyeuristic separation."[24] Forget, for a minute, that in "The Mirror Stage as Formative of the *I* Function" (1949), Lacan never uses *le regard* (gaze). In fact, do not forget it, for that is precisely the point: Lacan's mirror stage so overdetermines contemporary gaze theory that it hardly matters that his theory of the gaze developed elsewhere (in Seminar XI, given over a decade later, where the gaze names a look given by objects, not subjects).[25] In the mirror stage, the infant comes to identify with his mirror image and thereby *mis*identify himself in an image of an "ideal-I," a fictional ego that stabilizes his otherwise scattered sense of self. The imago, the "specular image" of self, comes to be the infant's "threshold of the visible world," a gestalt that splits the self from its alter ego and imaginary counterparts subsequently encountered out in the world.[26] To understand why the gaze is so powerful according to Mulvey requires understanding how the mirror stage became the theoretical mise-en-scène of visuality tout court.

Joining Lacan with Louis Althusser's account of ideological apparatuses (the social dimension of ideological misrecognition, the imaginary relation of individuals to the real conditions of their existence, represented materially through an institutional "apparatus"), Metz claims that as spectators we all reenter the mirror stage by analogy. We gain a sense of mastery over the image in front of us just as infants come to acquire mastery over their self-image. "The spectator is absent from the screen *as perceived*, but also (the two things inevitably go together) present there and even 'all-present' as perceiver. At every moment I am in the film by my look's caress." As we gaze at the screen, we achieve voyeur status, all-perceiving while ourselves unperceived. This is a highly pleasurable experience, as Mulvey too acknowledges. The pleasure reinforces our sense of mastery over the scene. We are of course duped, just as the infant was. We are not in control of that thing on the screen's nonmirror surface. And yet the mirror remains the basic figure of ideological illusion. The only one not fooled, at least in the time of writing, is the critic whose work attempts to "disengage the cinema-object from the imaginary and to win it for the symbolic, in the hope of extending the latter by a new province."[27] The critic disrupts our pleasure, revealing the symbolic and semiotic codes underlying our imaginary identifications. The critic is a killjoy, tossing golden apples into the parties culture throws for itself. Mulvey is the ultimate feminist killjoy, taking (presumptively male) pleasure in movies away from us. For the gaze is never innocent.

Beyond Mulvey and the Lacan-inflected apparatus theory out of which her essay springs, we encounter an extensive discourse on the gaze in all corners of the humanities. From art history to film studies, from literary theory to postcolonialism, from feminist theory to readings of the history of philosophy, people (real and imaginary) are gazing back and forth at one another. There are several other seminal twentieth-century texts where specific theoretical concerns motivate attention to this master trope of seeing, including but not limited to Jean-Paul Sartre's subject-object dramas of *le regard* in *Being and Nothingness* (1943), directly influenced by Alexandre Kojève's lectures on Hegel delivered between 1933 and 1939, which were also attended by Lacan, Maurice Merleau-Ponty, and Georges Bataille; Michel Foucault's analysis of the institutional power relations of the medical and the disciplinary gazes in *Birth of the Clinic* (1963) and *Discipline and Punish* (1975); John Berger's Benjaminian art history in *Ways of Seeing* (1972); Michael Fried's theory of painting's autonomy from the beholder in *Absorption and Theatricality* (1980); Svetlana Alpers's distinction between the perspective structures of Italian and Northern Renaissance painting in *The Art of Describing* (1983); and bell hooks's racialized oppositional gaze in *Black Looks* (1992). This list could be four times as long without sacrificing too much canonicity, but even here we see a dramatic range of concerns, subjects, and media. My contention is that the diversity is collapsed in most scholars' use of "the gaze," and that there has not been nearly enough reckoning about its free-floating, transdisciplinary, and value-shifting life.

In this way the gaze—as a concept, not as a phenomenological event—is like a hyperdexterous trapeze artist, flying with ease over every wall put up by the disciplines, even if the landing is sometimes awkward. The gaze is all around us not because it is so useful but because it has become rather meaningless, even ideological in T. J. Clark's description of its sneakiest manifestation, as "a set of limits to discourse; a set of resistances, repetitions, kinds of circularity."[28] If ideology sediments through forgetting, we have by now forgotten twice: we have forgotten the forgetting of the Mulveyan gaze and naturalized it by closing our language off to its others. I wish I could follow every path gaze theory takes us, take every trip to every dead end. But that would be beyond my expertise and beyond the scope of any readable book. The gaze, like the proverbial neighborhood milkman, makes too many progenies in its partial image. In what follows I limit myself to an American literary context.

But there is a reason for that choice beyond personal predilection and the limitations of competence: American literature of the long nineteenth century is a key locus for testing the underappreciated significance of the glance in art and world making. The American metaliterary stories of compact, settlement, and newness already referenced—whether they count conceptually for as much as scholars and authors often think they do—delineate the stakes of understanding how it is writers and artists really do branch into and occupy new aesthetic and representational territories. Novels, poems, and paintings contact social and political history in many ways, but in the United States at this time, how one sees—how one sees the land, the Other, the city—appears to be hopelessly wrapped up with a uniquely American ideology. So if we can complicate the theoretical picture underlying the overdetermination of the gaze in our readings and critiques, we will learn to see more in our field of study in the same way writers like Nathaniel Hawthorne, Frances Ellen Watkins Harper, Emily Dickinson, and Henry James learned to see more about their own worlds and about subjectivity through their work. And that "more" may not be foreclosed by those specific national ideologies of occupation, settlement, and accumulation we want and need to continually challenge as its guises shift through time.

Ralph Waldo Emerson is the central figure through which many central Americanist literary critics (including Bercovitch, Sherman Paul, and Carolyn Porter) read the development of an ecstatic, mastering, and disembodied seeing in secular form. But he presents a farrago of modes of poetic vision that differ according to mood and activity, and which might lead a literary tradition along alternative paths.[29] I will start with the one most heavily praised and critiqued.

When Emerson says, in *Nature*, that the eye "is the best of artists," he means that the eye takes a central role in man's "making," the dissolution of nature's brute facts into human forms. The eye's circle has a larger circumference than other bodily instruments, and its operation is wholly free to pick things up and drop them, join them or separate them, love them or hate them. Emerson's claim, in a Viconian moment, that "what we are, that only we can see," when coupled with the notion that "the whole of nature is a metaphor of the human mind," suggests that the function of the eye is not necessarily to perceive in the traditional sense—to gain access to the external object, the "Not Me"—but to become an eye turned inward.[30] Such is at least one direction in which Emerson leans in the spasmodic gait of his writing. Since natural facts signify spiritual facts, we can use nature's sign system to transcend nature, arriving at those higher laws that nature merely signifies.

But those "higher laws" are—at least when Emerson favors this leg over the other—the laws of mind, and the phenomena the eye discloses are things to see through, to re-collect into an interiorized landscape. Descartes lives in this version of Emerson. In *Nature*, Emerson's interiorization of vision, his "seeing" only the self in the final instance, is not a corollary to an ontological position but to an existential one: "Whether nature enjoy a substantial existence without, or is only in the apocalypse of the mind, it is alike useful and alike venerable to me."[31] Porter puts it quite succinctly, so I will follow her lead until the path twists: the Emersonian "Not Me" "acquires its meaning from its relationship to me, a relationship defined by the use Me makes of 'Not Me.'"[32]

When Emerson says that, as a "transparent eye-ball," "I am nothing; I see all," he attempts to resolve two different deadlocks: one is man's incompletion and his alienation from himself and the world, and the other is his inability to disappear from that world, to negate himself as a material thing in order to attain a godlike view of it. "By detaching one's self as an eye," Porter writes of a common strategy in classical American literature, "one assumes a perspective from which it becomes clear that nothing is permanent." The transparent eyeball projects an image of the "active relation between seer and seen" that *Nature* aims to describe. But this airborne eye ultimately "results from a beheading": "Standing on the bare ground,—my head bathed by the blithe air, and uplifted into infinite space,—all mean egotism vanishes."[33] Though Emerson means to feel his reified state dissolve into the ether, alienation percolates back into consciousness as one "me" sees nature and another "me" lives it.[34]

Emerson's Over-Soul leads our way through the American desert like a pillar of fire in the night. We are asked to build worlds by the imaginative, unencumbered light of the gaze. We are told to use the objectively given world as a semiotic system to progressively reunite our alienated selves with the inhuman real. But practically, this point of view is a vantage occupied by the most vulgar of speculators, of a man playing the stock market in a transformation Georg Lukács describes as the active craftsman or laborer turned "into a receptive organ ready to pounce on opportunities created by the system of laws," his activity narrowed down "to the adoption of a vantage point from which these laws function in his best interest."[35] Prospect easily turns into prospectus; the transparent eyeball into a general's coup d'oeil or, later, a moviegoer's invisibility. Emerson wants to make the alien world usable—as a sign, and particularly as a visible sign—but in doing so lubricates the reification of man's primitive state to a capitalistic function, the manager, the mastering consciousness with all its ideological baggage. When Christopher Pearse Cranch drafted Emerson's figure of the transparent eyeball, he made it a tall and gangly gentleman overseer clothed in hat, tailcoat, and cravat.

What literary critics gain from Emerson's celebration of the mind and eye of natural man—a secular break from the Puritanical-Edwardsean distinction between regenerate and unregenerate souls—is paid for through the loss of any rigorous understanding of the body, and specifically of vision's embodiment, which cannot be reified at a higher level of abstraction without remainder. Emerson identifies the cost later in the same essay: "The ruin or the blank, that we see when we look at nature, is in our own eye. The axis of vision is not coincident with the axis of things, and so they appear not transparent but opake."[36] Perhaps the closest thing to a gnomic truth in the entirety of *Nature*, visual opacity is conceived within the text as a problem to be dissolved rather than understood.

The theory of vision in Emerson's "Experience," by contrast, seems to follow Goethe's sober, early nineteenth-century acceptance of opacity as a crucial and productive component of vision. Whereas typical Enlightenment discourse on visuality represses and conceals whatever threatens the transparence of an optical system, Goethe's *Farbenlehre* reverses tack and describes vision as a process of navigating caliginosity. For Emerson now, the complexity of man's coming to self-consciousness involves the fall of our vision: "distorting lenses" that we are, we are reminded that "once we lived in what we saw." To see ourselves seeing is like looking at a window and looking through it at the same time. It is not that we can simply surrender to Spirit and repair the "blank" in our eye, like squeezing a few drops over a corneal abrasion. The wisdom of "Experience" comes in an aphorism that recognizes the centrality of the embodied glance: "We live amid surfaces, and the true art of life is to skate well on them."[37] Where *Nature* "promised American breadths of possession commensurate with their scope of imagination, 'Experience' shrinks the eye's empire to a swimming mote." Here, as in the lyrical line that Elisa New traces through Dickinson, Crane, Stevens, Frost, and Moore, fallenness is "more usable, more responsive, to Being than the pre-lapsarian innocence" that *Nature* had called poetry's "enabling condition."[38] Emerson's felix culpa is a slip and slide. But we feel the world's grains and grooves as we glissade. In "The Poet," another in Emerson's second series of essays, the "very high sort of seeing" he associates with the imagination accompanies the poet's resignation from the tasks of encompassing mastery or transparent representation in favor of "sharing the path, or circuit of things through forms, and so making them translucid to others."[39]

Even beyond the lyric poem (the ambit of New's analysis), nineteenth-century American writers traded "embattled, self-conscious visual figures like 'miles of stare'"—the title of Michelle Kohler's book on vision and transcendentalism, borrowed from a Dickinson poem that addresses the emptiness of metaphysical vision on the American landscape—which were "repeatedly tied to the task of 'signal[izing]' the seeing of literary language." Kohler argues, accurately to my mind, that the transcendentalist eye (traced back from Emerson's *Nature* to Sampson Reed's Swedenborgian correspondences) is not in fact an eye(ball) at all. It is hollow to the core. What's more, the transparent eye sees only itself: "Transcendentalist vision emerges, too, in a nation more broadly invested in mythologizing itself as a self-evident truth and a manifest destiny—a nation that had long justified itself by looking at itself, or that claimed it *could* justify itself by looking at itself." But as I have already suggested by positing two Emersons, I follow Kohler and New in my conviction that vision in American literature is in no way limited to the naive, uncritical, puritanical, or metaphysical-spiritual. Kohler inspires me in her further commitment to a "heterogeneity among ways of seeing" in American literature that "suggests a national identity driven less by consensus or a shared exceptionalist ideology and more by shared questions whose answers are significantly disputatious and provisional." Certainly, if we have "long been suspicious of the political and imaginative power of the transparent American eye," it is high time we did something about its commanding role in American literary history.[40] We must see beyond its horizon, see *through* the transparent eye, to glimpse something (or some things) else that was there all along. In this I follow these two critics who have already begun the long process of charting such richly heterogeneous territory, which includes visual forms of consent (New) and dissent (Kohler).[41]

Nevertheless, even as my work builds on theirs, I cannot help but note that both New and Kohler remain within the terminological boundaries of the gaze. Perhaps it is one of the shibboleths Americanists must learn to look at askance.[42] To that end, though I must use it many times in this book, I often write "gaze" as if under erasure, as denoting a concept that fails when pushed too far, and that we might eventually use less frequently.

While Goethe writes in the preface to his *Farbenlehre*, "in every attentive look [*Blick*] on nature we already theorise," not every attentive look amounts to the same thing, or to the same sort of theorizing.[43] Phenomenologist Edward Casey, playing at times with the vocabularies of critics Norman Bryson and Jean Starobinski, calls "the glance" the look that moves fast and touches lightly, that "caresses" the surface of things—indeed having "a genius for surfaces"—and that leads on toward understanding in the manner of Goethe's attentiveness.[44] Here is the full sentence from Goethe: "Every act of seeing leads to consideration, consideration to reflection, reflection to combination, and thus it may be said that in every attentive look on nature we already theorise." Glances—specifically those that advance from *ansehen* (looking at) to *aufmerksam* (looking up), from a mere flash to attentive cognitive motion—are reflective looks that read the surfaces of things but also tend to connect those surfaces together as they move. They proceed from part to part while also grasping a whole that does not necessarily develop according to those linear steps; for Goethe, when we see theoretically we get progressively closer to adapting our perceptions to the way nature itself proceeds. The glance is always already on the way to usable knowledge that acknowledges what the surface of the world affords us. It is a way of reading surfaces that activates our capacities to put those surfaces to good use.

Seeing's most adaptive form, glancing contributes to an active and bodily subjectivity: it is the mode of vision we use when running, walking, or working, where the posture of the body is used in a constructive, subtle way. The glance is particularly adept at picking out the peripheries and edges of objects, scenes, places, and landscapes. There is an affinity between the edge and the glance, the latter highly sensitive to the terminative edge of things. Indeed, the glance tends to go to the edge more than to the neutral and empty middle; it has a fascination with finding out how far a given stretch of space extends (not metrically, but in terms of its sensuous, qualitative presentation). The glance glides along a surface until that surface reaches a turning point, an edge, where the glance breaks off and pursues another surface. In this way, the subject of the glance learns what the environing world is like as a congeries of things, rather than as a single object: one learns what kind of complexity this world proffers, what the outlines and in-lines (the internal edges) of this world are like, and where its brute fracture lines exist, the joints that can be manipulated and reconstructed through forms of labor and artistry.

Casey explores the glance by tracking and recording his own visual experiences as his body turns, moves, and orients itself in place. As a starting point, embodied phenomenology is a version or extension of the Nietzschean ideal of philosophical practice, summarized by Elizabeth Grosz: "Philosophy itself was to be written walking—or, preferably, dancing."[45] Phenomenological attention to the distinction between the glance and the gaze, as well as the ubiquity of the former and its capabilities within a subject's encounter with a worldly environment, can also disclose the affordances the glance offers for imaginative constructions at the intersection of literary and artistic practice. Here, protoconceptual capacities of vision are at play in world-disclosing experiences, so that cognition and sensation are not separate abilities of the seeing subject, the former never entirely pioneering the latter. Rather, cognition only occurs through sensation, and sensation is always accompanied by cognition. The glance is a sort of reflection that senses, which accounts for its two-step operation, an ingress and egress or looping movement (out and back) that dissolves subject-object distinctions through acts of environmental engagement. The question, from a visual perspective, is the following: what is the perspective or point of view that would give me a maximum grip on something, that would most reveal the worldly object as it really is in the domain of my concern? Each concern is motivated by a desire to grip things and materials in sensuous excess of their two-dimensional, flattened profiles in a visual field of representation and thus by a productive blindness that engages the body in its protoconceptual attunement with the world.[46]

The blindness I speak of here is not procedural, not a geometrical calculation that goes on behind the backs of our conscious selves. It is a source of creativity, not a persistent state of illusion. An example is in order.

Robert Smithson writes, "A great artist can make art by simply casting a glance." The plurality of his next line may be closer to the truth: "A set of glances could be as solid as any thing or place."[47] In 1915, Claude Monet was filmed painting his water lilies *en plein air*. Anyone reading this can find a clip on YouTube. What you will see is an old, fat, grey-bearded artist making up for his inevitable decline in painterly dexterity with the quickness of his glance. His easel set perpendicularly to the live scene, Monet turns his eyes from the lilies to his canvas as quickly as he can in order to keep them in view. Even though there are moments of soft gazing at the pond, clearly this is not enough to retain what he needs in order to represent the lilies, light, and luminous reflections. If it were, he would not have to move quickly at all; his gaze would take the scene in at its depth and keep it there for as long as he needs. The painter's lithe glance does not serve memory but operates through a more ubiquitous, immediate, and routine form of retention, carrying into the present what was perceived directly prior to the instant where his visual field shifts. The lilies are not shelved in some storehouse in the brain only to be pulled out again when needed, but rather dance along through the sort of retinal play his Impressionism has been known to foreground.

Monet's glance thus quickens the relationship between nature and method, making painting a bodily relay somewhere between "instantaneous records of nature" and "deliberate products of some academic method." Art historian James Elkins encounters the gestures Monet made with a student as they attempted to copy one of his paintings and reproduce the singular effects of his brushstrokes. "Everything depended," he writes, "on the way [his student] moved in those few instants of contact. The best motions, the ones Monet must have made habitually, were violent attacks followed by impulsive twists and turns as the brush moved off. First the brush would scrape wildly, epileptically, against the canvas, jittering across its own trail, breaking it up, laying down thick paint alongside dry paint, and then it would abruptly lift and swivel, turning the jagged edges into little eddies. The gestures are a mixture of timidity and violence, of perfect control in the preparation and perfect abdication of control in the execution." Watching Monet work, I see that mixture of control in preparation and abdication of control in execution not only in his hand but, in a wholly connected way, in his eyes. That is what the glance does through a modulation between violent darts and softened caresses, habitually breaking its own habits, working with the hand to "keep turning the body against itself, so it never does quite what it wants to do—so it never falls into the routine of oval marks, all pelting down in one direction."[48] In that way Monet's glance is improvisational even as it is also typical and habitual, both preternatural and dissatisfied, just barely out of control but not so much that it ever leaves the body behind. It always returns, so the artist must find a way to let it shoot back out on new trajectories rather than along the same old grooves.

In "Eye and Mind," Merleau-Ponty considers the painter's inaugural gesture not as a cloistered, mysterious rite but as a prosthetic extension (through the brush) of the ordinary body-eye's worldly activity. Painting begins by setting a blank surface or canvas, which separates the painter's gaze from the scene or landscape that he aspires to represent, creating a break between the two visible dimensions. This break turns that gaze into a glance that must thenceforth traverse the minimal invisible gap between the saturated world and the blank space that will progressively be filled by movements of the artist's body. Painterly action then takes on the same two-beat character of any glance, which constructs "the diagram" of life in the body, "its pulp and carnal obverse" that bridges the gap between the "manifest visibility" of the world around the body and a "secret visibility" in the body that with minimal delay schematizes the former, preparing the body's movements in unison with the world's affordances.[49] The painter interfaces his perception of landscape and the gesture of painting, one bleeding into the other.

When the painter's brush begins its work—when it contacts the canvas and charts its colored trace, breaching forever the blankness of its surface—it starts encoding a transitional space between body and world, an intertwined chiasmus. The lineaments of the forming picture look back at the artist as his glance bridges his body's movements and his surrounds. Merleau-Ponty quotes Paul Klee as saying, while channeling this experience, "A certain fire pretends to be alive; it awakens. Working its way along the hand as conductor, it reaches the support and engulfs it; then a leaping spark closes the circle it was to trace, coming back to the eye, and beyond."[50] Klee describes a practical corollary to the state German Idealists sought in theory, the fusion of self-awareness and object-awareness. The embodied glance is like a "leaping spark," a darting probe that guides the hand through a quickened circuit between limb and eye.

Jacques Derrida's *Memoirs of the Blind* leaps out of Merleau-Ponty's painterly approach to define *le trait*—one of his many reformulations of the trace, of the supplement, of *différance*—as the mark, line, or stroke that "joins and adjoins only in separating," defining the way art thinks in its construction.[51] As an addendum to Merleau-Ponty's theory of the necessary power of the invisible, he says that drawing is blind, that in the interval where the artist's glance moves from the surrounding world to the support, there is a productive blindness, a shooting of a gap where eye and body construct a schematic picture together by interrupting the harmony of a prior visual field. The artist must turn from the object to the surface of his creation and work from memory, though the quickening of the glance and its consonance with the practiced movement of the arm, for instance, works asymptotically toward an elimination (though never complete) of the role of memory (or, more appropriately, retention). But where Derrida calls this productive blindness "transcendental," Merleau-Ponty more helpfully grounds this operation in the kinesthesis of the body, immersed in and with the world on view, intermingled with/in it, revealing a self not through "transparence, like thought, which only thinks its object by assimilating it" but "through inherence of the one who sees in that which he sees."[52]

Alva Noë's "enactive account" of seeing attempts to explain how we develop intuitive visual attunements to the shifting "sensorimotor profiles" of the world, how our physiological systems learn to cope with a world that is always shifting from our own moving perspectives: "When you move with respect to a plate, its profile changes. . . . Our appreciation of its actual shape consists in our perception of its profile and our understanding of the way the profile, or apparent shape, depends on movement. We may say, in a case such as this, that we are able to experience the shape of the plate, to see it, because we grasp, implicitly, the sensorimotor profile of the plate. Our grasp of the plate's sensorimotor profile makes its shape available in experience."[53] Developing such an implicit and automatic understanding of the sensorimotor profiles of concrete objects involves learning how to hone one's glance, how to consistently track objects as the body and eye move and (in doing so) repeatedly alter one's visual field. As we learn to see, we are all like the baseball player honing his ability to pick up and identify a curveball; it just takes far less time to learn to see things that don't move so fast.

Unreflective motor activities, like picking up a paint brush, chisel, or pen to work with (not to mention trained use of each), require an immediate bodily understanding of the gear's qualitative features, an understanding achieved not through a general concept or category but through the body's skill, through its ability to form a good grip.[54] Basic comportment is directed toward and responsive to the specific qualitative features of the object and is thus not merely the action of an internal circuit of reflexes (just as it isn't an experience of cold, critical distance). Visuality and tactility work together, joined in a kind of near-immediate sensorimotor understanding.[55] As Merleau-Ponty explains, the eye operates in ways structurally similar to the hand in its surprisingly effective and repeatable act of gripping: one's glance is constantly led to certain features of objects, the eye having an inclination to look at a thing in a particular way prereflectively and immediately tied to the visual context.[56] The eye and the hand are both directed toward and responsive to what my body takes to be the features of the object-world. The experienced eye leads the trained hand to the joint or cleavage in material reality that concentrates signals traveling from the body outward into the world and from the world back to the body. And so to theorize the glance in this way also means rejecting hylomorphic models that separate form and matter into a unidirectional imprint of the former onto the latter.

Hylomorphism, in the visual register, maps onto gaze theory, which imposes form onto an empty object that receives the action of the subject with barely any resistance. The glance instead occupies a fluid interspace between matter and form, material and formal cause. Because the world is not made up of a homogeneous substance, but is rather a mixed medium of actual and potential forms, artists and laborers proceed along a winding, trial-and-error path suspended in the time of the body, developing an improvisational comportment responsive to feedback from eye to world and back again rather than a linear progression of functional, cognitive steps. This winding path is the working curve of distributed subjectivity. It is my contention that the visual organ of purposive distribution is the glance, not the gaze, which works in the other direction, pulling an exterior image back to a concentrated interior point.[57]

To repeat what I already suggested: Emerson sometimes proves himself a thinker of the glance. "Do not attempt to be a great reader," he relates to a young protégé. "The glance reveals what the gaze obscures."[58] This Emerson, if we squint, seems to lend background support for what Stephen Best and Sharon Marcus call "surface reading," a descriptive apprehension of texts that intentionally forgoes long-celebrated promises of unlocking treasures in their hidden depths.[59] Or Heather Love's related call for modes of reading that are "close but not deep," an ultimately ethical practice "grounded in documentation and description" rather than critical motivation.[60] But the parallel is troubled. In "Experience," Emerson uses "glance" to celebrate indirection rather than minimal interpretation: "Direct strokes [nature] never gave us power to make; all our blows glance, all our hits are accidents."[61] Here Emerson holds two principles together that contemporary "reading wars" discourse tends to separate: surprise encounters and critical agency.[62] He says we make or create new things in our readings, but only through glancing blows, accidental connections, things the glance picks up as if haphazardly and without prior knowledge. And yet our impetus is still always to create.

Granted, Emerson rarely associates the glance with the eye of the traditional maker, the artist. In "Art," he describes the eye capable of tracking the ephemeral events of life in the city, "the eternal picture which nature paints in the street with moving men and children, beggars, and fine ladies, draped in red, and green, and blue, and gray; long-haired, grizzled, white-faced, black-faced, wrinkled, giant, dwarf, expanded, elfish,—capped and based by heaven, earth, and sea." Even reading that sentence requires nimble eyes, ones that Emerson believes are faster than the those of producers and beholders of painting or sculpture. Through the use of "coloring" or the "anatomy of form," the artist fixes "the momentary eminency of an object," slowing the motion of the eye until it turns into a gaze, so that even when the eye does move "we pass to some other object, which rounds itself into a whole, as did the first." The artist's eye has been primed so that the practices of painting and sculpture "are gymnastics of the eye, its training to the niceties and curiosities of its function" opposed to the natural, untrained glance Branka Arsić links to several other "natural" movements in Emerson's oeuvre: "It is able to see through a thing in the moment of its transformation; it is so fast that it escapes the control of the will, and so cannot be considered trained. . . . Glance sees the transition itself."[63]

In the end, this book is not primarily for artists. The training in question is literary, specifically of literary scholarship. More important for me than closing the distance Emerson held open between natural and aesthetic vision (a distinction I am skeptical of) is opening our eyes to a neglected problem in the history of American literature. Of course, while this book is historically and nationally situated, it adopts a far wider range of philosophical, literary, and artistic reference that hopefully recasts literatures, periods, and schools beyond my scope in a new light. Casting its lot with neither paranoid critique nor postcritique (terms hopefully nearing the exits of scholarly fashion anyway), its aim is to contribute to a body of knowledge Alexander Baumgarten calls "sensuous" (*cognitio sensitiva*) or examine what Jacques Rancière calls "distributions of the sensible" that open up underacknowledged visual worlds.[64] Though structured according to individual authors, no chapter should be taken as attempting the definitive word on their careers as artists or as an encompassing statement on a microperiod or intellectual-aesthetic movement. Rather, each is a "scene" or "a little optical machine that shows us thought weaving together perceptions, affects, names and ideas, constituting the sensible community that these links create, and the intellectual community that makes such weaving thinkable."[65]

If there is a historiographical method at work in this sort of scenography, it is in tracing a field of resonance in which aesthetic events expose or reveal underlying concepts and the development of "sensuous knowledge." There is no proposed inevitability to the examples this study engages with, and different inclusions would produce a different story, though I maintain that the study's canonicity is no accident or at least not only an overdetermination of my own socialized biases. I chose the writers I did because in each case, there exists a substantial body of scholarship on visuality in and around their work that has attained a level of convention. The force of my argument, as multivalent as it is beneath the organizing concept of "the glance," comes from canonicity, from the thesis that even as we've come to reject the inevitability of the American literary canon's historical shape, we have not yet gotten out from under some of its major organizing principles.

One of those principles might be an ethical one that guides the imposition of our organizational methods, though it is hardly unique to American literary studies: that we must choose ahead of time what kind of aesthetic politics we want to find in the phenomena we study. I want to resist this impulse for as long as I can. Think back to the Whitman poem I opened with, and its perhaps surprising performance of nonpossessive, even quietist perception. Sometimes the glance is more disruptive than that, scaling the limits of a visual field and straining against it to anticipate something not yet present or available to the eye. As I discuss in my chapter on Dickinson, glances both stitch and unstitch. If there is a difference between glancing and glimpsing, the word Whitman uses, it is that "glimpse" accents the momentary vision's static form while "glancing" (more commonly used as a participle) foregrounds its restlessness, its urge to always shuffle on. And because the glance is restless, it deconstructs the momentary visual fragment at the very same time as it constructs or concatenates a wider visual field.

This book is about how we make things, even as unmaking is a necessary part of any constructive process. Glances check out our surroundings, materials, and pregiven forms and turn them into "search spaces" where new possibilities for intervention emerge. Henry Staten calls this searching finding "join" or "fit," which is the first stage in finding form. Searching out new ways of making—whether in the fine arts, practical arts, or everyday tasks—is an ontological inquiry, for "any labor process must correctly come to grips with its object," as Lukács claims: "Each individual movement in the process of sharpening, grinding, etc. must be considered correctly (i.e., must be based on a correct reflection of reality), be correctly oriented to the posited goal, correctly carried out by hand, etc."[66] And Staten adds, along Lukácsian lines, that through these (bodily) movements "human purposes are slowly woven into the structure of natural being in such a way as to satisfy human needs, at the price of painstaking submission to the patterns of natural causality. Thus the realm of natural causality is intertwined with that of human purposes, giving rise to the distinctive ontological status of social being."[67] At this level of engaged activity, geared into material nature, there is no distinction between the human subject and the surrounding world (mediated as this intellectual distinction is by prosthetics and gestures encoded by intimate body-knowledge of the world's affordances, its material joints). We do not impose form from the inside out or from the top down; we enter the world's grooves and explore the direction of its grains, seeing how far we can push things to create something new without breaking it.

From a visual standpoint, the glance is indispensable for understanding how an embodied subject can get geared into the world through concrete labor practices. Just as "the tool writes the toolmaker as much as the toolmaker writes the tool," as Whitney Davis puts it, the glance constructs the subject as much as the subject controls the glance.[68] Which does not mean that the glancing subject is wholly determined by the world's current, present formal arrangement. What the glance seeks, when looking for something new, is adjacency. Noë, focusing on the hidden adjacencies of visual perception (the back of a tomato, for instance, pictorially hidden from view but nevertheless acknowledged as somehow present to us), argues that what is temporarily "out of view" remains available to us in "access space" because we implicitly understand how things will appear as we move our bodies or as the object moves itself in relation to us.[69] Analogously, when embarking on new designs for their objects, artists glance among the forms available to them and, in rare but famous cases, make small but significant leaps across traditional formal boundaries.[70] Whether we find ourselves in abstract "design space" or in perceptual "access space," the glance probes the boundaries of our world's layout and tests the possibilities for seeing and making it otherwise. It is both realistic and transformative; when we glance there is no distinction.

Each chapter to follow considers the phenomenological elements of the glance in an expanded context of visual artistry, focusing on specific American authors as well as contemporaneous developments in the visual arts. Intermedia comparisons do not aim to establish straight lines of influence or hierarchies of aesthetic subordination but to reveal the infrastructures of intellectual and experiential activity that affect art making, beneath differences in mode and form, as their unarticulated preconditions.

Chapter 1 traces Hawthorne's theory of the imagination from its initial analogical reliance, in "The Custom-House," on the camera obscura—a technology associated since the eighteenth century with an atemporal and interior model of vision—to a theory of visual mediation developed in *The House of the Seven Gables*. There, the daguerreotype provides a model for the artist's glancing attunement to environments undergoing constant change. The drama between the photographer Holgrave and the domestic Phoebe is not simply the bourgeois version of the old battle of aristocratic female and underclass male gazes that some critics have taken it to be, but rather a story of the photographer's learned ability to surrender mastery of a sitter's interior essence or personality, skimming instead surface details lost to the human eye's limitations. And then *The Marble Faun* further develops a theory of the artist's impersonal subjectivity by integrating the significance of the glance through a narrative of artistry that moves according to its rhythm (thus bridging the technical differences of the writer and the visual artist).

Chapter 2 focuses on Harper's poetry in the contexts of sentimental abolitionist literature and antebellum genre paintings of Black life. Vision in Harper's poetry toggles between gazes and glances to unsettle two competing forms of racialized seeing: the sentimental gaze and the slave trader's glance. While both gaze and glance carry ethical risks for Harper, neither can be completely disavowed as ingrained tools for understanding the way visual culture assists the sedimentation of racial hierarchies. Moreover, gazes and glances carry phenomenological weight in the conventional lyric forms Harper often uses, and so her poetry (through its shifts into modes of apostrophe and collective address) provokes a desire to interrupt events underway—slave auctions and fugitive slave hunts—and to resee the lyric present as containing latent possibilities for intervention beyond the limits of sentimental projection. This means borrowing an image, feeling, or experience rather than keeping, possessing, or owning it. Harper's poems, with their formal desires to attain the status of lyric, move rather than stand their ground. They do not unlock some sacred pathos contained in the suffering lyric subject but pull readers into Harper's address and reveal the lineaments of a lyricism beyond the horizon of her generic form. Scenes of anguish pull the epistemic ground from under our feet, and we begin to glimpse a future that would redeem its claims to justice by validating its lyric form.

Chapter 3 considers Dickinson's material practice from her early poems stitched into fascicles to her late scraps and fragments, charting an alternative to critical assumptions about her poetry's veils, formed to conceal herself from (masculine) gazes all around. Instead I read her development as an unstitching—a winding path of poetic construction that anticipates cognitive-visual models presented by the photographic motion studies of Thomas Eakins and Eadweard Muybridge. The turn from fascicles to scraps reveals Dickinson's metapoetic agon with visual sequence. Whereas her early poetics thematize the (material and visual) stitch as the ungrounded life's only defense against the abyss of nonbeing, her passage to "sets" and scraps, parallel with a renewed attention to animal life, are read as an attempt at more adequate environmental poiesis. I read her late practice as "animalian," founded on a theory of animal sight that was later articulated by Jakob von Uexküll and Maurice Merleau-Ponty and that contributes to a theory of extended mind. Dickinson shows how to ease the pains of separation and alienation through the glance, and through a poetics that embraces the niche-making capabilities of animal life.

Chapter 4 contextualizes James's theory of the novel within an increasingly portable technological regime and an aesthetic era committed to the "impression." I focus on the troubled role of portraiture in his fiction and the risks of the glance in a culture of portability. The "flattening" of Isabel Archer (in *The Portrait of a Lady*) as figure and seer through her catastrophic marriage arises in the midst of narratively charged glances circumscribed by bourgeois social habits. Despite James's general dislike of French Impressionism, his novel produces a dialectic of visual restraint and creativity characteristic of Édouard Manet and colleagues. Victorian restrictions on desire and decorum are (only) temporarily overcome by articulating subjectivity within an energetic visual field of glances. James's late style, evolving from a working relationship with photographer A. L. Coburn, then accommodated the turn-of-the-century portability craze standardized in the Kodak camera. In the *New York Edition* James experimented with image-texts that, by removing the human figure and negating his favored mode of portraiture, visualize the twentieth-century subject as anonymous, mobile, and radically exterior.

I end at the threshold of cinematic modernism, with the role of the cut in the development of twentieth-century avant-gardes. My coda conceives the Imagist movement in modernist poetry as both product of and response to early cinema's use of the cut as the basis for a new visual grammar. Describing and interpreting a selection of modernist fragments (Louis Lumière's short films, Ezra Pound's Imagism, *Un chien andalou,* William Carlos Williams's fractured verse, Robert Frank's *The Americans*), I show how cuts—between cinematic shots and between lines in a poem—are technical extensions of the glance. Filmmakers and poets alike are seen as directors of our visual attention, particularly when and where it is thought to be most fickle and fragile.

My book begins and ends with nothing more than a few glances, though a few glances are often enough to get a sense of the whole picture. The glance can sum things up, but it gives no pretense of absolute unity. I hope my readers embrace that, and that this book helps them dart off to encounter other scenes outside its circumference.

Eclipsing the Camera Obscura

Hawthorne's Glancing Imagination

"Foot-prints on the Sea-shore" (1838) is a story about improvisational wandering. It reads like a short daytrip away from the heavier fare in Hawthorne's collected tales. Summoned to the oceanside to rejuvenate his weary spirit, its narrator notes "a wet margin" along the water's edge "which glistens brightly in the sun-shine, and reflects objects like a mirror." This strip of sea-land dissolves into and out of form like a shifting, curvilinear pathway that "grows moist again as we lift our feet." The seaside stroller leaves temporary marks in the wet sand, impresses already disappearing out from under him the instant they are made. In appraising the trace of his walk, steps that (if only they would remain) might "recall the whole mood and occupation of the mind," every "unconscious wandering of thought and fancy," Hawthorne's narrator pursues an unstable image of the thinking and feeling self. "[By] tracking our footprints in the sand we track our own nature in its wayward course, and steal a glance upon it, when it never dreams of being so observed. Such glances always make us wiser."[1] But glances, like ghostly footprints in the wet margin, do not leave a resilient archive.

Andy Smith writes that many of Hawthorne's tales "exhibit a desire to stabilize phenomena in order to record human behavior accurately."[2] Smith mentions "Fancy's Show-Box" (1837) and "The Birth-mark" (1843), though one could also include the troubled epistemological scenarios of "Wakefield" (1835), "Young Goodman Brown" (1835), "Sights from a Steeple" (1837), and "My Kinsman, Major Molineaux" (1852) and at least a dozen more. For Hawthorne, though, the desire to stabilize and record is dangerous and prone to obsessive abuse. Each of those stories, when examined through their discourse and descriptive modes, testifies that the ephemeral image's unstable brilliance is just as important in an artist's visual reservoir (and might be ethically preferable). Henry James, reviewing Hawthorne's notebooks for *Nation* in 1872, calls his countryman "one of the gentlest, lightest and most leisurely of observers, strolling at his ease among foreign sights . . . weaving his chance impressions into a tissue as smooth as fireside gossip."[3]

"Foreign sights" and "fireside gossip" appear side by side only as montage, as in a summer vacation slideshow. I follow many strong readers of Hawthorne—including Susan Williams, Susan Stewart, and more recently Shelly Jarenski—in noting the significance of visual tourism in Hawthorne's late aesthetic (most explicitly in his *French and Italian Notebooks* and *The Marble Faun*). Much of the emphasis is on framing: tourism and travel writing, as in the Tauchnitz souvenir editions of *The Marble Faun* that afforded Roman tourists the opportunity to tip their own pictures into the text, selects, extracts, and visually possesses foreign territory (and, by extension, its inhabitants). Less attention has been paid to another word James uses: "chance." When we glance we also open ourselves up to chance encounters. Visual artists, especially photographers, cannot fully excise the real from their compositions. The eliminative property of framing never bounds and stabilizes the image for all time; the materiality of the picture, its propensity to fade and decay, signalizes the momentariness of the captured image, its unavoidable partiality.

This chapter traces an arc in Hawthorne's thinking across the 1850s. After *The Scarlet Letter* (1850), the visual arts come to the forefront of his work, floating to the surfaces of his narratives like a shape emerging in photographic developer. Anxieties about the aesthetic and commercial status of literature were behind Hawthorne's interest in photography, painting, and sculpture, as many scholars have already noted.[4] But behind those concerns, framed within frames, was a very basic epistemic problem encountered by just about every representational art in Hawthorne's lifetime, one at the core of the realism-romance distinction he so avidly championed.[5] Put in simple form, the problem is how artists can continue to construct a compelling effect of the real out of partial perceptions.

As Jonathan Crary has formidably shown, the Enlightenment-era construction of the camera obscura as a model of mind, offering an intuitive internalist account of how we turn embodied perspectives into universal knowledge, was waning in persuasiveness for philosophers, scientists, and artists alike.[6] New theories of the imagination and aesthetic vision were up for grabs. Because of the ontological distinctions Hawthorne was driven to assert between media, understanding his visual theory requires first thinking through the way different arts negotiate boundaries between reality and virtuality. Because of modern framing practices, the formative glance of the artist—which best reveals the interrelation between real and virtual phenomena, and which I described in my introduction by way of Monet's astonishing technique—was subtly hidden from view. But precisely because of that history we might recognize Hawthorne's scenic and narrative uses of the glance's finesse, his restless investigations into its receptive and creative capacities, as literary interventions into the ontology of art in general. Glances, in Hawthorne's work, serve to recoup a creative materialist aesthetic from his own dalliance with an idealist theory of the imagination. Let us begin, then, with how gazes and glances have been conceptualized in the history of visual art before looking at Hawthorne's refiguration of the glance as a writerly tool for contacting paradoxical visual phenomena, obscurities in plain sight.

Norman Bryson spins a comprehensive yarn about the triumph of "the Logic of the Gaze" over the "illogic of the glance" in Western art. The history of Western painting, according to Bryson, is a progressive effort by practitioners to hide all traces of their labor. Improbably for those who think primarily of the godliness of the historical past, the Byzantine image was once dramatically embodied, with the liturgical dimension of mosaic and glass distributed throughout an architectural space "where the body is enclosed on all sides and addressed in all dimensions . . . a theatre of religious ceremonial," the spectator solicited not as an individuated eye but as a "physical, ambient witness to the Sacred Word." The cathedral spectator was an "embodied presence in motion," moving through architectural space according to an ecclesiastical temporality, enfolded in a sequence of visual-sacramental events. A key shift occurs when the plasticity of mural space breaks up into individual, anti-architectural nonspaces. In other words, into pictures. The widespread use of easel support was the culminating infrastructural abstraction of installation space. At the same time, compositional advances like Renaissance perspective served to eliminate traces of the painter's gestures from the finished work and to present a frozen moment of sheer contemplation within an isolated window frame: "Suppression of deixis in the West operates by abstracting from the physical process of painting and viewing a valorized moment when the eye contemplates the world alone, in severance from the material body of labour. . . . In the Founding Perception, the gaze of the painter arrests the flux of phenomena, contemplates the visual field from a vantage-point outside the mobility of duration, in an eternal moment of disclosed presence. . . . [Such] vision as it is presented to the viewer is that of the Gaze victorious over the Glance, vision disembodied, vision decarnalized." For Bryson, concealing both painters' and viewers' bodies from the optical event of the displayed painting means eliminating "the diachronic movement of deixis" in a "synchronic instant of viewing that will eclipse the body, and the glance, in an infinitely extended Gaze of the image as pure idea."[7] Gaze over glance means the triumph of bloodless artistry and effete, overintellectualized reception.

But it does not necessarily follow that the "image as pure idea," as nice as it sounds, would or could ever be enough material and efficient cause to produce a work in the first place, or that it explains anything at all about how art is made outside of our ideologies about it. It sounds like dreaming up your cake and eating it at the same time. Still, Michael Fried's *Absorption and Theatricality* accounts for the way art can formally deny "the existence of the beholder, which is to say the primordial convention that paintings are made to be beheld," as in Chardin's figures absorbed in activities like reading, blowing bubbles, or playing with cards and giving the effect of having no conscious awareness of being observed.[8] Paintings like Chardin's are especially notable because they seem to do the impossible, overcoming the artform's implicit theatricality, the fact that paintings are made to be seen and that they assume the beholder as part of their presentational structure. Of course, the "primordial convention that paintings are made to be beheld" must first be assumed if it is to be formally denied. That's why Fried (and his theoretical protagonist, Diderot) draws our attention to human figures, those social and theatrical animals whom we might expect to pose for us in their pictures. Whether the beholder is effectively denied is fundamentally a question of "compositional unity." So Fried's account of the beholder—his dramatic translation of Diderot's *spectateur*—assumes a baseline ontological separation between seer and configured scene.

But how did we get to the point, well before the twentieth-century "theatrical" minimalisms Fried disparages, where we assumed the work of art to be a scene we might find ourselves inside or outside of, solicited by or denied a part in (even the part of spectator)? Erwin Panofsky's reformulation of Albrecht Dürer's definition of perspective is helpful here: "We shall speak of a fully 'perspectival' view of space . . . when the entire picture has been transformed—to cite another Renaissance theoretician—into a 'window,' and when we are meant to believe we are looking through this window into space." This is, of course, a common definition more or less recycled continuously since Alberti's *De Pictura*, but more interesting is where Panofsky goes from there: "For us, perspective is quite precisely the capacity to represent a number of objects together with a part of the space around them in such a way that the conception of the material picture support is completely supplanted by the conception of a transparent plane through which we believe we are looking into an imaginary space." That is, for perspective to really work, for the Albertian pyramid to achieve the proper syntactic arrangement producing the illusion of a window onto an absorptive alternate reality, an artist must present "a systematic abstraction from the structure of psychophysiological space" by concealing certain material aspects of the work's construction from view.[9]

One can hardly overrepeat how revolutionary it was when linen was first stretched over a wooden frame. After shedding its wooden, sculptural dermis, a painting could conceal its three-dimensionality behind a picture frame added on top of the apparatus's primary edge, now set back in a rabbet. As Hegel argues in his history of the individual arts, the features of painting's new form of physicality turn over into a display of physical lack, so that the art will now "appear outwardly *as* inner, will extinguish the spatial dimensions of the material and change it out of their immediate existence into something opposite, namely a pure appearance produced by the spirit."[10] Images appearing on the picture plane are "pure" because they seem to be visual phenomena only, apparitions suspended in a virtual space rather than the physically layered forms they actually are, made from viscous substances of water and stone applied to a three-dimensional support.

Gregory Schufreider, in a brief history of the rectangular painting through Mondrian, argues that painting's conversion from sculptural to virtual-optical form works only once the rectangle acquires the status of a neutral format. As painting produces its pure *Schein* by concealing the stretcher, along with its sculptural origins, behind the rabbet frame, the rectangle—"a spectral figure that is designed to neutralize the material shape of painting through the standardization of a format that effectively becomes *pro forma* and, as such, (dis)appears as a pure formality"—clinches the transformation of the picture plane into a "formless figure."[11] And, for the modern viewer, what was once a process of mediation becomes an immediately intuited formal given. Painting's modern mode of appearance qua disappearance is not trompe l'oeil, not perpetual heir to the famous contest between Zeuxis and Parrhasius, but a subtler kind of realism in that one knows one is looking at a representation and a configured scene while forgetting that the object in question is three-dimensional and continuous with the worldly surround it was made from, bearing traces of its material elements and its constructedness.[12]

Canvas painting emerged hesitantly in fourteenth-century Italy and exploded after the quattrocento, with the punch of a cardsharp turning over a full house. When Hawthorne walked through the Uffizi Gallery in June 1858, he called it "the most perfect collection, in a chronological series, that I have seen, comprehending specimens of all the masters since painting began to be an art."[13] What he surely noticed too in its chronology was the transition in painting's material form onto canvas and into the pro forma shape of the rectangle, which lost its abstractness through interminable repetition. Had he made his way to the Brancacci Chapel he would have seen something uncollectable by the Uffizi: there, Masaccio's fifteenth-century fresco *St. Peter Healing the Sick with His Shadow* exploits daytime light streaming in from a righthand window which, viewed in relation to the painted bodies on the wall, appears to generate the shadows cast *within* the biblical scene. Victor Stoichita notes that this spatial structure, impossible to create with a framed picture, allows for the natural light of the space of exhibition—which was also the artist's space of production, within which the artist followed Cennini's famous technical axiom to draw shadow "according to the arrangement of windows which you find in these places"—to "penetrate deep into the image, giving it a double structure that belongs to two worlds at the same time: that of fiction and that of reality."[14]

Too bad Hawthorne likely did not visit Masaccio's fresco.[15] One can imagine him seeing it and thinking analogously about the romance, and back to some remarks he made eight years earlier in "The Custom-House" introduction to *The Scarlet Letter*. There Hawthorne considers writing, particularly writing the romance, in spatial terms, in the language of metaphoric territories, like the famous "neutral territory" he's homesteading. Staking out an abstract space by way of a concrete enclosure, Hawthorne articulates a writerly project through visual description, and by borrowing a scenario associated with the formative moments of visual-artistic representation. The basic techniques of shadow and shade, particularly the projection of light that can join actual and virtual planes across an otherwise abyssal boundary (as in Masaccio's painting), motivate Hawthorne's desire to "dream strange things, and make them *look* like truth."[16]

Hawthorne's preface makes familiar Romantic distinctions between the real and the imaginary, matter and spirit, the quotidian and the ideal. And it contains a theory of the imagination that unites these realms in art, making them a sibling rivalry more than clans at war. But Hawthorne is also

FIGURE 2. Masaccio, *St. Peter Healing the Sick with His Shadow*, 1426–27, fresco, 230 cm × 162 cm, Cappella Brancacci, Santa Maria del Carmine, Florence

beginning to challenge latent metaphysical assumptions about the seeing subject, which would come to a head in heated debates between the Naturalists and the Pictorialists over the ontological status of photographic pictures. Hawthorne establishes an essentially philosophical scenario, familiar to readers of Descartes, where sitting at the fireside he appears to be ensconced in a camera obscura. His description of the moonlight entering through his casement, "falling so white upon the carpet, and showing all its figures so distinctly,—making every object so minutely visible, yet so unlike a morning or noontide visibility," initially seems to express competing sixteenth-century reactions to the camera obscura, where projected objects seem either part of a realm of magic or as scientifically useful images made objective to a disciplined gaze that has left its hat and umbrella by the door and locked itself in its study, blocking out the caterwaul of the outside world. Hawthorne's description of his room, with "magic moonshine" streaming in, applies for status as a third realm, "somewhere between the real world and fairy-land, where the Actual and the Imaginary may meet, and each imbue itself with the nature of the other."[17] Where the actual and imaginary could tryst, or at least play footsie under his table, without fear of prudish disapprobation.

Hawthorne thus insists he is not writing a (realist) novel, and so the intrigue of his set piece tends more toward Giambattista della Porta's description of mystical transport than the eighteenth century's fascination with the camera obscura as perfect copyist device. It is still worth understanding the philosophical appeal of the latter: on a superficial level, the confluence of the moonlight streaming through an aperture and the "dim coal-fire" rear-projected from within Hawthorne's writing space sounds much like John Locke's epistemological analogy of the "dark room" in *An Essay Concerning Human Understanding*, where he compares the understanding to "a closet wholly shut from light, with only some little openings left, to let in external visible resemblances, or ideas of things without."[18] Richard Rorty refers to Locke's theory of the subject as "the conception of the human mind as an inner space in which both pains and clear and distinct ideas passed in review before an Inner Eye." One imagines a single, unbroken, and flat inner space in which sensations are processed as "objects of quasi-observation." Rorty attributes this basic epistemological schema to both Locke and his empiricist followers and rationalists like Descartes, arguing that even the tabula rasa is "perpetually under the gaze of the unblinking Eye of the Mind," so that the physical eye's concrete imprint is of less interest than its second-order observation: "All the knowing gets done, so to speak, by the Eye which observes the imprinted tablet, rather than by the tablet itself."[19] From one angle, Hawthorne's preface dramatizes the artist's inner eye, which, removed for a brief but intense span of time from the workaday world, provides like dim fire the "heart and sensibilities of human tenderness to the forms which fancy summons up."[20] Fancy, in this scenario, is like the play of moonlight on the objects within the chamber. It estranges object-forms but doesn't yet enliven them. Thus the customhouse becomes the primal site of "that obsessive dark room which is always behind the focus of [Hawthorne's] vision," as Harry Levin first saw it, built throughout his twelve years of Salem solitude as his "mind itself became a *camera obscura*, a dark room which sensitively registered the infiltration of light from outside" and which heightened his sensitivity to chiaroscuro effects that join mind to world through visual style.[21]

To make the connection even more salient, the writer is depicted *sitting* in his parlor as a respite from his "sea-shore walks and rambles into the country." Taking a break from physical activities "which used to give [him] such freshness and activity of thought," he retires to an internal theater where unadorned furniture bought piece by piece like "the chairs, with each its separate individuality" and "the centre-table, sustaining a work-basket" are "so spiritualized by the unusual light, that they seem to lose their actual substance, and become *things of intellect*." But one must not miss Hawthorne's insistence that "nothing is too small or too trifling to undergo this change, and acquire dignity thereby." What prevents men like Hawthorne from achieving a vision in which the real and the imaginary "imbue" one another is not failure to access a carefully curated interior scene but the sort of deadened, habitual experience attached to customhouse work, wherein "moonlight and sunshine, and the glow of firelight, were just alike in my regard; and neither of them was of one whit more avail than the twinkle of a tallow-candle." Hawthorne claims to need a "different order of composition" in which his "faculties would not have been found so pointless and inefficacious" as they had become in daily life. He rejects as "folly" any insistence on "creating the semblance of a world out of airy matter"; imaginative vision must sustain its rude contact with reality. "The page of life that was spread out before me seemed dull and commonplace," he writes, "only because I had not fathomed its deeper import."[22] Hawthorne seeks a compositional principle by which any material can be placed into the artwork without losing its worldly character, like a collage piece holding on to a trace of life as part of a prior whole.

Take Masaccio's fresco, which dramatizes a passage from the Acts of the Apostles where Peter's shadow heals the wretched and infirm as it passes over them on the street. In the painting, Peter's shadow proceeds from a light source outside of the frame (on the picture's upper right), which is prefigured by daylight streaming in from the chapel's casement to the fresco's—and not just the imaginary scene's—upper right. Having the shadow fall from right to left contradicts Cennini's technical advice in *Libro dell' Arte* to "arrange to have the light diffused when you are drawing; and have the sun fall on your left side," so as to keep one's right-handed painterly gestures from interfering with the shape of the drawn shadow.[23] But Masaccio was working with the affordances of his taskscape: Stoichita notes that the Brancacci Chapel "only had one window that opened onto the apse," so that it would have been "out of the question to *envision* another source to the left of the image."[24] Standing in front of Masaccio's fresco one sees quite starkly how ambient conditions, which can be controlled by manner of degrees depending on the artist's workspace, give causal direction to the development of a made form.

But Masaccio's contemporary, Filippo Brunelleschi, bequeathed to practitioners his own more influential optical experiment that helped inaugurate the illusionistic era of monocular linear perspective that went hand in hand with the practice of concealing the material support of canvas and stretcher through the rabbet frame. The story popularized by Giorgio Vasari in his biography of the architect serves as a convenient origin for Florentine perspective as developed by the likes of Masaccio, Paolo Uccello, and Piero della Francesca.[25] One might call his ingenious use of a mirror on the steps of the Florence Baptistery around 1413 the Renaissance's mirror stage, inaugurating an optics of illusionistic alienation that conceptualized concrete, embodied making as a distanced and framed experience. Standing on the steps of Santa Maria del Fiore, facing the Baptistery, Brunelleschi's mechanical contraption—involving a mirror set up facing a painting of that same Baptistery, with a pinhole poked through the latter (like the single monocular pinhole of the camera obscura)—had the viewer peer through the painting's hole from the backside of the picture plane and gaze into the mirror opposite the painting. Lowering the apparatus, one could compare the real edifice to the painted version without moving one's body. Interpellated as the apparatus's organ, the eye is isolated from the viewer's other eye, from his other senses, and from the rest of his body, which Schufreider says is "literally backstage, as it is upstaged by a virtual displacement: not just placed behind the scene but, as such, displaced from the space in which the painted image is taking place."[26]

By the time linear perspective was more or less perfected and painters regularly used Brunelleschi's techniques and the mature camera obscura in service to their art, the spectator if not the artist himself was theorized as what Crary calls a "free-floating inhabitant of the darkness, a marginal supplementary presence independent of the machinery of representation," for the camera obscura diminishes the body a priori "into a phantom in order to establish a space of reason." Crary considers Vermeer's *Geographer* and *Astronomer*, who like Hawthorne's romancer have their eyes "averted from the aperture that opens onto the outside" of their interior spaces, turned into paradigms of the artist's mediated, obscura-style subjectivity. In Vermeer's paintings, the exterior world is known not by direct sensory examination but through a mental survey of its "clear and distinct" representation within the room (on the celestial globe or the nautical map): the "somber isolation of these meditative scholars within their walled interiors is not in the least an obstacle to apprehending the world outside, for the division between interiorized subject and exterior world is a pre-given condition of knowledge about the latter."[27]

Vermeer reveals modernity's contract between epistemological theory and practice in the arts and technical sciences.[28] Vermeer's eminent skills in the studio—monochromatic underpainting, semitransparent color work, uniform glaze, scumbled white paint in light value areas—dissolve the hard stuff of the external world in an atmosphere of solitary absorption and contemplation. The room becomes the site of inner-worldly projection, reality reproduced on the two dimensions of canvas and map. Art takes on the evidentiary function of confirming a rationalist theory of knowledge. Or at least it seems to, thematically. Hawthorne's own dim room, where moonlight rather than sunlight streams in through a single casement and casts bewitching shadows over ordinary objects, is like a locked box busted open, or a home bunker from which the writer can identify and pursue a new form of compositional seeing, eventually leaving the camera obscura and its correlative epistemic model of interior examination behind for good. Within a year he would write a novel where the daguerreotype functions as a key narrative apparatus, and he would, in so doing, complicate the relationship between his writerly practice and the visual arts. He would challenge the stubborn cultural-aesthetic inheritance of the solipsistic, phantom visionary subject.

The House of the Seven Gables (1851) presents a story about how Matthew Maule's "evil eye" is inherited by Holgrave in his photography. According to the romance's logic, Holgrave must use his camera's gaze to rearrange old, gendered class hierarchies into a new domestic form, as a way of building proper American homes. His ancestor Maule originally challenged the upper-class privilege of "beholding" the beautiful Alice Pyncheon by asserting his own male gaze; thus he defies the aristocracy's gender codes, but he does so too aggressively. Since the novel is an antebellum sentimental romance and obeys the genre's codes, Maule's catastrophic molestation of the aristocratic lady's class pride must be massaged and redeemed by a more welcome gender arrangement. The real trial for the Pyncheon and Maule families is in the transmutation of violent male rebellion into bourgeois masculine veneration for (and preservation of) domestic womanhood.

Actually, I just summarized Shawn Michelle Smith's powerful and elegant reading of Hawthorne's romance. Her discussion merits detailed attention both because it exemplifies how well-contextualized interpretations of character gazes can produce sophisticated readings of a novel's ethics or politics and because it demonstrates some of the costs of using a theory of the gaze to seek out political or ethical propositions that could be hung on an entire novel. It is a perfect example of the way visual-cultural studies have intersected with Americanist literary history. Smith's reading serves her larger historical project: the development of a cumulative photographic archive, "a catalogue of 'essential' facial types" (portraits), that over the course of the nineteenth century changed from images of middle-class gender to representations of white middle-class racial superiority. Bourgeois portraiture, whose initial claim to capture "interiority" was compromised by its wide dissemination and promiscuous display, prompted new criminological and eugenicist archives to police the borders of representation. Smith argues that visual regulation of identity was thwarted by "subversive self-portraits" made by white women at the turn of the century, images of women donning masks and wearing photo-encrusted dresses (which deflect the masculine gaze and express new modes of visual self-reception and self-production).[29] To understand the practices of visual culture that led to these experiments, Smith historicizes Hawthorne's novel alongside contemporaneous curiosities like "The Magnetic Daguerreotypes," a story published anonymously in the *Photographic Art-Journal* of June 1852 and which plays on misgivings associated with uncanny daguerreotype portraits and demonstrates the gendered nature of those anxieties.

That story's narrator wants a portrait of himself and his fiancé Elora, appealing to a mad professor whose pictures provide the viewer a window onto the subject's life. The professor, Dunkelheim, is a figure right out of Hawthorne's own stories—a Chillingworth, Rappaccini, Aylmer, or Westervelt, all artist-scientists of murky provenance. These masculine types possess a heart susceptible to any temptation promising power over mankind and the gods, and desire only the magnification of self, its power and dominion, without fear of a parallel dilation of its metaphysical, spiritual, and ethical blind spots.[30] The successful daguerreotypist must be both scientist and artist (a chemist and a composer), and Dunkelheim appears to embody (or disembody) what Lorraine Daston and Peter Galison identify as the nineteenth century's criterion for scientific reliability, a "mechanical objectivity" that requires an ascetic attitude toward objects of inquiry.[31]

Whereas the criterion for accurate analytic image making in the eighteenth century involved the willful intervention of the scientist, Daston and Galison argue that representation came to be judged based on the removal of the scientist's judgment in the recording of an image. This form of objectivity went together with increased reliance on recording instruments, which, like the camera, promised (and overstated) the possibility of eliminating human agency altogether. Treated as analytic ideals, daguerreotypists conjure exposures by merely preparing recording equipment rather than actively drawing figures, becoming the empty subject of a passive but all-consuming gaze. Dunkelheim's copies of Elora's portrait produce an "irresistible fascination" that "withheld" his look as he "continued to gaze and gaze with an intense and burning ardor that threatened to disorder [his] intelligence."[32] His photographs are mere means for lecherous, adulterous trespass. Smith attends to the way this story generates anxiety about women's public sexual vulnerability in order to establish the desire for a protective private sphere in which one man's (the right man's) prerogative can be claimed via public display. At the story's end, Elora is still an object of the male gaze, but happily of one man's, her husband's, whose claim on her body is justified.

Hawthorne is not the author of "The Magnetic Daguerreotypes," but in Smith's historicist reading he might as well be. Hence her claim that, in *Seven Gables*, feminine interiority is newly "envisioned," by Hawthorne and his readers by extension, through the visual technologies he embeds in his narrative logic. As a story of middle-class ascendance, it "poses the sacrosanct feminine interiority that anchors a middle-class 'private' sphere" through the conduit of a "violating masculine gaze that supernaturally sees that essence."[33] Holgrave, attempting to convince Phoebe Pyncheon to open herself up to his camera, says that he would like to test the "wonderful insight in heaven's broad and simple sunshine" on a "perfectly amiable face."[34] The gendered dynamic of this desire is passed down the generations. In a seeming reversal of causal expectation, "violation produces feminine interiorities that require protection" in the domestic sphere; the mask conceals nothing it doesn't put behind it when it's donned.[35] The stakes of gender politics in the romance hinge on the right kind of male gaze—transgressive or protectionist.[36] Class conflict turns on the microbattle over feminine interiority, and photography is the battle's tactical art. At the same time, the contest over women at the heart of this generational class power struggle takes us, via the daguerreotype, into a magical realm. As singular direct-positive objects, daguerreotypes were irreproducible. Their polished, reflective metallic surfaces were dangerously mesmeric. Their ultrasensitive images, when viewed from parallax angles, switched from positive to negative in what Marcy Dinius calls an "untranslatable multisensory experience."[37] The photographer is a "descendant of wizards who control magic mirrors."[38]

Matthew Maule and Alice Pyncheon engage in a high-stakes staring contest. "Alice's womanhood," Smith claims, even "her very soul, is penetrated by Maule's masculine mesmeric forces," and this ocular-phallic violation produces the aristocratic interiority it penetrates.[39] "Her spirit passed from beneath her own control, and bowed itself to Maule"; her free will is bound, gagged, and slipped into the wizard's back pocket. She is saved only if she accepts her reduction to a mannequin on the basic model of nineteenth-century middle-class femininity—humble, submissive, controllable, meek and mild—but since there is no place for *this* Alice in the world of the aristocracy, in her class and in her time, she wastes away. Generations later in the narrative present, Holgrave's "rare and high quality of reverence for another's individuality"[40] prevents him from wielding Matthew's brand of power over women: he "chooses to guard" Phoebe's feminine spirit-essence rather than overpower and possess it.[41]

And the choice supposedly ensures Holgrave's superiority over both the ambitious aristocratic patriarch and the working-class journeyman. He becomes a true middle-class bloke, saving Phoebe from her family's decay. Phoebe's humility—letting her eyes drop, she bows to Holgrave's gaze and says, "You know I love you"—compensates for the historic sin of Alice's haughty counterlook, the symptom of her class's diminishing structure of gendered feeling. Alice's look is described as an "admiring glance." But that conceals what Maule, like the "devil himself . . . so subtile in his perception," sees in it, a glance that unreflectively reduces him to a brute, physical, spiritless, working-class body.[42] Holgrave redeems his legacy by protecting and nourishing what Maule rent asunder. His phallic power over Phoebe is not hard or rough but soft and gentle. Alice's original sin, wrongfully asserting her class privilege by claiming an objectifying countergaze over the male body, is absolved in the creation of the true bourgeois family. On Smith's reading, then, the gender and class economy of the romance turns on what sort of gaze is proper to—and what sort of subject requires protection within—the domestic scene.[43]

I would not describe Smith's reading in such detail if it wasn't so smart. But associating the representation of daguerreotypy inside the story with the role of middle-class domesticity outside of it—the small-scale production and collection of family portraits that find their place in the album rather than the marketplace—is a bit like trapping Hawthorne's literary practice inside the epistemic model of the camera obscura his "Custom-House" introduction was wriggling its way out of. The preface to *Seven Gables* makes its own photographic analogy: the romancer, Hawthorne writes, "may so manage his atmospherical medium as to bring out or mellow the lights and deepen and enrich the shadows of the picture." But the "Author" also warns against readings that expose "the Romance to an inflexible and exceedingly dangerous species of criticism, by bringing [the author's] fancy-pictures almost into positive contact with the realities of the moment."[44] Alan Trachtenberg distinguishes "positive contact," a printing technique associated with new nondaguerreotypic paper photography like the calotype, from "another mode of fidelity to 'Present,' to 'realities of the moment'—that is, the mode of 'Romance,' which defines itself not by an absolute difference from 'Novel,' not by a rejection of mimesis but by the positing of another kind of mimesis, atmospheric, shadowed, faithful to that which flits away: a kind of mimesis that the narrative will apprehend with the help of its ambiguous and problematic daguerreotypes."[45] Reading a story and embarking on criticism as a form of contact printing means closing the gap between production and reception, attempting a perfect critical translation that dissolves the specific techne that encoded the work in the first place.[46] Like snapping a rabbet frame onto the work, pinning its meaning to its diegesis. But that's not the only lesson photography offers readers. Since daguerreotype images are built from silver surface granules, it takes, as Trachtenberg puts it, "a specific triangulation of viewer, image, and light" for it "to seem legible—or, as they said at the time, to 'come to life.'"[47] Viewing the picture demands a comportment that reenacts the photographer's angle-seeking view of the subject. The first step in seeing what's right in front of you is turning the plate so you can see what its maker saw first.

There are five portraits presented in the romance: two photographs of the Judge, one of Uncle Venner, a miniature painting of Clifford Pyncheon, and the keystone portrait of the Colonel that hangs on the wall like a monument to patriarchal authority. If Holgrave has special insight into the signs they contain, it is not necessarily (or solely) because of his class position and aspirations but also because he embodies the techne that produced them. He provides a model for reading and visual awareness that is not irreducibly possessive, that does not seize and reify what is directly in front of the eyes but opens first impressions onto their contextual surrounds through the glance. On the one hand, as Smith argues, Holgrave's way of looking can be associated with the rising middle-class protective male lover. But daguerrean seeing frames and unframes, proceeding via techniques of temporal sequencing that resist full-on recruitment as an allegorical model for either the bourgeois domestic romance or its formal-aesthetic opponents. With Holgrave, Hawthorne presents a new stage, ushered in by photography, in what Aaron Kunin calls gothic "depicture"—depicting and de-picturing—or the way the gothic genre reveals the animacy of the visual portrait behind or outside of its frame.[48]

Harriet Beecher Stowe calls *Seven Gables* "a succession of Rembrandt pictures, done in words instead of oils."[49] Successive "depicture" is fashioned not simply between the five portraits already mentioned, but in the life of each that refuses to be still, in the multiplication of images that flit by in the minds of Clifford and Hepzibah, and in the phantasmagoric holography Maule's Well projects. The Colonel's portrait virtually extends his expiration date. Holgrave sees the Colonel walking dead, in the zombie form of Jaffrey's likeness. But if depicture's form is occult, its content need not be. Clifford, whose peculiar way of seeing is mostly elided from accounts of the romance's logic that focus on the semiotic square Maule-Alice-Holgrave-Phoebe, is like a mannequin on which Hawthorne tries competing visual-subjective modes of being. His eye feeds images to his chaotic and broken mind, which struggles to gather sensual particulars into concepts. He is depicted both as a prismatic receptacle for unconceptualized sensations and as the ephemeral, ghostlike flicker on a daguerreotype's mirrored surface: "[He] faded away out of his place; or, in other words, his mind and consciousness took their departure, leaving his wasted, gray, and melancholy figure—a substantial emptiness, a material ghost—to occupy his seat at table. Again, after a blank moment, there would be a flickering taper-gleam in his eyeballs. It betokened that his spiritual part had returned, and was doing its best to kindle the house-hold fire, and light up intellectual lamps in the dark and ruinous mansion, where it was doomed to be a forlorn inhabitant."[50] Clifford's "dark and ruinous mansion" is both the gothic family home and the dark blankness of his interior life given over to an unfixed retinal flux, the empty support for a pure present deconstructed at every moment in the "flickering taper-gleam" of unprocessed sensations. His is a corporeal but not a unified lived body—described hauntologically as a "material ghost"—and his visual experience is conceived in terms disanalogous to a sense of touch. His visual field is as emptied of spatial depth as his "wasted, gray, and melancholy figure." It is as if Clifford has regressed to a reductio ad absurdum of Emerson's transparent eyeball, his mind a filmstrip pieced together by a child playing with scissors and tape.

Characters in the novel, in their concern for and horror at Clifford's nightmarish condition, want to experience reality from a distance, as a picture understood as something there before them, *Gegenständlich*, about which they are informed and for which they are adequately prepared. Those desires may be defensive reactions or epistemic foils to Clifford's ecstatic, absorptive, suicidal pull into the scene of a parade as viewed through the house's arched window(frame): "With a shivering repugnance at the idea of personal contact with the world, a powerful impulse still seized on Clifford, whenever the rush and roar of the human tide grew strongly audible to him . . . [he] would hardly be restrained from plunging into the surging stream of human sympathies." But, true to gothic style, pictures never stay safely within their frames. Several critics have read *Seven Gables* as a recapitulation or reformulation of G. E. Lessing's famous literary-visual distinction. Susan Williams, who pays careful attention to the novel's unframings, argues that Hawthorne "asserts the superiority of literature [over the visual arts] in part to protect it from the destabilizing proliferation of images that the market encourages," from the mise en abyme that characterizes Clifford's fragmented consciousness and Hepzibah's experience in her store as she views a "panorama, representing the great thoroughfare of a city, all astir with customers," a view that overwhelms her because the town's shops contain mirrors that endlessly expand commodity displays.[51] But if Hawthorne deregulates the borders between genres and forms, he does not glorify Clifford's inability to conceptualize and make distinctions. More precisely, he dissolves a long-standing (Puritanical) fear of imagery by reinstilling a sense of the picture's dynamism, opening the beholder's optical field to the practitioner's visual world.

Lessing's *Laocoön* was modern art criticism's pivotal challenge to the long-standing "Sister Arts" theory—commonly traced back to Horace's *ut pictura poesis*—that held an expressive equivalence between painting and literature. Lessing argues that while painting is instantaneously apprehended, in poetry meaning develops over time: "It remains true that succession of time is the province of the poet just as space is that of the painter."[52] To the extent that painting suggests action in time, it does so by intimating a fruitful moment in the middle of an implied arc of movement; time itself cannot be depicted.[53] The most common Romantic critiques of Lessing stress mental process, rather than the object of perception, as the locus of the temporal-spatial interchange. If the much-vaunted simultaneity of the painting or sculpture exists in the material artifact but not in its perception, then the latter is a matter of temporal processing, much like reading, with the difference that the ordering of perceptual sequence is not predetermined by the object itself. The path of this critique leads to a concept of inner time-consciousness, which aims to account for the subject's experience of change within immediate acts of perception. As a visual experience unfolds for us (or any perceptual experience for that matter), how do we retain and anticipate prior and posterior moments of the *now* while still staying within the immediacy of that *now*?[54] Edmund Husserl's explanation of how we unify an object as we walk around it is in principle no different than the way we unify a sculpture or a painting: the latter is in reality three-dimensional and plastic even if the material apparatus is concealed by a picture frame. And even if it weren't, the physiological limits of the human eye, which require us to foveate and refocus distinct phenomena that we don't have to turn our heads or move or bodies to see, require the retina to be capable of retention and the saccadic jerks of the eye primed to anticipate the formal conjunction or disjunction of spatial phenomena.[55]

Lessing's distinction between bodies and actions is a theoretical oversimplification even he is aware of as he makes it. After all, the *Augenblick* as portal to immediate apprehension has proven in modern painting to be a site of great experimentation, deconstruction, and critique.[56] It helps to read Lessing from the present because we know how obsessed visual artists became with the possibility (and inevitability) of moving images, seriality, sequence, and the epistemic limits entailed by static pictures. The assumption that the media specificity of all visual arts produces views of nature and man sub specie aeternitatis depends on another postulate: that encountering the art object bounds us, readers and viewers hunting for interpretive meaning, inside the outline of marble or frame and closes us off from every other attempt to render a similar representation.

Samuel Taylor Coleridge's discussion of *Paradise Lost* and "poetic painting" mediates Lessing and Hawthorne. Lessing would agree with the proscription that "the Poet should paint to the imagination, not to the fancy," but Coleridge continues: "Master-pieces of the former mode of poetic painting abound in the writings of Milton," whose work "is creation rather than painting, or if painting, yet such, and with such co-presence of the whole picture flash'd at once upon the eye, as the sun paints in a camera obscura." The camera is a consummate form of poetic imagination because of its power to capture the whole picture in a flash. Yet he knows the flash of insight demands interpretation and articulation, so he keeps going: "The poet must likewise understand and command what Bacon calls the *vestigia communia* of the senses, the latency of all in each, and more especially as a magical *penna duplex,* the excitement of vision by sound and the exponents of sound. Thus, [certain passages in Milton] may be almost said to reverse the fable in the tradition of the head of Memnon, in the Egyptian statue. Such may be deservedly entitled the creative words in the world of imagination." Coleridge seesaws throughout these passages. See: the camera obscura is unfortunately limited to and by the visual sense. Saw: visuality is not the problem, but rather a rigid and mechanistic way of seeing, describing, and fixing images programmed by the apparatus itself. One is inside the camera obscura, blocked on all sides by its walls, and thus its image is "fixed" not by a creative, synthesizing, mindful eye but through the camera's single, unmoving pinhole. Whereas the "dignity of poetic Imagination" comes from its "fusing power, that fixing unfixes & while it melts & bedims the Image, still leaves in the Soul its living meaning."[57]

Paradise Lost serves as a watershed in various histories of picture writing because of its revision of long-standing scholastic assumptions about the image's "likeness," which is ultimately a collection of its predicates and thus more of an intellectual model, definition, form, or schema than a sensual picture. W. J. T. Mitchell points out that Milton's images, like Adam and Eve presented as *imago dei* in the poem's fourth book, deliberately confuse "the visual, pictorial sense of the image with an invisible, spiritual, and verbal understanding of it," producing "radiance rather than reflection" by combining sensual appearances with undescribable predicates. Rather than joining one side of the tug of war between inner and outer images, of iconoclasm or iconophilia, Milton treated these relations—embodied in the masculine Adam whose "inner, spiritual image" accords with verbal and intellectual being, and the feminine Eve whose silent, "narcissistic idolatry" is really humanity's attraction to the divine image—as prolific contraries. For Milton poetry is "the scene of a struggle between iconoclastic distrust of the outward image and iconophilic fascination with its power, a struggle which manifests itself in his practice of proliferating visual images in order to prevent readers from focusing on any particular picture or scene."[58] Milton distrusts the static tableau and pinpoint perspective for theological reasons, and Hawthorne inherits some of them, including a wariness of man trying to see like God, falling prey to the very illusionism of disembodied neutrality he seeks to perfect through an artifice that can never really transcend finite particulars and contingencies.[59] Mitchell's astonishing insight into Milton's iconographical dialectic primes us to see his struggle over the image playing out in Hawthorne's romance, now salted and peppered with a few more dashes of historical anxiety since the daguerreotype is a reality instead of a vaguely nascent possibility.

Hawthorne, whose fictions are populated by Miltonic Satans, Adams, and Eves, was stuck on the necessity of "proliferating visual images" at a time when images were literally (or materially) proliferating in the marketplace.[60] His intuitions toward contrary iconoclastic and iconophilic energies exploding in the post-Daguerre world were hardly less complex than Milton's. Fiction enabled Hawthorne to create animated portraits, fiddling with the aesthetic knobs and turning the volume up on the word's role in giving indexical images their meaning and autonomy back—as pictures with encoded narrative dimensions rather than just bare, unembellished records of the real. When Henry James writes that the characters in *Seven Gables* "are all figures rather than characters—they are all pictures rather than persons," he recognizes Hawthorne's method as a romance writer grappling with the form's relation to visual art and technology even as he means to criticize his countryman's limitations as a novelist.[61] To put it more charitably than James, Hawthorne's pictures of people are like people *because* people conceal time-worn depths through surface presentation. They turn themselves into fixed, still images. Just like the case of the Colonel's portrait, whose frame and wall position conceal not only the event of its making but also the land deed Jaffrey has been hunting for and tormenting the innocent Clifford about, the written parchment that reveals a sordid family history and the original crime of displacement perpetrated by the Pyncheons against the Maules. Holgrave knows that his daguerreotypes, as much indexical truth as they contain, need linguistic supplement to frondesce into story. The fixed image never stands alone, full of meaning, because the image doesn't speak for itself. It just *is*, and it points back to a material arrangement that just *was*, and that's the source of both its allure and its insufficiency for meaning. A photograph is the product of a process that can be reconstructed or reverse engineered, but only through narrative.

So Holgrave's photographs play a necessary role in discovering the true story that backs or supports Hawthorne's presentation of the narrative present. The daguerreotypist is the author's silent partner, countering whatever conventional literary tendencies Phoebe brings with her into the romance. When Jaffrey's corpse is finally discovered, Phoebe is horrified that Holgrave has not called witnesses to the scene. But the photographer "did not feel the horror, which was proper to Phoebe's sweet and order-loving character, at thus finding herself at issue with society, and brought in contact with an event that transcended ordinary rules." Instead, he revels in "his present position," his "exclusive knowledge of Judge Pyncheon's mysterious death," in the secret that would be captured by his camera as "within the circle of a spell," in the spot of space and time where the exposure is made and that will inevitably be elided in the future story of the Judge told by a public that cannot reconstruct that "exclusive knowledge." Holgrave's perverse enjoyment at the scene cancels the heavy, gazing sobriety of his ancestor. As if gathering "a flower of strange beauty, growing in a desolate spot, and blossoming in the wind," his camera eye caresses the surface of his subject, the outermost external feature of the *thanatopsis* that horrifies Phoebe.[62] Photography, after all, is necrophilic, the mediated descendant of the Roman wax death mask that indexed the face of the deceased through the concavity of touch.[63] Maybe not to Holgrave, though, for whom portrait photography reaches into the crypts of human personalities only to pull out a "secret" already written on the "merest surface," of the "wonderful insight in heaven's broad and simple sunshine."[64]

Sometimes it is hard to get a grip on the tone of Holgrave's cheery proclamation, especially as part of a scene so apparently rife with feelings of desecration. And as readers we often side with Phoebe's disturbed interest in the man. It is hard too to know for sure whether we should take Holgrave as a cruel, coldly detached observer or one whose desire shapes his visual field every time he looks at a Pyncheon. This contradiction exists intractably on the level of narrative discourse. As the narrator notes, "In the artist's deep, thoughtful, all-observant eyes, there was now-and-then an expression, not sinister, but questionable; as if he had some other interest in the scene than a stranger, a youthful and unconnected adventurer might be supposed to have." But take this line that follows two chapters later: "He was too calm and cool an observer. Phoebe felt his eye often; his heart, seldom or never."[65] Holgrave is both too insensitive and too interested. Until its eighteenth-chapter tour de force, the narrator's discourse turns around on this contradiction, refusing resolution.

Quick comparisons are thematic realizations in seed form. Hawthorne's narrative "secret," which all his works contain in one way or another, is not an allegorical concept but a surface reflection of light lost by the human eye's limitations. Holgrave's camera catches a grimace on Jaffrey's visage that he had kept hidden, as if he had all this time been carefully posing for a picture to be captioned, "Judge: Fair and Balanced." In death, the photograph reveals all the rest, precisely because the mystery of the human heart has been extinguished. The corpse's "wide open eyes" penetrate because of their emptiness, because the corpse is all surface.[66] It sits as if posing for another exposure. What mystery is revealed? Simply that his grimace was there, a truth uncovered by photography's indexical tether to the real. But looking at a single image is never enough to reveal a lie. One must compare an exposure, the exposure of a soul, to the social and imaginary theater that conceals the true but hidden detail. The eye must submit to its supplementation and acknowledge its fleshiness, considering the snapshot not on its own but as part of a context of unaided glances, of the way things seemed to be. The photograph is the glance's prosthetic, doing in visual terms what the writer can do with descriptive language. It does not get inside the subject, exactly, and Hawthorne strives to respect the limits of other minds, keeping his characters' emotional states in qualified free indirect boundaries. But photography augments vision by amplifying the glance's probing qualities, strengthening its ability to fix revealing images out of durational flux. It magnetizes relations that the physical eye strains to hold on to as time passes. Hawthorne ties the metaphorical relation between human eye and camera shutter into an ethical-aesthetic knot: it is only in opening the camera eye that an exposure can be made, but the camera's set condition is closed and unseeing. The camera must ignore the lion's share of the world as the price for capturing a momentary surface in intense detail.

Once again, in the "Governor Pyncheon" chapter, Hawthorne takes us back to the artist's moonlit room as night falls on the death scene. But here he shows more critical acumen. As we enter the night of the world and the Judge is bathed in "infinite, inscrutable blackness," reality dissolves into near-formlessness where even shadows lose "distinctness of outline."[67] Dinius calls it a moment of overexposure: "At the literal level of the chapter, the Judge is no longer visible because of too little light rather than too much, but at the figurative level, it is the narrator's gaze—his 'too long and exclusive contemplation of that figure in the chair'—that causes his overexposure."[68] In the narrator's initial conceit the dead man has simply lost track of time, but really the narrator has lingered too long on the face. Made into a daguerreotypist like Holgrave, he momentarily forgets his role in the fiction: to keep things moving. Narrative progress comes to a standstill when he turns his playful glance into a cruel, sadistic gaze, coming awfully close to collapsing all ethical differences between the daguerreotypist and his ancestors. And just as realism in photography is hard won, the result of favorable lighting conditions, proper lenses, and good angles, so does the romance teeter on the edge of blurring fact and fiction into a dark, illegible sludge. In both cases we find evidence that, as Merleau-Ponty says, "for each object, as for each picture in an art gallery, there is an optimum distance from which it requires to be seen, a direction viewed from which it vouchsafes most of itself."[69] Everywhere we glance the world exceeds our presence even as it gives us hints about how we might see it better. We must continually tune our tools in the face of change. Hawthorne knows that the eye, the camera, and the pen must be tuned differently, supplemented by different material and conceptual toolkits.

If there are normative contradictions running throughout the novel, vacillating rapprochement and reproaches between written and visual reproduction, it is likely because Hawthorne has one foot in a residual model of subjectivity and one foot somewhere else, hanging like Buridan's ass between notions of the self as guarded private interior and as a disjointed collection of images or expressive surfaces. Like a picture developing out of darkness, spirit starts to reassert itself in Holgrave's dark chamber in tentative, half-formed shapes. But the visual tensions and competing perceptual epistemologies that run throughout most of the novel's discourse do not ever disappear from our sight. We note the contradictions along the way as features that might emerge beyond the end of this story. Hawthorne's concern throughout the novel about privacy and voyeurism—and the narrator's incessant questioning of Holgrave's motives as a beholder—is that a penetrating eye may heighten one particular detail of human life over all the rest, mutilating the inner life. In Michelle Kohler's account, as the narrator introduces Hepzibah, waiting for her to come out of her locked chamber (while at her toilet, putting on her public face) and over the "threshold" of the story, Hawthorne establishes a narrative vision "simultaneously propelled and constrained by the narrator's visual position: the narrator describes the physical conditions that limit his visual access to Hepzibah while for the most part retaining the transparency of the literary conventions that grant him access to the interior of the house."[70] Hepzibah is a descendant of the eighteenth-century stock prude, except that Hawthorne's narrator respects her dissimulation instead of cruelly conniving to crack it. Narrative decorum preserves the idea of deep interior privacy while turning the locked chamber inside out through a Holgravean camera eye, spreading the novel's psychological insights along exterior surfaces—of pictures, faces, and architectural cladding—which are not always directly available but flicker throughout the mise-en-scène.

And so Hawthorne's class drama describes and deconstructs the way a mode of vision, as Edward Casey claims for gazing more generally, "seeks to be the witness of the way things are as measured by how they were at some prior point," seeks the continual reenactment of a trauma, reinforcing the rules of the game rather than probing the way things could or should be, pinning events and people down as if "sticking a pin through a butterfly—thus at once depriving it of life, and causing it to stiffen in an ungainly and unnatural attitude."[71] Taxidermy, Hawthorne's metaphor for literary moralism and didactic directness, also stands for a critical gaze that fails to connect the partial object it fixes with the rest of its connecting surfaces, with the rest of the story: here, the logic of the explicitly conventionalized ending, the way portraits both obscure and reveal histories, the photographic process's ambivalent products. Hawthorne demands of us an interpretational suppleness to match the glance, a vision more attuned to what is *not* directly before one's eyes, what withdraws from immediate presence. Such are the shadows and reflections that drift through the gothic environment of a decaying mansion, the traces and lineaments on a picture or on the face of an object, all of which are not present as whole but point to something else not directly seen, a hidden source of light that enriches the visible. The mode of vision attuned to those horizons is not fixed staring but glancing, which delights in the visual ambiguities Hawthorne prizes. Hawthorne anticipates a critic still to come, one beyond my modest efforts, who would shade in so many more of the romance's half-tones that "Maule's Well" will appear not as the narrative exception but its compositional rule.

The drama of Holgrave and Phoebe is not only a bourgeois version of the old battle of aristocratic female and underclass male gazes. If Frank Kermode is right to claim that the novel registers "a transition from one structure of society, and one system of belief and knowledge, to another," those epistemes do not reduce to face-to-face gazing contests.[72] They include the intertwined histories of the crafts of painting, photography, writing, and storytelling, each more than symptoms or correlations of a sociopolitical habitus. *The House of the Seven Gables* occasions a collision of forms drawn from each art as well as from social life more broadly. Its jarring visual encounters pry Hawthorne's imaginative practice from the stultifying form of the camera obscura's black box, opening his and his readers' eyes in preparation for an ars poetica still to come.

I have tried to show, suggestively at least, that *The House of the Seven Gables* was Hawthorne's tentative but significant step beyond a theory of aesthetic imagination married to the epistemic model of the camera obscura. That model was proving inert to a writer who saw equally exciting and disturbing formal possibilities in realist technologies that, attuned to ever-shifting surface phenomena uncaptured by the human sensorium, provided counterpressure to the romance's generic interest in interiors and soul-making expressions. Hawthorne found much in that dialectic to occupy his craft. But at the time, questions about the status of writing amid a newly crowded media landscape sounded and surrounded like white noise. Was writing fiction a craft like other arts, especially the visual? The increasing intermediality of Hawthorne's narratives compels the question and desires an answer.

In *Talking Shop*, Peter Betjemann analyzes the literary and print discourse on artisanship in the nineteenth century as "a Gordian knot which, in its intricacy, made text the most visible artisanal medium in Anglo-American culture and reconstructed the cultural meaning of workmanship." He argues that Benvenuto Cellini's nineteenth-century canonization—generated by a cottage industry made up of fiction writers, translators, and art critics—created "an account of artisanal sensibility that cohered around the example of his range and charisma." The contradictions in Cellini's autobiography (printed for the first time in English in 1771), particularly the paucity of references to the craftsman's concrete labors in a narrative largely constructed around heroic feats, society anecdotes, and the winning of commissions, placed the period's cult of Renaissance craft "on the dystopian trajectory of history summarized by Karl Marx as the 'division and sub-division of labor,'" with the practical work concealed behind numerous social abstractions. Most importantly for literary studies, however, is the more modest claim that—as in Cellini's autobiography—craft became a privileged site for literature as it tested its own limits as "both icon of a restored relation with the body and a misleading, dodgy narrative" about its own "potential to incarnate, to vitalize." Hawthorne, who made a number of references in his fiction and in his journals to Cellini, is said by Betjemann to desire "to ground craft and its texts in durability, singularity, and centripetal relations with objects even as he recognizes the forces . . . that draw craft toward mutability and embed its narrative interest in the sense of possibility it offers."[73]

Betjemann writes belatedly, after much commentary on Hawthorne's romances in the context of nineteenth-century modes of production and consumption.[74] On *The House of the Seven Gables* specifically, Michael Gilmore and Walter Benn Michaels exemplify two sides of this dialogue: Gilmore, in *American Romanticism and the Marketplace*, argues that the novel directly critiques an economic system wherein "appearance matters more than substance," while Michaels, in *The Gold Standard and the Logic of Naturalism*, holds that Hawthorne's focus on intangible property and ghostly imagery is a strategy that allows the author to escape from contemporary modes of capitalist appropriation and exchange.[75] But instead of positioning craft as either a material haven from capitalistic fantasy or an idealistic activity separate from capitalistic materialism, Betjemann chooses to show how, for Hawthorne, craft is not a refuge but a problem to be worked out. His reading of the scarlet letter in "The Custom-House" is a case in point: "Craft's mandate reverses and reverses again depending on whether it is understood from the perspective of the repressive structures of history and the 'unimaginative sagacity' of the trades (in which case artisanship's higher potential lies in subjectivity, contingency, and the inimitable aspect of handmade objects) or from the perspective of nineteenth-century trade and manufacture (in which case artisanship signifies objectivity, durability, completion, and the longevity accorded to a prior material culture)." And yet craft's promise to incarnate something either beautifully subjective or solidly objective often disappoints inside the story world of Hawthorne's fictions. Those fictions use craft's signifiers less as a "critique of manual labor's limitations than as a critique of the false promises about craft's incarnating potential peddled in written, read, and oral forms," which tend to sneak in claims linking the craftsman's product to incarnations of the godlike genius's intellectual intuition.[76] Imagine a dog trying to get through a narrow door with a stick in its mouth—that is the technician trying to get something transcendently beautiful out of his trade's humble tools. Craft, for Hawthorne, both solicits and resists problematic Romantic shibboleths.

So several of Hawthorne's stories allegorize the battle between artisanal craft and abstract labor. Betjemann begins, for instance, with "Rappaccini's Daughter" (1844)—and its contest between the evil scientist and his rival Baglioni, who comes bearing the story's tragic antidote in a vial "wrought by the hands of the renowned Benvenuto Cellini"—while also pointing to less celebrated tales like "Drowne's Wooden Image" (1844) and "The Artist of the Beautiful" (1844). But no work is more invested in the nuances of craft and its relation to the visual than *The Marble Faun* (1860). By focusing on a community of artists, it directly considers an ethos of material production as the domain of imaginative, aestheticized vision. The novel's American personae are somewhat more insulated from the economies of Hawthorne's other stories; they are artists rather than merchants, of course, but they are also expatriates in Rome. One might speculate that his characters' privileged class positions allowed the author to focus on visual phenomena in the practice of art making, evading the question of craft's standing in an individualistic and increasingly consumerist market society.

In the 1860 romance, Hawthorne conceives visual art's material production as the result of a felix culpa, as both symptom and glory of our condition as imperfect, embodied seers. From the beginning, Hawthorne promises the reader that his Rome, an arena constructed by and for artists, will be built descriptively through glances: "We glance hastily at these things—at this bright sky, and those blue, distant mountains, and at the ruins, Etruscan, Roman, Christian, venerable with a threefold antiquity, and at the company of world-famous statues in the saloon—in the hope of putting the reader into that state of feeling which is experienced oftenest at Rome." Even while promising a return to experiences of the utmost "weight and density," the narrator describes the narrative to come as woven through with "some airy and unsubstantial threads, intermixed with others, twisted out of the commonest stuff of human existence," ultimately built out of perceptions "not widely different from the texture of all our lives."[77] In its paradoxical conflation of the weightiest with the airiest, of the antique beauties of Rome with the everyday, the glance forges its way as the connective tissue grafting ordinary lifeworlds to the expert practice of fine artists. What appears to be superficial and evanescent elsewhere, experience's "airy and unsubstantial threads," is foundational to experience in Rome, where one cannot fail to be touched and influenced by art.[78]

For that matter, in Hawthorne's conception, nineteenth-century Rome is the place where one cannot avoid Romantic aesthetic commonplaces. And the novel's true Rousseauean Romantic is the narrator, posing as an art critic always looking for the expressions of genius behind mere craftwork, for whom "there is an effluence of divinity in the first sketch . . . the pure light of inspiration, which the subsequent toil of the artist serves to bring out in stronger luster, indeed, but likewise adulterates it with what belongs to an inferior mood." If we know Hawthorne at all we know his narrator is a pose; taken as a whole, the novel shows us that those inferior moods, recorded in the artwork's drift on its way through material craft, are the very substance of any art we might call human. Still, the narrator piles up Romantic distinctions to the point of parody: in addition to the expressive versus the technical, we find repeated schematic binaries like innocence versus experience, animal versus human, original versus copy, the naive versus the sentimental. At first, the Acadian Donatello expresses himself as spontaneously as Keats's nightingale, "by the natural language of gesture, the instinctive movement of his agile frame, and the unconscious play of his features" in a living art unsevered from the childish body. No wonder the artist's studio is too dark and gloomy for him. When we first find ourselves there, we are pulled as if back into Hawthorne's moonlit parlor with its single pinhole: "The windows were closed with shutters, or deeply curtained, except one, which was partly open to a sunless portion of the sky, admitting only from high upward that partial light which, with its strongly marked contrast of shadow, is the first requisite towards seeing objects pictorially." But now Hawthorne clutters the space, filling it with "glimpses, sketches, and half-developed hints of beings and objects. . . . Pencil-drawings were pinned against the wall or scattered on the tables. Unframed canvases turned their backs on the spectator." The dark room is now a taskscape, the "outward type of a poet's haunted imagination," a model for aesthetic form as a dark material process rather than an immediate projection of the illuminating imagination.[79]

Through the competing visual registers of the novel's artists, their various preferences of color, form, and plasticity, Hawthorne develops a narrative of a (literal) fall, an ambiguous cliffside murder, whose subtext and ultimate subject is art making. Hawthorne's chatty artists spend as much time theorizing art as they do making it. Kenyon, the sculptor, privileges physical and moral "standstill," states of repose either prior or posterior to all intervals of change. Sculpting is negation, an act of removing transition until there is none: "Flitting moments, imminent emergencies, imperceptible intervals between two breaths, ought not to be incrusted with the eternal repose of marble." Miriam, a painter, pokes at the lack of visionary freedom in sculpture's "fossilizing process": "In painting there is no similar objection to the representation of brief snatches of time; perhaps because a story can be so much more fully told in picture, and buttressed about with circumstances that give it an epoch."[80] Sculpture presents "substantial fact, and may be tested by absolute touch and measurement," Miriam earlier admits, whereas in pictorial arts resemblance is always "half allusive and imaginary." Stone bears the "massiveness" of the past, Roman or geological; drawn line and mixed color offer less and more, fancifully tapping into experience's more fragile qualities, flowing ephemerally in the "dreamy character of the present."[81]

Each character's perceptiveness is constrained by their art's mediatic disadvantages. Jonathan Auerbach notices that the narrative's climax, Miriam's and Donatello's murder of the haunting body of the model, "imitates and illuminates other acts of artistic creation in the novel, such as Kenyon's execution of Cleopatra ('with a word') and Hilda's execution of the Old Masters, who continue totally to 'enslave' the virgin Puritan precisely because her copies are too exact duplicates of the originals."[82] Each character, in their participation in the homicide, freezes into frieze figures, like Stations of the Cross on the way to a smashing success: Miriam commissions it, Donatello gets his hands dirty, Hilda gets a sneak peek. If the model is a rough-hewn copy of the aesthetic idea, the artist's product is also an imperfect copy of the model: in the novel, the actual model dwells obscurely in the dark zone between conception and execution, a half-formed grotesque figure "on the doubtful limit of obscurity."[83] He is the drift of art techne personified, the frightening between-state where both plan and product recede from view.

In a number of scenes that depict art making, iterative transformations from model to plastic product are conveyed visually, as series of glances between world, model, and aesthetic object, just like when Hawthorne's cast looks back and forth, in the opening scene, between their friend Donatello and the Faun of Praxiteles.[84] But thinking back to *Seven Gables*, one is impressed by an ontological difference between the status of the model in photography and the representational (rather than indexical) arts: the model's literal presence dissolves in painting or sculpture in a way it cannot in a photograph. The model's presence is not even necessary in a painting, though this became more obvious in the photographic age. Which leads Hawthorne to smuggle the logic of photography into the romance's background, turning it into a causal absence, the engine for an aesthetic inquest rigged out in moralistic regalia.

Miriam's crime, as Kenyon says in Hawthorne's postscript, "'lay merely in a glance.'" But we are already aware that glances can tip the virtual into the real, as in Miriam's sketch of Salome receiving John the Baptist's severed head, which casts a "miraculous glance" that awakens the former's "whole womanhood . . . to love and endless remorse." A single glance communicates Miriam's murderous wish to Donatello. The glance's supreme power is suggestiveness, its ability to convey allusive and otherwise suppressed feeling, which is also the artist's lever for capturing the real detail, stain, or tic around which the imagined work falls into place. But vision's enabling condition is also a symptom of finitude, as Hilda finally realizes at the Basilica of St. Peters, where her dream of overwhelming vastness and transcendence gives way to an anamorphic series of architectural remnants: "You see an aisle, or a transept; you see the nave, or the tribune; but on account of its ponderous piers and other obstructions, it is only by this fragmentary process that you get an idea of the Cathedral."[85]

This is not Hilda's first experience of St. Peter's. Earlier in the novel, with Kenyon, she sees its "grandeur" from such a distance that "the entire outline of the world's cathedral . . . is taken in at once." From a fortunate vantage, where the imagination lends its assistance to "the weakness of human sense," one's aesthetic sensibility becomes receptive rather than productive, like Reason in Kant's account of the sublime (giving us intimations of our infinitude). But as the prospective vision returns to narrative form, as Hilda and Kenyon "let their glances fall into the piazza at their feet," looking down and away from the perfectly framed basilica, they find Miriam and her model. The former in turn looks down, "as if she were counting those little, square, uncomfortable paving stones that make it a penitential pilgrimage to walk in Rome."[86] Miriam appears to be counting the historically weighty visual cues of an Italian painting in linear perspective—how many there are, their visual pyramids constructed through an urban piazza, its paving stones fortuitous steps tracing its orthogonals—taking the measure of the cold geometrical form Kenyon calls the prison of her thought. As if to say: the artist must descend into the prison house of historical form, must trade the fortuitous gaze of the complete picture for the dissatisfied glance of form in process in order to even think about challenging the power of compositional convention.

Hilda's preparation for her own anti-transcendent vision is a run of Coleridgean dejection in the "long galleries": "Heretofore, her sympathy went deeply into a picture, yet seemed to leave a depth which it was inadequate to sound; now, on the contrary, her perceptive faculty penetrated the canvas like a steel probe, and found but a crust of paint over emptiness." Taken literally, the emptiness Hilda finds is the material ground of painting, its absent surface. The return of the artwork's ground as void or emptiness is a dramatic reinstatement of what Hilda's "steel probe" gaze repressed through her sympathy with the spirit of the work of art as seen through "angel's eyes": the corruption that inheres in everything made. Hilda had always looked at art with "the faculty of seeing it in its pristine glory," beneath its injuries, neglect, retouches, and decay.[87] It makes her a good copyist but a failed artist, enslaved to the Masters, unable to venture into the murky materia prima of unmixed pigment and half-formed figures slouching toward being.

I disagree with Susan Stewart's claim that Hilda is a vehicle for Hawthorne's ideal of New World art, her "metonymic relation to the Old Masters" a suggested "technique" for spiritually remaking Italian classics "under the conditions of a Protestant novelty."[88] Rather, Hilda's visual innocence, a transcendent (and theological) equivalent of the ideal of blind sight, is shown to be not only impossible but an intellectual dead end: we may attempt to see the world redeemed, but in unfamiliar territory we must measure our current experience against other pictures, against stored memory, against the images reality itself discloses. We never look at just one thing in isolation.

Our vision continuously compares what's happening against what once happened, against existing forms, against conventional aesthetic preferences and taste, and glancing actively through these archives teaches us to perceive and visually construct a world. When Kenyon tries to reassemble a dismembered Venus de Medici discovered in the ground, replacing its severed head onto its marmoreal body, he attempts an imaginative abracadabra: "It immediately lighted up and vivified the whole figure, endowing it with personality, soul, and intelligence. The beautiful Idea at once asserted its immortality, and converted that heap of forlorn fragments into a whole, *as perfect to the mind, if not to the eye*, as when the new marble gleamed with snowy luster." But the "beautiful Idea" that marries the sculpture's soul with its "earth-stained" body is not enough, for without a material form commensurate with its fragmentation, without a formal cause imbued by the material (rather than an internalized ideal, here of Woman, or Kenyon's image of Hilda), the object falls back into a "heap of worthless fragments."[89] Even from a narrative standpoint the archaeological discovery, somehow missed by everyone actually working on the dig, was absurdly fortuitous, too good to be true.

And even if one takes the process of artistic construction to be an aeolian incarnation of spirit in matter, Hawthorne lays the artist's prestidigitation bare in moments of technical reveal. In the *American Notebooks*, Hawthorne writes of portraiture: "The pursuit has always interested my imagination more than any other; and I remember, before having my first portrait taken, there was a great bewitchery in the idea, as if it were a magic process." But this "magic process" consists, specifically, of the way a painter captures a moment by struggling in and with time, "casting quick, keen glances at me, and then making hasty touches on the picture, as if to secure with his brush what he had caught with his eye."[90] Painting through a series of glances produces, in the belated viewer of a portrait, a new series of glances (what Hawthorne here calls glimpses) that work to catch the representation at the highest moment of the artist's insight into his reticent, withholding model: "It is a peculiarity of this picture [of Beatrice Cenci], that its profoundest expression eludes a straightforward glance, and can only be caught by side glimpses, or when the eye falls casually upon it; even as if the painted face had a life and consciousness of its own, and, resolving not to betray its secret of grief and guilt, permitted the true tokens to come forth only when it imagined itself unseen."[91] For Hawthorne, the question of art is a question of value, how out of the infinity of forms that can be generated mechanically an individual makes judgments of representational adequacy. But when the mechanics of vision in the process of making and execution are forgotten in the act of aesthetic appreciation, we also forget that the product is not an object with an aura, a portal to the Ideal, but a visual event of the here and now. It is an invitation to understand the way we see not just the art object but the world, how we construct worlds by glancing, how we order them by arranging and rearranging the materials they offer.

Hawthorne's anxieties about his career as a writer include questions about how real the material he works with really is. His concern was widespread in the nineteenth century, when distinctions like romantic-real or America-Europe (or more dramatic geocultural oppositions than that) threatened to balkanize literary activity through competing viewpoints on the ontological status of fictions. *The Marble Faun* continued Hawthorne's long train of thought on the relation between the Imaginary and the Actual (and the imagination and the body), mediated and even incarnated in so many representations of the insights and breakdowns of optical life. But the work stands at the end of a career that was also a threshold on which further technological advances in mechanized seeing were still to arrive, significant visual prostheses that would motivate, in turn, further writerly experimentation. Even more than early photographic apparatuses that would develop, with the Pictorialist and Naturalist movements, into practices of fine arts to imitate or rival painting, "philosophical toys" like the thaumatrope, phenakistoscope, stereoscope, kaleidoscope, and zoetrope would generate new theories of the image that relied on a temporary interface between the human body and an imprinted picture. Because the moving images depend existentially on the limits of the human eye (mechanisms of retinal retention that feed to the optic nerve a simplified version of the movement of the eye's visual field), the mystery of their location in optical space—neither wholly *in* reality nor *in* the eye—would feed back into considerations of metaphor, techne, and the imagination by authors, like Hawthorne, already grappling with those meta-problems in literary fiction.

Despite making much of Hilda's technique as a copyist, a trade that came to demand photographic training as part of its techne, the novel makes only one reference to photography (surprising in comparison with *Seven Gables*). Because the Roman galleries forbid easels, Hilda explains, regarding her unlikely success with the portrait of Beatrice Cenci, "I had no resource but to sit down before the picture, day after day, and let it sink into my heart. I do believe it is now photographed there."[92] Dan Clinton notes the curious fact that, in the novel, "optical devices like the camera appear only in figures of speech," in analogies for artistic impersonality, with copyists described as "Guido machines, or Raphaelic machines" and sculptor's assistants as "some nameless machine[s] in human shape."[93] This rhetorical display occurs at a moment in Hawthorne's career when he dispensed with the narrative significance of photography. But when Hilda refers to a photograph fixed on her heart, while she might be limiting photography to a mere figure of speech, she is also repeating Hawthorne's own desire, spelled out in a letter to Sophia, to find "something in the intellectual world analogous to the Daguerreotype in the visible—something which should print off our deepest, and subtlest, and delicatest thoughts and feelings, as minutely as the above-mentioned instrument paints the various aspects of Nature."[94] In other words, the path from *Seven Gables* to *Marble Faun* involves a turn from the use of photography as the romance's explicit content to a more deeply embedded formal principle, less diegetic actant than one side of an analogy of compositional process.

At the same time, while the daguerreotype sinks into the metaphorical background of Hawthorne's romance, evanescent optical illusions proceed downstage. These are visual events Kant calls "charms" or attractions; they are not substantial enough to be part of a shared aesthetic.[95] Miriam is said to resemble "one of those images of light, which conjurors evoke and cause to shine before us, in apparent tangibility, only an arm's length beyond our grasp; we make a step in advance, expecting to seize the illusion, but find it still precisely so far out of our reach."[96] An 1860 readership might have associated "one of those images of light" with the airy pictures produced by a popular philosophical toy (often described as optical magic tricks) like the thaumatrope, which synthesized two different images printed on either side of a spinning disc; common examples include a bird and its cage or a horse and rider, though one could easily imagine Donatello sprouting faun's ears through stroboscopic effect. The synthesized image of the thaumatrope was certainly real—it was not a hallucination, since it was shared intersubjectively by those operating the device. But it could not be located in measurable space, inside any frame, because it was an effect of perceptual change.[97] In contrast to a painting or a photograph, the "philosophical" image depends on both viewer and device for its existence, neither fixed in the mind nor on canvas or paper by dry paint or sodium thiosulfate.

Besides the climactic event of the murder, Hawthorne structures what plot *The Marble Faun* has around moments of image fixation, like the model's face that threatened to become "fixed ineffaceably on [Miriam's] brain."[98] The processes of fixing and dissolving images invade Hawthorne's narrational style, including his choice to limit use of free indirect omniscience, thinning it down further than he ever had before.[99] Hawthorne's narrator can describe works of art, but not the animating, private images or charms that set their creations in motion. He thereby establishes an ontological distinction between the material and immaterial, the fixed and the unfixed image. Hawthorne marks an abyssal difference between what can and cannot be represented and communicated in language and for public criticism or judgmental reflection, which is always narrative and retrospective because it tells a story about an object's conception, gestation, and birth. Hawthorne's narration, one might then say, tries to cohere with and respect the principles of techne expressed by his characters' work and in the climactic execution of the model, which depends on a murderous glance open to psychological conjecture even as it proves indubitably efficient in action. What happens passes too quickly for the conscious actor, observer, and even the narrator to adequately narrate, but the result is an accomplished, fixed act that cannot be wished away, for it provides a trace or index of reality: "Hilda had looked into the courtyard, and saw the whole quick passage of a deed, which took but that little time to grave itself in the eternal adamant."[100] Adamantine judgment may be morally unfair when applied to fleeting acts. But for Hawthorne that asymmetry is a basic fact of aesthetics and criticism, and his allegorical method aims to capture the dynamics of art making inside the frame of a morality tale, thereby heightening the tensions between the modes of intention governing each domain.

Contained within the apparent contradiction between a momentary glance and an eternal engraving is the budding transformation of the seeing subject unfolding in theories of the arts, the optical sciences, and philosophy just as it was taking place within Hawthorne's fictions. This was a time, as Crary's history of nineteenth-century visual culture establishes, when the observer or viewer wriggled out of its conceptual pillories, loosed from the spatial relations "presupposed by the camera obscura and into an undemarcated terrain on which the distinction between internal sensation and external signs is irrevocably blurred."[101] And as one sees through the so-called magic of the thaumatrope or phenakistoscope, the introduction of temporality as an inescapable component of observation challenged classical optical presuppositions. Classical optics assumed instantaneous image transmission, which led to the premises of subject-object simultaneity and an ontological bond between the image in the camera obscura and the object of representation *out there*. But once shifting, fluctuating, and shuffling temporal experience was acknowledged as seeing's sine qua non, the mediatory foundation of perceptual experience as continuous self-difference, visual theory was delivered from the most reductive accounts of the Cartesian observer locked in on objects made transparent by mind's inner powers.

The hard sciences were providing evidence that the human subject constructs a perceptual world through the embodied glance. Xavier Bichat decentralized and scattered the body's living systems, beginning the process of piecing the interlocking mechanisms of sensory and motor nerves back together. Augustin-Jean Fresnel found that light waves were transverse rather than longitudinal, calling into question light's independence from the human sensory apparatus. Johannes Müller posited a seeing subject analogous to the photographic camera, with a physiological apparatus susceptible to external procedures of manipulation that continuously produce new experiences for a subject suspended within a circuit of circulating energy. Finally, Hermann von Helmholtz asserted that since perception begins with small reality "effects" rather than complete images, the eye's truths were ultimately "practical truths" depending on the interests of the perceiver who, while never able to overcome the physical distortions of the bodily eye, can manage them the way a person who looks "through a prism and executes movements of his body and hands as they appear in his field of view soon learns to see through the prism correctly."[102] As the sciences gutted the mansion of eighteenth-century optics room by room, instituting physiological optics at the center of visual inquiry, artists and writers were left to grapple with a difficult question: How does one create an image of lasting value if visions are evanescent operations of the finite human body?

If the time of the glance is a sheer instant, its intentional body like a skittering searchlight of minimal dimension, Hawthorne came to understand that its diminutive dimension made it so powerful, because—unlike the penetrating gaze with its heavy psychic baggage, carried along by Matthew and Alice in *Seven Gables*—it was fundamentally prosthetic and impersonal, and thus open to novelty. Despite Hawthorne's longtime interest in the camera obscura and his familiarity with the clunky apparatuses and long, penetrating exposure times of the contemporary daguerreotype, he was able to imagine more nimble photographic practices as the technology was being developed elsewhere, and as a menagerie of optical toys were heralding the future of moving pictures and stimulating new ontologies of the image. Throughout his oeuvre Hawthorne demonstrated the unique power of the fleeting vision on a subject trained (or even simply reduced) to receive and work with them. Like Goodman Parker's lantern in "The Wives of the Dead" revealing indistinct fragments out of chaos, like the meteor that briefly illuminates the dark sky Dimmesdale's gaze couldn't otherwise penetrate, or Ethan Brand's flaming lime kiln that flickers and momentarily transforms figures in the surrounding darkness, real illumination comes through the impersonal glances of subjects who have become empty, receptive bodies "in harmony with the low relief and dimness of outline of the objects that surrounded them."[103]

What *The Marble Faun* does more exquisitely than any of Hawthorne's preceding works is embody this impersonal subjectivity in the figure of the artist while integrating the glance's significance in a narrative that moves according to its rhythm (thus bridging, at least tentatively, technical differences between writing and visual art). The painter Miriam, whose instantaneous glance is the axis on which the novel's epic form turns, appears as an "image of light" at one moment, beholds herself "as in a dim show" when the model enters, turns into a waifish actor with no clear memory of the deed when she bids Donatello to murder, assures him that the act "was no more than . . . a dream; there was as little substance in what you fancied yourself doing," and finally appears to Hilda and Kenyon as a disguised image "kneeling on the pavement, just beneath the great central Eye" of the Pantheon.[104] She is both a fleeting figure in a magic lantern show, unable to be looked upon directly and dissolving with each scene, as well as an artist whose being is staked on the transformative potential of these liminal moments, the impersonality that inheres in the gestures and glances that cross the finest boundaries between subject and object, self and world, imagination and reality.

Fugitive Address

Harper's Glancing Lyrics

Let us briefly compare two of the most famous slave auction scenes in American literature. First, from the opening chapter of Harriet Beecher Stowe's *Uncle Tom's Cabin* (1852), is the slave trader Haley's initial appraisal of Eliza:

> There needed only a glance from the child to her, to identify [Eliza] as its mother. There was the same rich, full, dark eye, with its long lashes; the same ripples of silky black hair. The brown of her complexion gave way on the cheek to a perceptible flush, which deepened as she saw the gaze of the strange man fixed upon her in bold and undisguised admiration. Her dress was of the neatest possible fit, and set off to advantage her finely moulded shape;—a delicately formed hand and a trim foot and ankle were items of appearance that did not escape the quick eye of the trader, well used to run up at a glance the points of a fine female article.[1]

And here, reproduced in full, is Frances Ellen Watkins Harper's "The Slave Auction" (1854):

> The sale began—young girls were there,
> Defenceless in their wretchedness,
> Whose stifled sobs of deep despair
> Revealed their anguish and distress.
>
> And mothers stood, with streaming eyes,
> And saw their dearest children sold;

Unheeded rose their bitter cries,
While tyrants bartered them for gold.

And woman, with her love and truth—
For these in sable forms may dwell—
Gaz'd on the husband of her youth,
With anguish none may paint or tell.

And men, whose sole crime was their hue,
The impress of their Maker's hand,
And frail and shrinking children, too,
Were gathered in that mournful band.

Ye who have laid your lov'd to rest,
And wept above their lifeless clay,
Know not the anguish of that breast,
Whose lov'd are rudely torn away.

Ye may not know how desolate
Are bosoms rudely forced to part,
And how a dull and heavy weight
Will press the life-drops from the heart.[2]

At the level of representation, these are both "scenes of subjection," Saidiya Hartman's term for largely unexceptional and ubiquitous sites of everyday terror faced by African Americans (both before and after emancipation).[3] In Stowe's scene, the line about the slave trader's "quick eye," which has been trained to "run up at a glance the points of a fine female article"—likely appraising the exploitable reproductive potential of her body—follows directly upon a distinction between glance and gaze, the latter giving way to the former while momentarily suggesting a more sentimental and less overtly violent "undisguised admiration." Throughout the novel, in fact, glancing is mostly associated with slaveholding capital, racial hierarchy, and socialized misogyny, while a softened gaze figures the oppositional work of the female novelist, a nurturing and mothering look that dissolves racial difference and thereby teaches us all how to "feel right," to see and feel morally and abolitionally.

Harper, as poet of verses like "The Slave Auction," as novelist of the influential Reconstruction-era *Iola Leroy* (1892), and as a public lecturer, is typically aligned with sentimentalist abolitionism, connected to Stowe in particular through her own doing, with poems like "To Mrs. Harriet Beecher Stowe" (1854) that thank the author of *Uncle Tom's Cabin* "for [her] pleading / For the helpless of our race."[4] Hazel Carby, in her important reading of *Iola Leroy*, argues that Harper "intended to hand her readership a political weapon," to "morally rearm the black intellectual," a project perhaps tempered in its militancy by the prior claim that Harper ultimately meant to "aid in the uplifting of the [black] race."[5] Carby's initial one-foot-in, one-foot-out view of Harper's sentimental racial politics has been taken up and progressively sharpened by critics, even as challenges to the assumption that her poetry, prose, and public speeches fit neatly in the context of mainstream antebellum abolitionism (and its routine sentimentalist epistemology) have been knapped to a fine point. Carla Peterson's commentary on Harper's poetry has been an engine for continually rethinking its legacy: on the one hand, she says Harper promotes in her readers and listeners "those emotions that would elevate moral consciousness and bring about social transformation" while also "decorporealiz[ing] the body," producing *both* immediate, revolutionary affect and an equally transformative (if risky) abstraction.[6] This is an apparently contradictory hybrid effect I want to consider further through the possibilities of lyric.[7] Ultimately, this chapter follows all those scholars who have begun thinking through Harper's work as a rejoinder to nineteenth-century racial sentimentalism (shaped so much by Stowe), with a focus on competing visual dynamics that shape lyric poems and genres of the visual arts marked for the public as irreducibly Black.[8]

I will not seek to theorize the difference between racialized gazes and glances per se;[9] I draw on W. E. B. DuBois's influential (visual) theory of double consciousness even as I take a select few examples from Harper's poetic oeuvre and contemporaneous American visual culture to guide the forms of seeing at issue. bell hooks's concept of a Black female "oppositional gaze" explains much about the limits of "the gaze" as it has been passed down in visual theory through Laura Mulvey's "Visual Pleasure and Narrative Cinema," connecting contemporary modes of spectatorship to the "politics of slavery, of racialized power relations . . . such that the slaves were denied their right to gaze." hooks insists, in a way that might startle with the force of saying what should be quite obvious, that the enslaved nevertheless looked, and that "all attempts to repress our/black people's right to gaze had produced in us an overwhelming longing to look, a rebellious desire, an oppositional gaze." The oppositional gaze thus opens "the possibility of agency" within the "face of structures of domination that would contain it."[10]

But "The Slave Auction" provokes hooks's reader in part because its use of gaze is not resistant or oppositional. The woman who gazes is not explicitly registering the implied look of the slaver or even the reader. Vision in Harper's poetry and prose toggles between gazes and glances to unsettle two competing forms of racialized seeing: the sentimental gaze and the trader's glance. Stark opposition between gaze and countergaze does not fully explain the range of looks her poems construct and activate. Both poles of seeing—gaze and glance—carry ethical risks for Harper (albeit of differing significance and urgency), even as neither can be dispensed with as ingrained tools for attentional comportment and, at a certain level of abstraction, political understanding. Moreover, gazes and glances carry phenomenological weight in the conventional lyric forms Harper often uses, and so her poetry (through its modes of collective address) provokes a desire to interrupt the events underway and to resee the lyric present as containing latent possibilities for nonpossessive intervention. This means—when put in the language of nineteenth-century sentiment—borrowing an image, feeling, or experience rather than keeping, possessing, or owning it.

Harper's poems, with their built-in formal desires to attain the status of lyric, move rather than stand their ground. If they move us, it is not because we unlock some sacred pathos contained in the suffering lyric subject. We are pulled into Harper's address and allowed to see both the generic limits of the form in which she writes and the lineaments of a lyricism beyond the horizon of those limits. As in Hawthorne the glance connects real and virtual domains across the boundaries of otherwise conventional aesthetic forms. As we gaze upon a scene of anguish, we find the epistemic ground on which we stand pulled from under our feet, and we begin to glance at the world's edge, the boundary that shields the poem's content from a future that would redeem us, all of us *here* looking *now*.[11] Who is this "we" or "us"? That is a question Harper's poetry aims to answer by producing a wholly new answer, by creating a "we" that would change over the course of the struggle for freedom that, in her case, is also a struggle for lyricism. Harper's creation of a new first-person plural in the otherwise restricted domain of lyric occurs in and through the time of the glance, which reflects in miniature Gregory Laski's account of "untimely democracy," which "untether[s] the politics of racial progress from the precepts of progressive time."[12] I aim to show how Harper's lyricism engages the possibility of racial justice without reifying or merely reflecting a contemporaneous stage in its historical development. That's why Harper draws so resourcefully, and carefully, from the futurity embedded in every glance.

When Harper writes of the woman who "Gaz'd on the husband of her youth, / With anguish none may paint or tell," she places us inside a visual dialectic of vicarious suffering while negating the sentimental access we expect the lyric to offer.[13] As Harper of course knew, many artists and writers have painted or told of slave auctions. Often anguish is absent from scenes of visual representation; antebellum America was flooded with paintings and engravings of slave auctions with comedic elements.[14] But many similar scenes of subjection in sentimental prose and slave narratives attempt to reproduce the affective register Harper bars them from. Perhaps those accounts are closer to the children's "stifled sobs of deep despair" that *do* reveal their "anguish and distress." Whereof one cannot speak is the specific feeling—what philosophers of mind call the qualia—behind the woman's gaze. And what the addressee does not know is the felt densities of affective life—"the anguish of that breast," the desolate "bosoms rudely forced to part," the "dull and heavy weight" that "press[es] the life-drops from the heart"—that dwell just like love and truth in "sable forms."

By rhyming *dwell* and *tell*, Harper establishes a direct opposition, as if once suffering is told it has already vacated the shell of the sable form replicated on page or canvas even as it remains uncaptured, dwelling in the flesh. Harper knows too that most of her readers have never seen a slave auction beyond representations of print or pen. In fact, many of the writers who sought to depict slave auction scenes had not either. Such was painter Eyre Crowe's frustration as he attempted to accurately depict several auctions during his time in the United States. His goal was to do better, "as no pen, we think, can adequately delineate the choking sense of horror which overcomes one on first witnessing these degrading spectacles."[15] And yet in his initial attempts he did not fare much better, as Maurie McInnis notes in a comparison to Stowe: "Whether it was Stowe in *Uncle Tom's Cabin* or Crowe in his series of sketches, artists tended to portray slaves as a series of types that conformed to notions of black inferiority. For the most part, the slaves in these publications are largely infantilized, represented as being worthy of white empathy and protection . . . [In Crowe's initial sketches] the trader appears fiendish and the slaves almost comical as they are shown either devoid of emotion or amused."[16] In other words, either enjoying themselves despite their situation—a sign of a threatening Black propensity to continuously enjoy—or utterly ignorant of it, often appearing blank and bored without much inner life to express. His mature and much-celebrated 1861 oil painting *Slaves Waiting for Sale, Richmond, Virginia* has "comical" elements, most notably the young woman and child striking playful poses near the composition's center. But the man at the far right has sloughed off aspects of his conventional role as compliant property. A brief, close look at this figure will help us understand the heightened stakes of looking and counterlooking in the fraught, hemmed-in moments of danger and mourning for the enslaved. Why we need to consider the status of glances as much as gazes here, despite overwhelming critical attention to the latter in African Americanist scholarship, may then become clear.

The man in Crowe's prior 1853 sketch is a caricature, similar to standard contemporaneous visual depictions of Stowe's Uncle Tom.[17] Indeed, McInnis puts it strongly: "The man waiting to be sold in 1853 *was* Uncle Tom."[18] So what specifically makes for a graphic Uncle Tom? Jo-Ann Morgan summarizes Uncle Tom's common compositional position in popular engravings (most often pictured with little Eva): "As a favorite slave on Eva St. Clare's plantation, Tom is a cloistered being, dressed in finery, dolled up by the child, and placed not on a pedestal exactly but on a little perch in the cultivated garden." Tom is depicted as possessing a few admirable traits—he is passively well dressed, looking good in white man's clothes—that do not threaten because he is clearly lorded over (by a cherubic white female child, no less). Morgan judges the convention a "successful image precisely because the sight was dangerous yet contained, courting the unmentionable and then so unequivocally squelching any chance that a dark, attractive African American man would ever live up to his masculine potential."[19] This is precisely the implied dynamic offered by the man in Crowe's sketch. Since the drawing is colorless, diagonal hatching marks his skin's hue as equivalent to his suit's, linking Blackness to clothing in a semiotic gesture shared with early runaway slave ads designed to help whites construct visual keys for identifying specific fugitives wearing their masters' clothes as disguise (of which more later).[20] Here, the man's exaggerated facial features break the visual chiasmus established between skin and suit, producing a racist visual irony that "squelches" the threat of dandified "masculine potential." His hat, removed and on the floor, is a small but revealing draughtsman's touch that signifies the artist's revelation of telling prognathic features beneath all sartorial cover.

In the 1861 painting, the detail of the hat on the floor (coupled with the absence of suit jacket) takes on an entirely different meaning as objective correlative to the "suffused indignant scorn, mingled with defiance" one contemporary reviewer saw in the man's face.[21] The hat now seems tossed aside in silent protest rather than removed by a caricaturist standing in for the examining slaver. "He has demonstrated his unwillingness to comply with the usual costuming that was a central element of his commodification."[22] His defiance, as helpless as it is in the context of the framed scene, builds a possible affective world outside the genre of the enslaved awaiting sale, providing a hint or even threatening promise of future resistance against whoever demands that he put his hat back on (and, of course, whoever demands that he uncross his arms, get to work, or smile). Of course, far more critical readings of the painting are available given the Black man's position, blocked off from the central group of women and children and balanced by the playful smile and inquisitive pose in the composition's center. But Crowe's sfumato technique, blending white hagglers and overseer so that they nearly blend into the built surroundings—with the latter at ease but ready to whip the enslaved into "shape" should they deviate from their places in the composed scene—literally foregrounds the restrictive and disciplinary economy of the racist commercial institution at work. The development of the male character from sketch to painting reinforces its compositional depthwise split by affecting a distance *within* the enslaved body (taken in both individual and collective aspects).

I took this brief detour to show how one visual artist refined his work when abolitionist and secessionist clamor was coming to a head, but also to mark a distinction between Harper's poem and its visual-cultural context. For one thing, any effort to supply the sort of description critics apply to the

FIGURE 3. Eyre Crowe, *Slaves Waiting for Sale, Richmond, Virginia*, 1861, oil on canvas, 76.3 cm × 107 cm, Heinz Collection, Washington, DC

individual men and women of antebellum genre paintings and engravings—realistic or exaggerated, blank or expressive—fails with a poem intentionally light on visual detail. Harper's premise is that affective communicability fails on one level but might yet succeed on another, though explaining precisely how it might succeed is the critic's task. The poem establishes active visual-bodily relations within a written tableau of arranged and blocked figures *as if* in a period genre painting that most readers would have relied on to get a thickened sense of the scene. Likening skin color to the impress of the "Maker's hand," Harper figures God as a painter who gives some creatures a shade more weight, an ethically neutral (or even positive) gesture that nonetheless supplies the fallen world with the opportunity to mark criminal difference. But the poem's ultimate lyrical gesture negates the epistemic crutch that would set the poem inside the visual-cultural imaginary to which it refers. The poem admits that something is missing from its picture but importantly refuses to specify what. The missing detail that would connect all subjects via feeling, no matter what race, ethnicity, or gender, is invisible. Indeed, for Harper it needs to be shown to be invisible, to be lacking in the visual field (and unable to be told in descriptive terms). Thus "The Slave Auction" is anti-ekphrastic, suggesting the visual tableau the poem fails to congeal into, arousing but not fulfilling the reader's desire for static, framed representation. There is no monument to suffering via enslavement here, nothing to stand in for and thus punctuate the time of institutional pain. Rather, the anguish is ongoing and repetitive, so that at the end of the poem the eye blinks, the reader's countergaze is broken, and the insufficiency of sentimental communion sets something else in motion. That "something else" is, if Harper's life is any indication, the stuff of abolitionist politics, articulated more directly on the lecture circuits where she first gained notoriety. But considering the distinction between lyric and lecture (or, alternatively, politics proper) raises the question of attention, or how we must attend to suffering to make a difference.

As the poem moves inexorably toward its end, its spot of time dilates and contracts like an eye opening onto the scene and then closing. As the women gaze upon their lovers, we glance. Uncomfortably, we might feel the deficiency of our feeling, the very thing Harper insists on by provoking a sympathy that falls short of empathy. Or we might call it, along with Martha Cutter, "parallel empathy" rather than "hierarchical," a mode of feeling that leads the reader to "vicarious introspection" rather than voyeuristic projection, a "spiraling" and even glancing process "between self and other" that does not collapse difference but does promote recognition that "but for the luck of birthplace, wealth, or skin color, the other could be the viewing self."[23] Parallel empathy includes a recognizable gap in the interpersonal connection, a bit like Adam Smith's well-known theory of sympathy where, "as we have no immediate experience of what other men feel, we can form no idea of the manner in which they are affected, but by conceiving what we ourselves should feel in the like situation."[24] Smith says that we supply a supplemental narrative to imagine the causal-contextual condition of another person's experience. And we may try to imagine not only how it would feel to be us in another's situation, but how it would feel to be that other person in that situation. We approach an unbridgeable, even unthinkable ontological divide armed with conjecture.

For Harper, imaginary sympathetic narratives can be experienced *as* imaginary through lyric encounter. The encounter's result is therefore ambiguous: if Stowe's sentimentalism contrasts the lingering empathetic gaze with the profiteer's quickened glance, Harper's poem remains unsettled in such a firm, moralistic distinction. It draws our attention from the enslaved's anguished gaze to a restlessness that exceeds the bounds of the sentimental (readerly) gaze's mirroring identification: "Ye who have laid your lov'd to rest, / And wept above their lifeless clay, / Know not the anguish of that breast, / Whose lov'd are rudely torn away." Feeling is sensuous knowledge; the addressed may feel stirred, may feel a parallel, but she *knows not* the anguish. The stanza is a broken chiasmus, twisted to deconstruct a presumed equivalence (and rhetorical parallelism) between the "lov'd" laid to rest and the "lov'd" torn away. These are not the same types of a universal form of mourning or melancholia.[25] Alone, feeling does not connect even when it parallels.

I mean that, for Harper, *interiorized* feeling does not connect. The promise of the sentimental gaze is that it connects two *souls*, that the absorptive look can change our feeling (verb) so that we come to possess the right feelings (plural objective). Hence Stowe's famous plea at the close of *Uncle Tom's Cabin*, with italics included in the original to help readers feel the right emphasis: "But, what can any individual do? Of that, every individual can judge. There is one thing that every individual can do—they can see to it that *they feel right*. An atmosphere of sympathetic influence encircles every human being; and the man or woman who *feels* strongly, healthily and justly, on the great interests of humanity, is a constant benefactor to the human race. See, then, to your sympathies in this matter! Are they in harmony with the sympathies of Christ? or are they swayed and perverted by the sophistries of worldly policy?" Feeling right in *Uncle Tom's Cabin* also means feeling better. And the absorptive gaze is the instrument that plays feelings to the tune of Christ's sympathies, the channel for rays of "heavenly love" that connect souls across the color line. Little Eva redeems the irascible Topsy in a mere moment:

> "O Topsy, poor child, *I* love you!" said Eva, with a sudden burst of feeling, and laying her little thin, white hand on Topsy's shoulder. . . . The round, keen eyes of the black child were overcast with tears;—large, bright drops rolled heavily down, one by one, and fell on the little white hand. Yes, in that moment, a ray of real belief, a ray of heavenly love, had penetrated the darkness of her heathen soul! She laid her head down between her knees, and wept and sobbed,—while the beautiful child, bending over her, looked like the picture of some bright angel stooping to reclaim a sinner.[26]

Tears, as Jane Tompkins acknowledges, are the "sign of redemption" in the novel.[27] We might say, adapting Wordsworth, that they are the spontaneous overflow of powerful (redemptive) feelings, the leaking out of an interior form in the process of forming, at the site where two souls meet: the eyes. The picture of Eva as stooping angel compresses racialized condescension in empathetic visuality. Hammatt Billings's illustrations for the novel's first edition replicate what Cutter calls hierarchical empathy, most striking in little Eva's "mediational glance" toward Tom in the arbor, a look that constructs our (pale) gaze, leading us to views of the novel's Black characters through white sightlines.[28]

The illustrations' kitschy iconography puts us in the affective register of antebellum social reform movements, which Christopher Castiglia analyzes through a Foucauldian disciplinary framework. "How social order became understood in relation to the description and reform of specific types of citizens' interiority (their 'natures' or 'characters,' emanations of the 'deep' self)," Castiglia writes, "is central to how social reform affected public opinion in the nineteenth-century United States and how it continues to shape American understanding of 'race' and of social identities more broadly to this day." At a time when the enslaved were still routinely disciplined through immediate attacks on the body, reform movements recast the "bodily coercions" of state and plantation system "as the apparently voluntary and internally managed orders of what Michel Foucault calls governmentality, an interior state that is both consensual and self-managing," offering a new interior battleground where good and bad affects battle and good and bad citizens are made.[29]

Glenn Hendler opens his study of nineteenth-century American structures of feeling with reference to Eliza Harris's conversation with Mrs. Bird, a "classic example of [the] gesture" of sympathetic identification "predicated on the fashioning of a 'significant analogy' between two egos."[30] His "classic example" is Eliza's question, "Have you ever lost a child?" The question provokes tears in Mrs. Bird and, more to the point, "every one around her" shines forth "signs of hearty sympathy." The narrator's subsequent address partakes in the lyric technique of apostrophe—a rhetorical trope we must think about in Harper's poem—to draw us into a present tense: "And oh! mother that reads this, has there never been in your house a drawer, or a closet, the opening of which has been to you like the opening again of a little grave?"[31] Hendler's point is that Stowe's question-begging performs the possibility of entering into emotional communion with the enslaved mother, a "fantasy of experiential equivalence" that marks sentimental literature's affective puissance, put toward making liberal reader-citizens. "The Slave Auction," Hendler recognizes, trades on the power of sentimental address while explicitly critiquing the politics of sympathy and its "drive to turn all differences into equivalences, all analogies into coincidences."[32] His brief comparison points us to Hartman's piercing question: "Does [making the suffering of others one's own] not only exacerbate the idea that black sentience is inconceivable and unimaginable but, in the very ease of possessing the abased and enslaved body, ultimately elide an understanding and acknowledgement of the slave's pain?"[33] And in what way does sentimentalism's a priori construction (or illusion) of the self and its pathways of feeling hide the gaps or lacks in the liberal subject's constitution to naturalize public hierarchies of experiential capacity?[34]

Although Harper posits a deep self in the poem, by denying the reader access to it she evades constructing what Castiglia calls "abolition's racial interiors," the appropriation of African American suffering that "supplied the intimate pain that entitled more privileged citizens to engage in public debate with an authorized moral authority."[35] But her lyric also intimates a positive visual logic—the flipside of its more explicitly negative stance—that takes us away from the biopolitical overdetermination of racialized seeing. Even Foucault himself, in *The Birth of the Clinic*, reveals the productive ambiguity of invisible life exceeding the death-dealing diagnostic gaze that takes the body in its purview as "disease itself, with shadow and relief, modulations, nuances, depth," viewed as a framed pictorial figure.[36] As in the nineteenth-century medical clinic, what was previously unseen and unfelt in the "mournful band" at auction is seen and felt because reduced and managed as (abolitionist, diagnostic) spectacle. And yet, the poem ends with an insistence on affective excess, articulated through an embodied metaphor that relies on an invisible felt difference in the otherwise universal trope of the heartbeat.

The "dull and heavy weight" of the poem's final stanza parallels the extra weight of the Maker's hand that darkened the skin of some of His children. Put together we have another rhetorical chiasmus: the visible outside folds into the invisible inside. Thus for all its didacticism, the lyric only uneasily participates in the reformist distinction between silent, suffering (Black) interior and vocal, public (white) representation. It posits an excess of anguish as the public's prod, but also implies that acknowledging one's epistemic deficit rather than mirroring the right feelings in white reformers (readers) is the first step toward structural change. In this implication Harper foreshadows W. E. B. Du Bois's visual-theoretical analysis of the color line in *The Souls of Black Folk* (1903). For Du Bois, like Harper's lyric persona in "The Slave Auction," the psychological damage of the color line manifests through asymmetrical relationships to the self's primordial lack—asymmetrical because acquired in a hierarchical social world. And the substance of the color line is learned through primal visual scenarios much like the auction scenes constructed by Harper and antebellum artists.

Du Bois recalls the moment when the "shadow" of the color line first "swept across" him: "In a wee wooden schoolhouse, something put it into the boys' and girls' heads to buy gorgeous visiting-cards—ten cents a package—and exchange. The exchange was merry, till one girl, a tall newcomer, refused my card,—refused it peremptorily, with a glance. Then it dawned upon me with a certain suddenness that I was different from the others; or like, mayhap, in heart and life and longing, but shut out from their world by a vast veil."[37] Peremptorily, "with a glance," Du Bois's white classmate lowered the veil behind which—or more accurately, through which—his marked difference and double consciousness was introjected. Her glance, perhaps because so light and therefore dismissive, initiated a process whereby the great weight of a originary illusion (the self-sufficiency of the internalized ego) was shattered in the Black child. Understanding the nuances of this moment—and the painful but perspicacious birth of the child's "second sight" in the encounter—can help complete our reading of Harper's poem and the specific form of lyric address it takes in light of its visual grammar and interior-exterior dialectic.

Du Bois uses an autobiographical example to illustrate white supremacy's common sense: sight. It is common enough to be reinforced by one momentary glance that pierces the child's self-image of wholeness. Shawn

Michelle Smith reinforces the relationship between the self-image shattered by the color line and psychoanalytic theories of the ego as imago, for "in the white girl's eyes [Du Bois] sees an image that he does not, and cannot, recognize in relation to himself, an image that fractures the illusion of the ideal and complete ego. This first encounter with the color line troubles the cornerstone of initial misrecognition of self as image in the mirror stage."[38] Her glance is a blast upon a shrouded bruise: it destroys the self-mastery built in the early stages of his life, a mastery that (from the Lacanian perspective Smith refers to) was an illusion anyway. So the Black child learns a painful truth that the white child is shielded from: we are not equal to our self-images, our egos.[39] They are always prone to destruction or deflation at the hands of other people. Hence Du Bois's "second sight," which is as self-reflexive as it is socially astute. The problem is that racial hierarchy, reinforced by a white supremacist common sense that turns glances into veiling gestures and acts of separation, offers white subjects the privilege of not having to come to terms with the illusory nature of their self-images. The delicate suture that ties ego to ideal image remains largely intact for white subjects de facto unchallenged in their self-mastery. At first cozier and more at home than split subjects who sense their irreconcilable twoness, white subjects are doomed to repress and thus misunderstand their own internal contradictions. Like the self-satisfied but ill-fated Hegelian lord, they underrate their vulnerability to delusion. The Black subjects who perceive their own self-insufficiencies, then, come closer to recognizing subjectivity's universal structures in their own persons.

Du Boisian double consciousness, built on an ontological split in the subject's image(s) of self but reinforced by sedimented racial hierarchies, is a poisonous gift that disarms the sentimental gaze and renders it ineffective. Or more to the point, the sentimental gaze cannot undo the damage wrought by a stray, piercing glance. And the condescension of the sentimental gesture, its visual economy, in fact reinforces the self-blindness of the sympathetic gazer by feeding the originary illusion of the image as ego, the fact that whiteness, "culturally, legally, socially, economically, and institutionally privileged as an *unmarked* racial category . . . enables the 'white' ego to remain blind to the suturing effects of its own fundamental misrecognition."[40] Which means that the supposed timelessness and subjective stability of the gaze is imaginary, propping up illusions about both subject and object poles of the sentimental pair, the liberal flipside of the dismissive white supremacist glance. It "sees" in the enslaved an interior affective state it can claim and possess, nurturing the wound as a necessary part of reformist politics. It assumes that it sees and assumes that it can share in the interior state of anguish because it fails to recognize its own a priori complicity in the state of affairs structured around identitarian misrecognition. The sentimental subject assumes a burden it pretends it does not already have. It negotiates and sympathizes with the racialized other's incompleteness—the rift and lack at the core of its existence—while implicitly maintaining its own wholeness.

Thus when Harper's speaker addresses the reader, insisting that she "Know[s] not the anguish of that breast, / Whose lov'd are rudely torn away," she is not urging the reader to try harder to know or appropriate the specific feeling of separation on the part of the enslaved. In fact, she leaves the door a crack open for the reader in the following, final stanza: "Ye may not know how desolate / Are bosoms rudely forced to part." Harper tempers the sentimentalist adynaton to suggest that while her (white) reader does not know the anguish of that breast, the specific affective character of the experience of the soul's auction under a white supremacist system, she may in fact know a little something of the larger subjective desolation that pertains to the rude departure of one's counterpart. While the so-called sentimental gaze attempts to connect with the wretched individual sufferer based on the former bit of knowledge, the possible but barely available epistemic insight of the desolation—and the corresponding dull and heavy weight, associated with the pressed markedness of the self in the eyes of the social other (the Lacanian Other)—could be understood. But a major shift in visual perspective would be needed.

If you think you have felt an emotional pain equivalent to the enslaved mother's—the poem seems to say when reviewed through Du Bois's theory of the veil—you have not yet interrogated the way your own interior affects are mediated by more primordial losses shielded from consciousness by, among other things, reformist rhetoric and contemporary visual culture. But even without imposing dialectical Du Boisian insights from the future, we can see how "The Slave Auction" promotes a visual alternative to the sentimental gaze in the form of its lyrical intervention into a tense time (or time's tense), which shifts the ground under the empathic stance of liberal affectivity. The shift often happens in Harper poems, as it does here, with a turn to the present tense in the final stanzas, which Monique-Adelle Callahan characterizes as "a type of polyphony that models the [operative] relationship between text and reader."[41] It is the moment when the poem attains the ontological status of lyric through what Jonathan Culler has identified as the mode's central rhetorical trope: apostrophe, which "remov[es] the opposition between presence and absence from empirical time and locat[es] it in a discursive time." In Harper, one common apostrophic address is the American national public, turning the reader into a political representative hearing an appeal not in the empirical time of the represented scene but in the fictive time of the lyric now. The reader qua liberal public persona becomes an element "of the event which the poem is attempting to be."[42]

Harper's lyric event crosses temporal spans, beginning with the indifferent speed of the auction and struggling to decelerate time by glancing through coordinating conjunction: "And mothers . . . And woman . . . And men . . . And frail and shrinking children . . ." The glance, in this case, slows time against the unseen but felt backdrop of callous slavers at work by stretching synchronous moments into consecutive states. G. E. Lessing thought such stretching the exclusive province of poetry, but it is perhaps more helpful to say that glancing consecutiveness marks the difference between being inside and outside a work of art. They may gaze, but we glance. And glancing does not come set with its political baggage, as if the (sentimental) gaze connects souls that live in different bodies while the glance is automatically the profit-oriented tool of those who would commodify and trade lives. The retiming of time itself through the progressive lyricization of "The Slave Auction" dialectically alters that sentimental distinction. As Dana Luciano subtly notes by way of the same comparison Hendler and I are making, "For although 'The Slave Auction' also pits the profit-oriented indifference of public time against the regenerative appeal of interior temporalities, the poem eschews the (re)productive rebalancing of contemporary forms of time seen in *Uncle Tom's Cabin*, instead suggesting new forms of temporal connection as the necessary solution to the problem(s) of history."[43] The glance's function in constructing "new forms of temporal connection" within and not outside history is technically lyrical but not disembodied, solipsistic, or asocial.

In saying so I implicitly reference protests articulated by Yopie Prins and Virginia Jackson, specifically the implications of the founding rhetorical gesture of "new lyric theory": turning the phrase "reading lyric" around into "lyric reading." Prins explains the distinction: "If 'reading lyric' implies that lyric is already defined as an object to be read, 'lyric reading' implies an act of lyrical reading, or reading lyrically, that poses the possibility of lyric without presuming its objective existence or assuming it to be a form of subjective expression." As actual historical material ("objective existence"), what counts most for Prins and Jackson are lyric poetry's subgenres with their specific occasions of legibility—odes, hymns, funeral elegies, and many more—whereas twentieth-century criticism and its habits of "lyric reading" subsumed all that material under the baggy category "lyric." There is much tension between the circulation of actual lyric subgenres and their post facto academic reception: "A great deal of lyric reading in the twentieth century attempted to restore lyrics to the social or historical resonance that the circulation of lyrics as such tends to suppress."[44] Essentially, for practitioners of the new lyric theory, lyric names a mode and act of reading rather than a genre or act of writing.

Jackson and Prins often maintain that the vocal abstractions we associate with lyric poetry—a speaker overheard, a stable and centered enunciating subject, an "I" always already disassociated from any empirical person—are acts of violence done to a poet's body (clearest in their seminal monographs, *Victorian Sappho* and *Dickinson's Misery*, where gendered bodies and corresponding modes of address are shown to work, speak, and circulate underneath the leveling umbrella of the lyric voice). Anthony Reed further argues that the lyric is racially coded in its "hermeneutic enclosure, which figures the expressions and experiences of a singular intending consciousness that is in turn metonymic for race." Making the lyric a universal expressive category "has played an important role in what kinds of things we say about poetry, what kinds of things we think poetry says (especially when it says 'I'), which techniques we consider significant and worth study, and ultimately which poems are worth serious attention."[45] By unmarking and universalizing the lyric values of timelessness, consciousness, and the singular voice, critics of lyric reading enumerate its implicit exclusions. G. Gabrielle Starr writes of the ultimate effect of lyric reading, "where readers are placed in close contact with a speaking 'I'": "Bodies disappear."[46]

The disembodied generalization granted poems we call lyric, a dominant readerly presupposition often blamed on the New Critics, is, for Jackson, Prins, and historicists critiquing the lyric in their wake, tainted with the guilt of avoidance. Although it is not necessarily part of their purview, especially given its generic association with the novel rather than verse, one can see how sentimentalism (or sentimental reading) connects to their argument: in generalizing the claims of the suffering body beyond socialized difference, we risk ideological blindness to the material conditions that underwrite that suffering. Peterson's account of Harper's public performances helps us understand the risk: she was celebrated as a speaker in reviews (quoted here directly) for her "quiet" appearance, a manner "marked by dignity and composure," a delivery that was "never theatrical."[47] Peterson's point, which only reinforces critics of the lyric's skepticism that our poetic-theoretical categories discipline bodies, is that Harper's persona was made to be quiet, unassuming, neutral, and chaste, all to keep her Blackness from infiltrating her public voice.[48]

But is there another side to lyricization on this front, not just to the act of lyric reading but to the promise (whether fulfilled or unfulfilled) of *writing* lyric?[49] Looking back at our poem in question, Harper makes a so-called lyric spot of time not to promote universalized empathy via interior pain but to point to the invisible, to what we miss when passive empathic identification lets the slave auction start again and again. The point is to change this scene, not identify with it, and therefore to traverse the epistemic and visual lacks readers bring as nominal outsiders to the scene rather than to seek the other's redemption by mirroring their trauma. In this chapter's next section I will expand on this point—on the sentimental subject's need to dress fugitivity in its own clothing to relate to it—but finding oneself in the other is sentimentalism's primary speculative strategy reinforced by the introjective character of gazing. "Rather than teaching readers to appreciate difference," Elizabeth Barnes writes, "sentimental lessons reinforce for readers the idea that recognition relies on likeness—that one is bound to love whatever or whomever appears most like one's own."[50] Specious identification is certainly a lesson the aforementioned lyric theorists take from the ideological operation of lyric overhearing. But apostrophe in "The Slave Auction" specifically works against identitarian collapse, marking and maintaining difference (including drawing attention to the Maker's mark on the enslaved's skin) and foregrounding the struggle to make lyric work—rather than the result of attaining a work of lyricism—through direct second-person address.

To achieve its supposed timelessness, its time of enunciation that exceeds and displaces the empirical time of the historical near-present, overfilling its synchronic container, lyric strives to make its own context disappear. The poem's unfulfilled promise, the promise of lyric time as a regulative ideal, contains the implicit conviction that "a future oriented present," as Frank Kirkland defines "modernity in black," can be "the fortunate occasion in which culturally distinctive innovations are historically redemptive of a sense of past."[51] It is the poem's wish that its affective resonance will become universal even as it accepts and insists that its unfolding in time—its very reason for being made now, but maybe not its reason for remaining to be read later—depends on embodied difference, on a now-irreducible though not ontological concept of Blackness. The future tense "The Slave Auction" settles on, even as settling remains a distant ideal, is a gnomic future: Harper creates an axiom—a "dull and heavy weight" *will* "press the life-drops from the heart"—that everyone should hold, and in holding it we might dispense of it as metaphorical description. We could even (maybe) forget it, its use as a racially specific principle put under erasure in the very act of gnomic abstraction. That might be one example of June Jordan's "difficult miracles of black poetry in America," a persistence in writing at the juncture of that writing's impossibility, laying down its own conditions for legibility at the same time the poems are born.[52]

Luciano reads difference in the poem as postsentimental because the "'private' temporalities" of the emotions—the incessant movement inward and the lyric displacement of (the slave auction's) empirical time by a slow time of grief, anguish, and mourning—"displace, but cannot delay or undo, the linear motion of the commercial event, as its inexorable onward movement effectively deprives emotion of any regenerative capacity."[53] The poem moves through mourning toward death, not toward revival and salvation.[54] Nevertheless, there is a crack left open to the scene's outside, and not simply to the time of slave commerce or what Eric Lott calls (in a Mulveyan metalepsis) the "pale gaze."[55] The lyric's final second-person address refuses to reproduce, as Lauren Berlant writes in defining "postsentimentality," "the sublimation of sub-altern struggles into conventions of narrative satisfaction and redemptive fantasy."[56] But it also sets in motion, in its very refusal of emotional transubstantiation, a process of restless lyric reading that might unsettle the sentimental tendency to naturalize suffering and the time of mourning—the time, within the lyric narrative, of gazing—in favor of a contrapuntal poetics of fugitivity. Let us see how that might be.

Sentimentality, James Baldwin writes, or "the ostentatious parading of excessive and spurious emotion, is the mark of dishonesty, the inability to feel."[57] Harper's "The Slave Auction," as I have already suggested, achieves postsentimentality by tarrying with the negativity of excessive, unrepresentable emotion while projecting future readings that, in a different sociopolitical context, "may" or "may not" allow the poem to attain the lyricism it seeks. Meanwhile, the poem's visual dynamics, pure relation without description, train readerly attention on the imminent severing of family ties by slowing the inevitable progress of the inhumane sale. The poem does not make readers feel the anguish of the enslaved (such cannot be told, much less painted); instead, it clears a time for mourning in which the "dull and heavy weight" that presses on the hearts of the inconsolable can be temporarily slowed (but only temporarily, for now). In the dilated span of lyric time, the gaze figures prominently as a resigned expression of the pain of separation, a limited resource of the suffering woman from which we are nevertheless barred.

Noticing the lack in our visual field and feeling the lack in our affective bodies, we are pushed away from psychologistic identification and toward scenes that might be constructed otherwise.

And Harper constructs other lyrics otherwise. "Eliza Harris" (1853) analogizes Stowe's central character as "Like a fawn from the arrow, startled and wild," sweeping by an initially unidentified "us" with her child in tow.[58] As several Harper critics have noted, her distinct use of ballad form integrates lyric urgency with collective, folk experience.[59] The poem's plural address does not easily fit into either first- or third-person African American lyric traditions catalogued by Kevin Young and concisely sorted by Christopher Spaide into lyrics "drawn towards the pole of 'I,' the freedman or -woman of the slave narrative, the solitary soul singing the blues, the Baldwinian witness, the Invisible Man, and the self-aggrandising MC; [and those] drawn towards 'we,' the singers of work and protest songs, choruses, congregations, testifiers to a shared black experience, or activists uniting to proclaim 'We Shall Overcome,' 'Yes We Can,' or 'Black Lives Matter.'"[60] Harper's "us" does not clearly demarcate a racialized group, Black or white, and the woozy ambiguity of address positions an earnest reader uncomfortably from the beginning.

Each of the poem's twelve quatrains rhyme *aabb*, and in all but two stanzas the first couplet opens the field of Eliza's flight while the second momentarily closes it down through signs of imminent danger. Take the full opening quatrain that I just cited in part:

> Like a fawn from the arrow, startled and wild,
> A woman swept by us, bearing a child;
> In her eye was the night of a settled despair,
> And her brow was o'ershaded with anguish and care.[61]

Heretofore ignored is a basic dissonance set up by this stanza along the imaginary line separating the couplets at the semicolon: the first two lines suggest the quickened presence of a darting flash past whatever group the speaker counts herself part of, while the latter impossibly focus on facial details (metaphorical as they are) in a way that belies the conceit of the initial image. The stanza advances from the implied plural eyes of an interpellated community of readers, moving along the page as if tracking Eliza's skittish path: like a scared fawn the line's step is brisk but irregular, with shifting syllable counts ranging between ten and twelve throughout and a wild meter stuttering through tension and release.[62] Then all of a sudden we are brought close to Eliza's eye and brow, where the flash of blackness (on her light-brown skin, one might know) is internalized and "settled" as the mark of despair and as a covering shade that imposes itself on her movements.[63]

Harper, knowledgeable about biblical *figura*, captures the ambiguity of the covering shade, at once protection (as in Psalms' shelter "in [or under] the shadow of thy wings"), transience and mortality (Job's "Our days upon earth are a shadow" or Psalms' "Though I walk through the valley of the shadow of death"), and the long tradition of foreshadowing *umbra futurorum* where earthly shadows predict the afterlife and redemption to come.[64] Rhetorically, Harper's overshade links despair (of the eye), anguish, and care in a nonrepresentational mode, since the speaker would likely not be able to see a shadow on the brow of a fleeting Black woman. Thus another possible way to read "o'er" is as *extra*, Eliza being shaded black twice as a result of her fugitive condition, so that her quickened pace actually reveals her to the imagined public and her pursuers to be Blackness itself in motion. Harper would then be troping on fugitive slave iconography, the semiosis of antebellum Blackness. And that semiosis is another way of (retroactively) reading the eye's "night of a settled despair," a recapturing of the Black body in the static image of fugitivity, an icon of property on the run.[65] At stake, as Fred Moten theorizes, "is fugitive movement in and out of the frame . . . a movement of escape, the stealth of the stolen that can be said, since it inheres in every closed circle, to break every enclosure."[66] Harper's poem is structured—through its rhyme scheme and oppositional stanzas—to reveal the two-sidedness of Black fugitivity, the freedom in flight and a corresponding danger of openness that threatens those marked by slave iconography (and thus closes and bounds the body at the very moment it is opened to the elements).[67]

So what is the difference between the tracking glance of the lyric's "us" and the slave trader's glancing containment of Eliza's "finely moulded shape" in *Uncle Tom's Cabin*? Ultimately, the assigned place of the reader in either scene differs dramatically, and in such a way that challenges certain assumptions we may have about the lyric: that it is a closed form, ideological in the completeness of overheard interior presentation offered. The lyric poem must be rewritten just as Eliza Harris is rewritten, allowed to become the darting presence not quite amenable to either sentimental projection and introjection or straightforward, violent objectification. Meanwhile, the plurality and mobility of the poem's speaker and addressee constantly shifts modes, so that *we* are put in motion alongside Eliza, unmoored from a ground only barely stable at the poem's open. The subject-pole of our visual experience—when reading the poem and as implied within the poem—shifts in glancing relays that suggest acts of tracking (as the slave hunters and/or their animals), watching (as an interested liberal nation that supposes itself to be outside the scene), and making (art and poetry).

The glance's fugitivity opens the forms of lyric poetry and painting alike. Witness Eastman Johnson's *A Ride for Liberty*, exhibited during the Civil War in 1862, three years after his blockbuster genre painting, *Negro Life at the South*. Whereas the latter formally bounds Black life in an urban slave yard, the former articulates Blackness as a line of flight, unbounded by a landscape equally in motion and transition, its contours bleeding out of shape. The urban slave yard, even as a scene of subjection, appears kinder (or at least more secure) in its compositional values. We might build on Hartman's analysis of the enslaved's "innocent amusements" and note Johnson's crafting of racial boundaries in *Negro Life*—our eye perhaps moving from the white-passing young woman at the far right also passing through the threshold separating house and yard to the edifice's other apertures looking onto the leisurely scene—as a "liberal extension of feeling . . . [that] serves to efface violence and circumscribe the captives' sentience through such attributions of contentment or evaluations of the bearable."[68] In such a critical judgment our evaluative eyes move in a way the enslaved cannot, tracing and testing the formal-architectural boundaries of the scene, glancing but in as absorbed a way as the painting's grouped and individual Black figures. All of a sudden we find ourselves at the top of a hierarchy of passing, for as Eleanor Jones Harvey argues, the collection of vignettes in the painting "form a narrative that challenges the very idea of race as a means of determining a person's status," with skin color and the fineries of class allowing for specifically circumscribed means of (literal and social) movement.[69] Who can move from house to yard and who cannot? Who has a high vantage and who has a low? More reflectively: Are genre scenes of enslaved life depicting bearable amusements and pleasures in hierarchically circumscribed space immediately participating in the limitations of sentimental liberalism?

Hartman answered the last question for us in impressive detail, so I will draw out the significance of the initial ones. These are questions about form. When we ask them, we are asking after the relation—or, to use a popular relational term, imbrication—between aesthetic and social forms. That does not mean that they are one and the same, that the distributions of formal arrangements on canvas (or in a poem) translate directly to equivalent formal networks of the sociopolitical world from which they spring. But as Caroline Levine states so bluntly: "It is the work of form to make order. And this means that forms are the stuff of politics."[70] While remaining agnostic about

FIGURE 4. Eastman Johnson, *Negro Life at the South*, 1859, oil on linen, 94 cm × 116.8 cm, New-York Historical Society, New York

the critical value of translating one definition of form into the other, I aim in my brief reading of Johnson's *Negro Life* to set a way of looking at painting and poetry in motion, one that links their production to their reception to better understand the stakes of making art whose address automatically solicits a political stance in the audience. Fugitivity is the name of such a stance when the ground of spectatorial stability is taken away.

Following Harvey, I said that in glancing between *Negro Life*'s grouped figures—particularly between those in relative compositional freedom and those bound by their station in the painting—we experience a freedom of passing/passage.[71] Now look at Johnson's aforementioned *A Ride for Liberty*, a painting that puts us in a position similar to the "us" at the beginning of Harper's "Eliza Harris." Compositionally open as if its scene extends beyond the material frame, the painting throws us into the midst of fugitive precarity. For the runaway family on horseback, openness is dangerous. From a literary vantage, we are here on the open road as described by Douglass, not Whitman. A manifesto for leaving all shackles behind, for breaking "Out of the dark confinement!," Whitman's "Song of the Open Road"—with its almost all-inclusive catalogue of journeyers in section 12—assumes interlocutors bound by habit rather than chattel chains. When Whitman assures that the road "is safe—I have tried it—my own feet have tried it well," an uneasy sense of unconscious privilege pervades his itinerant ethos.[72]

Trish Loughran's account of the representations, in abolitionist societies, of fugitive slave experiences on the open road seemingly supports Whitman's celebration of detachment, endless transition, and fluid mapping as a nomadic ideal: "[The] figure of the mobile, sometimes 'fugitive,' slave—of Dred Scott and William Wells Brown—casts in stark relief the stakes of such travel: the disintegrative potential of bodies moving too quickly through space, making disparate populations finally feel somatically connected not just to their racial others but also to their regional others—North and South, East and West."[73] But enslaved fugitives' recorded experiences on the American road often tell the story of openness as a condition of terror, the unmapped as a condition of vulnerability, and nighttime landscapes as the complete inverse

FIGURE 5. Eastman Johnson, *A Ride for Liberty—The Fugitive Slaves*, 1862, oil on paperboard, 55 cm × 66 cm, Brooklyn Museum, New York

of Whitman's "efflux of the soul" (a happiness that "pervades the open air," waiting at "all times" to flow into us). The "formless and wordless" open can be a horizon of extreme violence and danger.[74] Nineteenth-century slave narratives thus contain all manner of negative space, marked as both figurative and literal distances between bondage and freedom.[75]

So as Frederick Douglass's *My Bondage and My Freedom* (1855) describes the attempted escape to the North by "our little band," it dissolves the official cartographic map of the Atlantic corridor into what Robert Abrams calls an "alternative spatial experience of the enslaved."[76] Douglass characterizes escapees' experience through "vague and indistinct notions of the geography of the country":

> We had heard of Canada, the real Canaan of the American bondmen, simply as a country to which the wild goose and the swan repaired at the end of winter, to escape the heat of summer, but not as the home of man. . . . I really did not, at that time, know that there was a state of New York, or . . . of Massachusetts. On the one hand there stood slavery . . . the evil from which to escape. On the other hand, far away, back in the hazy distance, where all forms seemed but shadows [stood] the untrodden road . . . conjecture.

As Douglass reports, on the railroad, people of color "must be measured and carefully examined, before they were allowed to enter the cars," "steamboats were under regulations equally stringent," and "the great turnpikes . . . were beset with kidnappers." Space and transportation for the runaway slave were not vectors shooting out into the distance, open roads of pure locomotive potential that linked the subject to a burgeoning national imaginary, but checkpoints one struggled to pass through, with the penalty of failure reenslavement or death. "At every bridge" the enslaved person "saw a watchman" rather than a rite of passage: "We were hemmed in on every side."[77]

Harper and Johnson turn Douglass's topography of open and enclosed space into a contest with(in) the limits of their media. In *The Ride for Liberty*, our glance looks for something to latch on to as we find ourselves in the uncomfortable epistemic position of the watchman (albeit secretly, as the presumptive mother glances backward at the felt absence of the "real" pursuit). The placeless liminality of the landscape at what seems like dawn or dusk—the right time for flight, when the traceable shape of the fugitive can attain a visual fugitivity of its own—puts every conceivable look out into the open, Janus-facing the work's compositional freedom as simultaneously turned toward the past and future, unmoored from the picture's frozen but pregnant present. Silhouetted like a cluster of fugitive slave icons found on advertisements for their capture, the speed implied by horizons blurred into wash unbounds the group silhouette "as a mechanism of repossession," unseating what Michael A. Chaney notes as the contradictory truth of the runaway advertisement: the way it "envisions the denial of its own proscription, suspending the figure in a visual field of stasis and density that belies the likelihood that anything so inert and cumbersome could escape, let alone move, in the first place."[78]

Motion itself may be radical when everything—from the withholding of cartographical knowledge to the art historical overdetermination of Blackness bound by generic convention—is set against it. Hence poet-critic Nathaniel Mackey links the "fugitive spirit" of Black music to "African American literary practice . . . [in] the alliance of writing with fugitivity":

> One recalls that in 1829 George Moses Horton hoped to buy his freedom with money made from sales of his book of poems, *Hope of Liberty*. One thinks of the role played by literacy in Frederick Douglass's escape, of Harriet Jacobs's denunciations of the Fugitive Slave Law, of the importance of the slave narratives to the anti-slavery movement. W. E. B. Dubois referred to the essays in *The Souls of Black Folk* as "fugitive pieces," and the impact of fugitive spirit can be found in the work of William Melvin Kelley (the mass exodus in *A Different Drummer*, the bending and reshaping of language in *Dunfords Travels Everywhere*), Ishmael Reed (Quickskill in *Flight to Canada*), Toni Morrison (the flying African in *Song of Solomon*, the "lickety-split, lickety-split" at the end of *Tar Baby*, Sethe's escape in *Beloved*), and others.[79]

Harper is not mentioned in Mackey's study, likely because of her poetry's lyric conventionality and the "expectant" future it projects.[80] Her poetry always seems to run toward something, perhaps ultimately toward a new nation form in which her lyrics will come to be, finally, lyrics. That horizon of possibility generates the fugitive spirit in her work, actualized (or embodied) in a poetics of flight that leaks out from the enclosed structure of the poem through a restlessness of address. "Eliza Harris," a poem whose title coincides with its central persona, flees on two levels: the poem stretches itself between present and future to generate a circulatory context in which the text, like Eliza, would overcome its sculptural reification as a "statue of fear and despair." It is as if Harper foresaw Sharon Cameron's definition of lyric, which "insist[s] that meaning depends upon the severing of incident from context" and whose formal achievement—"the stunning articulation of the isolated moment"—is underwritten by despair, "the despair of the possibility of complete stories, of stories whose conclusions are known."[81] "Eliza Harris" as protolyric begins by despairing of a futurity framed by a lack of knowledge about and control over its own generic status. The metapoetic question raised is how the empirical present can be made into the past tense and, in the process of that transformation, how to end a poem with a renewed present and exclamation to no one in particular: "For the child of her love is no longer a slave!"[82]

The anticipated nonsite of lyric circulation was, for Harper, an achievement that went hand in hand with abolition. Meredith McGill tracks the public transformation of Harper's poetics in her authorial name change, traveling and publishing on the abolitionist lecture circuit in the 1850s as Frances Ellen Watkins, leaving the circuit after her marriage for roughly the span of the Civil War, and returning as Harper (often called "Mrs. Harper") in 1864. "The end of the Civil War also brought her greater geographical mobility and a revitalized career lecturing to mixed audiences in churches and public buildings throughout the South."[83] But McGill's point is that stressing the difference between her personae—and the differences in her poetry's public networks associated with each name and the contextual factors involved—allows us to account for the changing status accorded her lyric texts. In my readings so far, I have linked the glance to fugitivity and the futural possibility of attaining lyric form, a form that requires a shift in attitude toward the subjects of Harper's poetry (a shift that would universalize suffering in a way "The Slave Auction" does not yet countenance). It is also worth stressing that the glance, a probe for ascertaining forms of motion and circulation, is a two-sided affair, as my initial comparison meant to show: it can aid in the flattening, commodification, and dismissal of persons and bodies or it can be turned into a feeler for avenues of flight at the edge of the present as it shuffles toward open futures. It is the tool through which we can *see* differences in the textual forms of Watkins's and Harper's lyrics across relatively small but decisive temporal boundaries.

Referring to Harper's (really Watkins's) 1860 "To Charles Sumner"—an apostrophic poem from start to finish—McGill argues that the "conceit that the poem is itself speech . . . creates a sense of intimacy without the individuation we are accustomed to find in lyric poems." Ultimately, McGill argues that when contextualized in abolitionist discourse, Watkins's/Harper's poetry leaves us with a "figurative rescattering" rather than "a generalizable lyric inwardness," a circulatory potential for rhetorical *effect* out in the world beyond the poem.[84] My point is that this figurative rescattering—which must include her poetry's participation in the recirculation of characters from Stowe—does not take us away from lyric but moves us toward it, does not de-generalize lyric inwardness but witnesses its difficulty for Black poetry while articulating a lyric future. Since Harper always seems to be chasing something, pressing toward the abolitionist victory that would complete her poems' modulations into the lyric present, her work does not easily fit under Amiri Baraka's concept of the "changing same" in Black musical expression, in which the "Negro's music changed as he changed, reflecting shifting attitudes or (and this is equally important) *consistent attitudes within changed contexts*."[85] In choosing lyric possibility, Harper scatters our attention in the service of Black fugitivity while maintaining an expectant futurity of universal subjecthood. But there is one element of the changing same in her poetry, one that might gather her authorial names, lyric personae, and visual unsettledness in an ontology of Blackness: the hue or Maker's impress that would remain even as the status of her poems shift perceptibly into full lyric mode.

Black, that special hue of the God-maker's palette, will not easily be made to signify something other than a mark or a wound, but in a metonymic displacement in the tenth stanza of "Eliza Harris" (which begins with the announcement of Eliza's freedom), slavery's "scourges and chains" stain "our banner," our flag, the symbolic body of the nation.[86] Harper leaves hue out of it, except by the implication that the stain is in the dye that paints our national colors. Noting such a displacement is common in extant Harper scholarship. What remains to be thought is how the transferential movement of her poetry in trope and in address perform the glancing relays—the subjective visions to be borrowed and passed on rather than held and identified with—that energize antiracist activism and art making alike. "Eliza Harris" circulated widely, following the path of Eliza the character through American abolitionist networks. Thus another kind of "changing same": the utopian attainment of lyric form and lyric persona that, far from being only a cultural watchword to be questioned and destroyed in the subsequent century, must be considered (in some cases) a measure of freedom *from* context. Lyric form qua abstraction can liberate as much as constrain, providing experiential vessels that lighten a body's load, address those who are absent but accountable, and open private temporalities to public history.[87]

Glances pull objects and other people into our visual flow only to relinquish them; thus they prefer to borrow rather than hoard. Glances concatenate sequential images and draw them into a spot of time—slowing the inevitable progress of an auction, tracing the path of a fugitive's speedy escape—but dislocate temporal unity at the same time, reinforcing "the contradiction between social and personal time," the very tension Sharon Cameron designates "the lyric's generating impulse."[88] What I have claimed as Harper's lyric futurity (the attainment of lyric as grafted onto the attainment of liberty and social equality) subsists in the poem's joints, in the gap between "I" and "we" only tentatively sutured by apostrophe. In her poems, the tension between social and personal time is generative, founding the rhetorical basis of the lyric's trajectory, but still contradictory.

The contradictions of sentimentalism that generate the poems in the first place set the glance in motion, making the implied audience stretch their visual imaginaries beyond the reification of marked flesh and suffering soul, beyond an endless scene of Black subjection. Glances always seek the edges or limits of fields constructed for the eye's facile, passive consumption; Harper's would-be lyrics use the glance to renew the activity of selves straddling the boundary between a presented scene's inside and outside. Glancing goads. It remakes the subject as it goes, straining against its epistemic complacencies, its easy ways out of culpability in the state of the world as found. McGill calls Harper's poems "an invocation of a better world to come," though they stop short of willing that world into being. Instead, as they turn into lyrics they shoot a glance toward the future and the "larger public" they apostrophize, "one of indeterminate extent."[89] Proper maternal sentiment aside, the "mother's fond kiss" that ends "Eliza Harris" is glimpsed outside of empirical time, for we are at this impossible moment neither bystanders on the southern bank nor members of the small escaped band on the north.[90] We have shot the icy gap with Eliza, attentive to the pathos-laden kiss and witness to the utopian promise of lyric to de-mark the marked body without redomesticating fugitivity for our own redemptive purposes. What we see, ever so briefly, is the troubled, uneven, and endlessly historical—but shimmering—promise of lyricization as an unsettled form of freedom from the boundedness of the abjected self, a mode of aesthetic justice whose accomplishment has always yet to arrive in final form.

Plashless as She Sees

Dickinson's Glancing Stitch

Emily Dickinson's fourth letter to Thomas Wentworth Higginson reveals that her mentor asked her to provide a photographic self-portrait. She answers, "I had no portrait, now, but am small, like the Wren, and my Hair is bold, like the Chestnut Bur - and my eyes, like the Sherry in the Glass, that the Guest leaves - Would this do just as well?"[1] Her response gestures toward the post-Lessing, nineteenth-century *paragone* taken up by Hawthorne and many others, here as a friendly competition between language and light as means of representation. Marta Werner concludes from this epistolary episode, "By withholding/canceling the 1847 daguerreotype from Higginson's gaze and offering instead a discourse of ekphrasis, Dickinson the thirty-two-year-old writer at last escapes the subject-position of 'target,' acting, instead, as the 'operator' or controller of the scene (of writing)."[2] That Dickinson actively wriggles away from the object-position of the photographic act is all the more intriguing when one looks closely at her one sure photographic likeness.

That picture, which Mary Bernhard claims was taken by William C. North and which her siblings Austin and Lavinia rejected as "too solemn," was made when the poet was either sixteen or seventeen, during her time at the Mount Holyoke Female Seminary.[3] That means when many of us recall Dickinson's face, we recall the schoolgirl rather than the mature poet. We sense her looking to the future, both at us, at her unknown future readers who will take obsessive, even pettifogging interest in her weird poetry and desire to unearth more likenesses from a dearth of "authorized" pictures,[4] and more immediately at her own future productivity as an artist. Between her and us lies a century and a half, though as big a gulf—the gulf over which she looks and we look back—is her poems, little mysteries for us as well as for her adolescent self. But upon close inspection, she does not appear to be gazing straight at us, or at her future. Her visage is ever so slightly walleyed: according to Richard Sewall and ophthalmologist Martin Wand, applying the Hirschberg measurement, her right cornea deviated at least fifteen degrees from true.[5] They take this as evidence that the mysterious optical illness she suffered from—referenced several times in her letters—was the effect of exotropia, the outward turn of the eye. Before she ever put her pen to paper, Emily Dickinson's eyes were just a bit wide of the mark. She could not look at things straight on; she literally saw them slant.

Slantwise poetics and vision come together in a poem that begins with the injunction to "Tell all the truth but tell it slant":

> Tell all the truth
> but tell it slant -
> Success in Circuit
> lies
> Too bright for our
> infirm Delight
> The Truth's superb
> surprise
> As Lightning to
> the Children eased
> With explanation kind
> The Truth must
> dazzle gradually†
> Or every man be
> blind -
>
>]moderately
>
> (F1263)[6]

Dickinson's slants—her half-rhymes, her oft-ungrammatical dashes, her metrical stutters, her irregular line lengths unfixed on many of her manuscript pages—succeed, in the terms of this poem, as parts of a "Circuit." One simple name for a circuit of slants is a poem, an argument that reveals a truth gradually and indirectly (though not always moderately, as Dickinson's weaker variant offers). This poem, as a performance of telling and seeing slantwise, begins with a maxim only to proliferate metaphoric substitutions: telling the truth slant means establishing a circuit or circuitous discourse *as if* shielding us from a bright light *just as* we protect children from the violent surprise of lightning with a kind story *or else* the shock would strike us blind.

If "Delight" is "infirm," if our bodies are too small and fragile to take in blinding truths all at once, we must approach scenes of revelation at glancing angles. Every poem and every part of a poem offers a glance at a truth, and like a circuit of glances they are stitched together to form a whole, though the wholes in question retain their holes. We do not always see best or most poetically, in other words, when we try to see everything at once, as if panoramically. There are several other poems in which Dickinson relates seeing and blindness to the size and directness of a truth or image, including "Before I got my eye put out" (F336), a curious lyric whose speaker comes to prefer (as "safer") spiritual sight over the physical, unconventionally marking the latter more dangerous to the infirm seer. And yet, even as she chooses the seeing of the soul over the visual capacities of her "finite eyes," it is physical sight that contains—even as it struggles to not be overwhelmed by—all the poem's treasures, not least "The Motions of the Dipping Birds" which return again and again (like birds themselves, in their endless migratory "Circuit"[7]) in Dickinson's poetry. The question remains how best to see given our visual limitations, and how best to make poetry at the boundaries that separate and join the seen and the unseen. What follows is an extended look at these boundaries, these stitching points, which join Dickinson's immediate physical materials to a distributed ecological awareness.[8]

The ideal of perceptual distribution, one that this chapter approaches much as it claims Dickinson does, along the path from fascicle form to scattered scraps, is animal life. I will argue that Dickinson both thematizes "plashless" glancing vision, associated for her with the animal difference, and metabolizes it as a poetic technique over time so that it comes to inform her most interesting form and media choices after she stopped binding her poems together. Like Harper, Dickinson was searching for poetic forms that might deconstruct the poisonous privileges of ocular-subjective stability, but unlike her contemporary, Dickinson's moving target was not a universalizable lyric form. She charted a path toward ecological-textual distribution, with the glance as both a thread of sequential progress and eventually a means of dissolving the perceptual and cognitive traces of lyric humanism. The glance's two affordances for Dickinson, its capacity to stitch and unstitch, recur as she continually tests new possibilities for approaching the impossible: seeing without imposing one's sight on the environing world.

During Dickinson's lifetime, and as I suggested too about Hawthorne's, photography was the biggest technical provocation to the question of what and how else we might be able to see. So I will start there before exploring the perceptual, thematic, and formal relationship between the glance and the stitch. For Dickinson, ultimately, the stitching and unstitching of a glancing poetics gathers its resources in attunement to animal craft, like the wren's. But that's an insight attained on the other side of Higginson's request. When Dickinson contrasts the circuit of slant truth to a flash of light(ning) that overwhelms the seer, we might first think that she's restating the conflict Higginson provoked: A photograph or a poem? Which sees best?

Circling back to Higginson's request after her circuit of metaphorical descriptors, Dickinson writes that in any case, in her experience, "the Quick wore off those things, in a few days," likely referring to the albumen gloss on a freshly printed photograph.[9] The technical term *quick* also referred at the time to a chemical accelerator (originally for daguerreotypes) that "increased the sensitivity of the light-recording compound and thus very materially reduced the time of exposure in the camera . . . from minutes to seconds."[10] If the quickening brought signifier and signified into more immediate relation—was what appeared to collapse the gap between object and image that was so apparent in longer exposures—Dickinson's disparaging comment suggests her knowing skepticism about such immediacy, that photography's magic had already worn off, for her if not for everyone else. But while Judith Farr argues like Werner that, in this letter, Dickinson demonstrates her "preference for capturing images in the suggestive language of poetry rather than by strict graphic means,"[11] her extensive use of the word "quick" throughout her poetic corpus—for instance, in "The Soul's distinct connection" (F901)—instead suggests a far more complicated working relationship to photography's mechanical process:

> The Soul's distinct
> Connection
> With immortality
> Is best disclosed by
> Danger
> Or quick Calamity -
>
> As Lightning on a
> Landscape

Exhibits† Sheets of Place -
Not yet suspected† - but
for Flash† -
And Click† - and Suddenness.

]Developes
]still unsuspected]Fork
]Bolt

(F901)

This poem, likely written in 1865 and never bound, is considered part of Dickinson's Set 5. The poem's second stanza makes a subordinate clause, its "As" cordoning off two sides of an analogy and thereby splitting the poem in half according to the logic of likeness. Internally, within the second stanza, her diction splits custody of the "quick Calamity" in which the Soul meets immortality between natural and mechanical phenomena. She plays off then-commonplace associations between the camera's flash and lightning strikes, the latter "seen as capable of 'photographing' outlines onto natural objects" and "often regarded, like photography, as an amalgamation of the mystical and the scientific."[12] "Quick," "Sheets," "Flash," "Click," and her variant "Developes" all bring the photographic process into the domain of existential crisis, with interior and exterior "Landscape[s]" revealed in an expectant glance. The short poem, its dashes increasing in number as it rushes to a sudden conclusion and exposure, produces epiphany's interruption within the flow of thought and in the breakdown of common meter. One of Dickinson's characteristically tense moments of the soul's proximity to the eternal is transformed into the rhythms of photographic revelation, of the camera eye's "Suddenness" as it pulls a decisive "Place" out of time.[13]

One can perfectly imagine a coherent reading of this verse that plays up the violence, the lurking "Danger" and achieved "Calamity" inflicted by the flash and click on the unsuspecting "Soul." Indeed, few Dickinson lyrics overlook the hazards of revelation, violent and self-destructive by definition. One might ground a poem like this within a general economy of agoraphobic aversion, thinking that the "Danger" of the camera's flash and click is its threat to the self-contained (lyric) self, scattering and disseminating its mien throughout an unfeeling, gaping, critical public. Several critics have reached such a conclusion—about Dickinson's poetry if not specifically about her feelings on photography—as they attempt to explain the mystery of her extremely sparse publication record (only about twelve out of her nearly two thousand poem-like objects appeared in print during her lifetime). Often these claims suggest Dickinson's passivity in the face of some threatening cultural monolith: the critic, the market, print culture, eternity, God. Werner, focusing on the aforementioned photograph's "final presentation format," a "sixth-plate portrait under glass, set in a velvet-lined leather case bearing a clasp," suggests that the daguerreotype materializes the "ideals of bourgeois existence and gender politics in mid-nineteenth-century America: the young woman gazing out into space is first miniaturized and then withdrawn from the public sphere, enclosed in the family home that would soon become the scene for an emerging interior life."[14]

But Dickinson envisions interior life differently.[15] Ultimately photography falls away as a central visual analogy; something else will have to "do just as well," something closer to home and to her own craft. As Diana Fuss notes, her progressive retreat indoors has been "variously pathologized and romanticized, overdramatized and idealized." At the same time, there can be no doubt that the forms of the homestead inform her poetics, that "House" named "fairer" than prose, "More numerous of Windows - / Superior - for Doors -" (F466). Poetry is a house not only because it is bounded and contained but because it is "The Finite - furnished / With the Infinite -" (F830). Her lyrics are not gaudily furnished but largely spare of bric-a-brac. Referencing a late two-line poem, "All things swept / sole away / This - is immensity -" (F1548), Fuss writes that Dickinson "alliteratively sweeps the poem free of internal clutter, exposing in the process the sheer immensity of a minimalist space."[16] The poem's minimalist design means the interior detail is set in infinite intellectual space, allowing the eye to jump from a part to a whole in the course of its motion. Limited domestic spaces become little worlds of the glance, thickened through ordinary acts of poetic attention.

"There's a certain Slant of light" (F320) provides one such little world. The last poem in Fascicle 13, it was copied with no variants:

> There's a certain Slant of light,
> Winter Afternoons -
> That oppresses, like the Heft
> Of Cathedral Tunes -
>
> Heavenly Hurt, it gives us -
> We can find no scar,
> But internal difference -
> Where the Meanings, are -

None may teach it - Any -
'Tis the seal Despair -
An imperial affliction
Sent us of the Air -

When it comes, the Landscape listens -
Shadows - hold their breath -
When it goes, 'tis like the Distance
On the look of Death -

(F320)

Many Dickinson poems begin in the aftermath of some crisis or event, but this one starts closer to the middle of a temporal sequence. By beginning with the afternoon light, eliding the day's origin in sunrise, Dickinson orients us to a moment pregnant with atmospheric rather than narrative meaning. As the stanzas roll, this poem describes the irreversible effect of an ordinary diurnal perception that gains in tangibility as the subject takes in the layout of a visual environment, grasping a surface's constituent detail as continuous with a more encompassing whole. Though light is diffuse and does not typically resolve into graspable substance, this is a "certain" slant of light, an image of light, reflected at least twice from its source, its crooked face on the wall a concrete abstraction that parallels despair's mysterious imprint on the soul. In the first stanza, light quickly converts into sound as ground contracts into figure, gaining physical and lyrical weight.

Nowhere in the rest of the poem does the slant return as an image, though it will in other ocularcentric lyrics like "The Angle of a Landscape" (F578). But here, Dickinson's view of the slant is a joint or scar on the world's surface (as on the wall's) that returns to her as her glance comes and goes like the light does. In between the glances, which are all we are spared of the light's longer and slower path from nothingness to nothingness, the image leaves an "internal difference, / Where the Meanings, are": pain produces knowledge that cannot be refunded, as its temporal dimensions cut diagonals through linear sequence. Glances are nonlinear too, bearing extra weight in their return loops as they drink from the past's reservoirs, a whole heritage of perceptions, thoughts, desires, intentions, and patterns stored in the body and affecting the next glance the subject will send out. The concluding stanza returns to the surface level of the winter afternoon: the slant is now recognized as a symptom of the sun's decline from our earthly vantage, for "When it comes, the Landscape listens - / Shadows - hold their breath -," and the quiet of approaching dusk binds subject and world in nervous apprehension of their disappearance in a shroud of darkness. This vision of the final and complete desolation of the landscape—concurrent with the disappearance of the poem's founding image—is a manifestation of the "internal difference" that the action of the poem brings about in the speaker, in the dramatic shift in Dickinson's visual attention.

Though this single lyric does not offer a complete Dickinsonian theory of vision, the "shift" I reference above is not another example of the most common analogy for thinkers of the gaze: the moving searchlight taken to characterize consciousness's intentional-visual access to the world. Indeed, if there is a gaze in the poem, it is on the side of the object rather than the subject, in the slant that moves across the wall as the absent, panoptic sun moves. In terms of the eye's mechanics, an "internal difference" is opened by each saccade, in the minute parallax distance between the eye's positions as it jumps fitfully whenever its target object is located within the central twenty degrees of our visual field (when we do not need to turn our heads or bodies to track it). The general function of saccadic movements, as James J. Gibson puts it, "is to establish a new fixation . . . in the act of scanning the environment [or] in reading."[17]

"I watched the Moon around the House" (F593) extends Dickinson's insight into the fixation-shifting character of the glance. As the moon moves around the house like a nocturnal counterpoint to the certain slant of light, it temporarily rests "opon a Pane" which allows the speaker to gaze upon it until it slides "carelessly away." Each window onto the moon is a temporary "Rest" in a world of shifting phenomena, and so the poet must shift her lunar metaphor constantly, turning the poem into what Michelle Kohler calls "discursive formation in action, as the speaker makes a series of fine metaphorical or grammatical revisions that reconfigure eye, moon, and metaphor in relation to each other."[18] The speaker finds that she cannot hold the moon fast through her gaze, through a look that sees into the life of things and produces the perfect metaphor: "The privilege to scrutinize / Was scarce opon my Eyes / When, with a Silver practise - / She vaulted out of Gaze - ." I will return to Dickinson's use of silver, but for now it suffices to note that the moon's "Silver practise," its "Superior Road - / Or it's Advantage," is precisely what escapes the gaze, and so the meaning-making quality of the poem depends primarily on the glance as it tracks the tenor's "finer Gravitations." Although she does not make the distinction between gaze and glance, Kohler notes that Dickinson's vision of vision is here "a brief means of access that falls 'opon' the speaker's eyes for the scarce moment before the moon 'vault[s] out of Gaze.'"[19] I would emphasize "scarce," following Dickinson's meter.

And so the glance stitches a visual fabric out of the eye's fragmentary movements. Spasmodic, the eye does not smoothly scan a visual field and capture the object it rests on as an organic whole. Instead, it loops back on itself bearing small, perishable gifts from its surroundings, opening an "internal difference": "there is a critical moment just before a given saccade is wholly under way when its direction and speed can be altered significantly" by new, immediately felt information.[20] The moving glance's trajectory is attuned to respond to sudden changes in the visual environment and can be trained to account for (and even overplan for) expected movements of a given target object.[21] And the smaller the scale of the visual field, and the finer the motor skills needed to perform a given task, the more crucial each saccade's accuracy is. The glance makes its home at the scale of fine-grained activity, crafted and perfected through a feel for the small world it moves in.

Hermann von Helmholtz's *Treatise on Physiological Optics*, which synthesizes data gleaned from several experiments on eye movement, was published in Dickinson's lifetime, its final volume released in 1867.[22] In it, Helmholtz describes ordinary vision as a series of "unconscious conclusions derived from sensation," formed through a combination of perceptual data and experience and through physiological solutions to the eye's limitations, particularly the fact that the retina's center (the fovea) contains far more densely packed photoreceptor cells than its periphery.[23] Helmholtz and his colleagues consolidated their empirical findings into laws describing the eye's miraculous ability to track objects in time and stitch together coherent sequences out of worldly flux. Donders' Law and Listing's Law (named after two such colleagues) explain the development of regular saccadic principles, the rules of the eye's angles of torsion depending on attentional demands. The time of the eye's movements, Helmholtz argued, was a time of construction and experimentation in which we "test whether we have correctly interpreted the lawful behavior of the phenomenon in question, i.e. its postulated existence in a definite spatial arrangement."[24]

I call the glance and its saccadic, disjointed temporal structure a "stitching operation" for a good, though perhaps predictable, reason. It is well known that, beginning in 1858, Dickinson copied many of her poems onto folded stationery sheets and sewed them together into small booklets (fascicles) with red string. The great villain of Dickinson criticism, Mabel Loomis Todd—the adulteress who cut the sacred string, unbinding the fascicles for individual, anthological consumption—in fact helped produce a scholarly cottage industry devoted to reconstituting the context of the poems' material production. As we scorn Todd and other early publishers, we engage in a Neoplatonic spiral of procession from and return to the source: Dickinson's craft. One might argue that it was because the string was cut, turning the originally bound poems into individual lyrics, that the critical desire to understand them otherwise, as more than a collection of mysterious fragments, was generated. The Dickinson critic became a sewer, a binder, a *glancer*, one who tries to replicate the poet's vision as a maker rather than a prophet, as someone who stitches a world together through materials rather than Ideals. And when we attempt to recapture the Dickinson family's home economics, the sewing and unsewing of the poems—and how Dickinson repurposes household scraps and fragments through the later innings of her life—we find that glancing attunements are far more capacious than homely, as much ontological as domestic.

Of the many interpretations of Dickinson's poiesis generated by the fascicle form's centrality in her writing life, two stand out as stark alternatives. Werner compares them to "forty locked doors [that] attest to the power of enclosedness," each binding an "enclosed textual space in which Dickinson explored the contents of privacy and power."[25] Sharon Cameron suggests, on the other hand, that while binding signals a "desire for the limit," a door locked against endless scattering and textual proliferation, the inclusion of variants on the fascicle sheets in effect resuscitates such proliferation, making it virtually "impossible to say where the text ends because the variants extend the text's identity in ways that make it seem potentially limitless."[26] I wonder, though, if these are indeed the primary hermeneutic alternatives. Certainly Werner's position rhymes comfortably with readings of the individual poems that emphasize privacy and formal-domestic veiling operations as a defense against the male gaze and its critical counterpart in the literary marketplace. And sustained attention to Dickinson's intricate drafting and sketching process actually reveals the fascicles to be, as Alexandra Socarides formidably argues, "flexible, ever-developing objects whose methods of construction ask us to consider them in those terms."[27] At the same time, Cameron's appeal to the limitless still enacts a formalism as textualism, a consideration of words on the page and the production of meaning through their relations, potentially unconcerned with the poetry's material support and the way Dickinson makes objects by gathering worldly forms. In other words, my view of Dickinson's development and material practice in some important ways agrees with Cameron's but in other equally important ways departs. Like Cameron, I think we must include devices like the variants as internal to and integral to the texts and individual poems, and that doing so in fact troubles the very distinction between the "inside" and "outside" of a poem. But, especially when we move beyond the fascicle form, as I will later in this chapter, we also find that the frames, edges, and limits of the object-text (the very thing Cameron deconstructs) do come to matter with a new kind of force. The most productive form of criticism, then, might involve Cameron's insights about the potential limitlessness of the fascicle to bear specifically on the changes in the material supports and techniques of craft Dickinson chooses. Because she does choose those.

Ultimately, I think only by joining textual and theoretical readings can we truly make sense of the visual economies of Dickinson's poiesis, and the way Dickinson's omnipresent thematic of vision threads her praxis through her poems' speculative meanings. "I saw no Way - The Heavens were stitched -" (F633) combines stitching and seeing at its open, and its first dash performs an enjambment internal to the line like a hem, allowing us to read the phrase either in rhythm or broken by a caesura: she either sees no way forward because the heavens were stitched, or she does not see how the heavens were stitched. The seam in the line introduces Dickinson's sense of how stitching-together can be a mode of completion or alienation. The heavens, sewn together, exclude her. But also, if she could see how they were stitched, how the heavens were made—just like poetry critics who might see how this poem was made—they might open back up for her. Stitching implies unstitching; making implies unmaking; seeing implies unseeing. The last lyric on Fascicle 23's second sheet references the sewing and unsewing of the poem:

> From Blank to Blank -
> A Threadless Way†
> I pushed Mechanic feet -
> To stop - or perish -
> or advance -
> Alike indifferent -
>
> If end I gained†
> It ends beyond
> Indefinite disclosed -
> I shut my eyes - and
> groped as well
> 'Twas lighter† - to be Blind -
>
>]Course
>]reached
>]firmer
>
> (F484)

"From Blank to Blank -" hems and folds vision into a textual landscape. The writing of the poem, pushing "Mechanic feet" from "Blank to Blank" (a phrase reminiscent of verse meter, a loom, and even a presser's progression in a sewing machine), is an obstacle-ridden hike over a "Threadless" or pathless abyss. The poem's forward thrust is as troubled as the dangerous course, halting and advancing in equal two-beat measure. The caesuras at the end of the first stanza break the convention of the "Mechanic" meter and resolve into an "indifferent" end rhyme. Here the dashes are both compositional stutters, places where the flow of Dickinson's hand halts, and markers or pitons laid down for support.[28] If she pressed her hand a bit harder, she would have rent the page and produced new sites for her string to thread. Ariadne must lay her thread in order to create a traceable path to the end of the labyrinth, but there is no Theseus here to benefit from the task, at least not until the finished poem is read. So it is not just "lighter" but "firmer," as the last variant has it, to advance blindly toward an end or close that does not appear as final form until it is reached. One travels better without a backpack, though here the carry-on would be preshaped *light*, which is too heavy to bring along. Wrapped together in Dickinson's taskscape are stitches and glances, blind gestures and looks—modes of touch and sight that feel their way along without firm conceptual frames to arrest them—that are nonetheless productive in the poem's formation and the achievement of material relation to the other poems it is bound with.

The thematic stitch linking "From Blank to Blank -" to the other poems in Fascicle 23—death, death's personifications, and the end of the poem as *the* end—and then outward to the techne of the fascicle form itself suggests that it is too restrictive to conceive Dickinson's bounded sequences as locked doors.[29] And the knot that ties the poet's vision (often conceived by her readers in sublime, prophetic terms) to the working of her hands (typically a sign of her material craft, her "narrow" grasp of verse's "Paradise" [F466]) suggests that Dickinson charted the foundations and limits of meaning in both language and physical material. Branka Arsić refers to the poet, in this sense, as "someone who in order to exercise poetics and versify words, must also create an object—form matter—that will then generate and sustain the form of the poem." Is this what the hand and the glance conspire to do together, and what the temporality of Dickinson's poem—inserting a word here and a thread there, halting so as not to proceed too quickly, closing one's eyes to the misleading image that arrests the body—replicates at the level of techne? Dickinson glances between the object-form of her poetry and the individual page like a sewer checking the progress of her local pattern against the whole.

She practices poiesis "not as a weak form of creation—where the creation of the poem is analogous to, but does not coincide with, the creation of a material thing—but instead as a strong form of creation that produces something palpable and embodied . . . a question not only of aesthetical but also ontological generation."[30]

Dickinson's palpable objects change over time.[31] She was not always stitching pages together. But in her fascicle stage, in part because she *was* then stitching pages together, the form of her poetry and the visual language contained therein accord with the techne of stitching movements, which Anthony Tuck has traced back to the origins of some Indo-European verse in weaving song (though there on the principle of loom-made patterns).[32] In "All overgrown by cunning moss" (F146), one of the first poems in Fascicle 7 and an elegy to Charlotte Brontë, Dickinson inserted an "Or" in between the third and fourth stanzas:

> All overgrown by cunning moss,
> All interspersed with weed,
> The little cage of "Currer Bell"
> In quiet "Haworth" laid.
>
> This Bird - observing others
> When frosts too sharp became
> Retire to other latitudes -
> Quietly did the same -
>
> But differed in returning -
> Since Yorkshire hills are green -
> Yet not in all the nests I meet -
> Can Nightingale be seen -
>
> Or
>
> Gathered from many wanderings -
> Gethsemane can tell
> Thro' what transporting anguish
> She reached the Asphodel!
>
> Soft fall the sounds of Eden
> Upon her puzzled ear -

Oh, what an afternoon for
Heaven,
When "Brontë" entered there!

(F146)

Dickinson's publishers have not known what to do with the "Or," as Socarides notes: "The 'Or' disrupts the temporal ordering of the poem's experience, a disruption that both Todd and Franklin avoided when they published the poem as stanzas 1, 2, 3, 4, and 5 and as 1, 2, and 3 respectively."[33] It's as if she took a Miltonic conjunction, proliferating vehicles in one of *Paradise Lost*'s layered similes, and made the impossible choice a format feature of her poem. If one wishes to treat the "Or" not as legitimate poetic content but as an extraneous note for future use, it could mean a variety of things: choose between stanzas three and four, perhaps, or between stanzas two and three and four and five. One can, of course, print all five stanzas and simply cut the "Or." But assuming that Dickinson's poetry should be read according to its possibilities for future print regulation is alien to her very project.[34] And the richness of Dickinson's poetic process reveals itself precisely when one includes devices like the "Or" as elements of and keys to Dickinson's object construction.

While Socarides focuses on the genre of the elegy, and on the temporal confusions inherent to the experience of (narrating) loss and death, Dickinson's "Or" is just as relevant to the temporal structure of the glance and the scene of material production. The "Or" opens a Möbius track internal to the poem that also, through its disruptive emplacement on the page, serves as another rent or hole for tying its multiple meaning relations to the wider economy of the fascicle. First, the "Or" troubles the static image of the bird preceding the break, foregrounding the poem's alternative tropes of a bird returning to its nest and the "transporting anguish" that signifies not cyclical return but unknowable termination. But even as the poem "provides the bird a way out of the stasis that the poem might have otherwise produced for it,"[35] pushing against both the natural time of cyclical return and the lyric moment of interior clarity and stillness, it produces a temporal node on the page consistent with many of Dickinson's other unusual practices, like embedding variants between the poem's lines or utilizing material page breaks to make the act of turning the sheet relevant to the pacing of the poem. These nodes work by forcing readers to glance back and forth as they progress linearly through the poem from beginning to end (for how else can one adequately judge the options produced by the "Or" or by internal variants?), turning the text itself into a recursive, nonlinear, and endlessly branching event.

Jerome McGann, in his reading of Dickinson's "textual invasions," writes that the parallel shifts in our attention demanded by many of her poems ask us to learn to "'better see' what the print conventions of poetry work to keep us from seeing."[36] They also force us to see, through the glance, the netherworld of the poet's enactive vision, the variations that crop up as the poem is being sketched on the page. Like the unconscious saccades of the human eye from the perspective of the coherent moving scan, the internal, nonlinear variations of poiesis are often passed over by a retrospective critical gaze and what Dickinson scathingly calls publication's "Auction" (F788). The construction of a nodal object—gaining in complexity when one moves from the individual lyric to the sheet, from the sheet to the bound fascicle—is like the "weaver's masterpiece" in *Faust* I.4: "Unseen the threads are knit together, and an infinite combination grows."[37] And in encountering the fascicles' combinations, the threads that both bind the whole and unbind the poems from within, the reader's glance subverts the reading subject in ways often narrated by Dickinson herself, most obviously in her postfascicle lyrics that loosen the stitch holding the mind together just as she was loosening the stitches holding her poetry together.[38] Just as the glance is flung from the subject, thrown rather than cautiously and delicately aimed, Dickinson's practice constructs the object by displacing its center of gravity. "Where the gaze consolidates its gains, the glance acts to dispel and disconnect," Casey writes. The glance alters "its course at every opportunity"; whereas the gaze seeks "a fixed point of attachment," the glance is an "agent of displacement."[39] As the glance stitches images together in concatenated sequence, each new image alters the store from inside, reshuffles the stock. Each new glance, like each new sheet, momentarily scatters the archive before it settles back into a new sequence. As if acknowledging this fluttering dialectic, one already contained in the simplicity of her "Or," Dickinson began to scatter her pages.

Dickinson's final project, I aim to show, was an attempt to undo the sequence as an experiment in becoming-animal, in seeing and working like an animal. Animals, for a poet who always observed critters with keen interest, presented a hard but radically productive problem in that they appear to human eyes as "plashless" (Dickinson's term of art, which I will discuss shortly). That is, any question of human relation or even community with animals must deal with the sense that animals seem to live unreflectively within their narrow(er) niches, and appear to perceive their worlds immediately, seeing and acting in unbroken circuits. Plashless living would be analogous to seamless or stitchless writing. Watching an animal simply be, we might speculate, would be like seeing one's own lack or insufficiency as a seeing subject and as a poet, and thus like seeing one's deepest desire for an art that sacrifices the stitch as an outmoded way of gathering a world acted out by a lucky nonhuman who does not even know how fortunate it is to exist as it does.

Let us jump forward in time for a minute. In 1886, Emily Dickinson died. In 1886, Eadweard Muybridge was completing a series of animal motion sequences following his 1878 series *The Horse in Motion*. Muybridge had been working on this project, which would revolutionize motion studies, since Leland Stanford approached him about a bet in 1872 (are all four of a galloping horse's feet ever off the ground at the same time?). He went on to build a menagerie of locomotive animal studies, from birds in flight to elephants in slow motion. Dickinson had been exclusively writing unbound poetry since 1871, a large percentage of which were fragments of animal lyrics. Muybridge and Dickinson approach their animals from opposite directions—observing from without and inhabiting from within—though both strived to operate on an ocular level separate from commonsense anthropocentric visual paradigms. In so doing, both generated fresh insights about the peculiarities and possibilities of human environmental manipulation and the distinction between human and animal seeing. But whereas Muybridge demonstrated the power of rational, procedural, and trigonometric analysis for overcoming our embodied visual limitations, Dickinson began collecting man-made scraps for her nest like a resourceful bird, picking things up and letting them happily fall like a being already seamlessly integrated into the world.

In order to complete this comparison, I will continue to track the development of Dickinson's poiesis while glancing at the work of another contemporary visual artist (painter and photographer Thomas Eakins) who reached maturity around the key moment of transition in the poet's career. There is no direct, immediate, and unproblematic line between Dickinson's fascicles and her late scrap poems. The path can be evaluated as either a progression or regression in her art, just as developments in the contemporary visual arts—the transition between realism and Impressionism concomitant with the growing use of naturalistic and scientific photography—were seen as cultural progressions and regressions in almost equal measure. Just as Dickinson was reviewing her poetic practice in terms of more fragmentary modes of construction, Impressionists were rethinking the ground of artistic

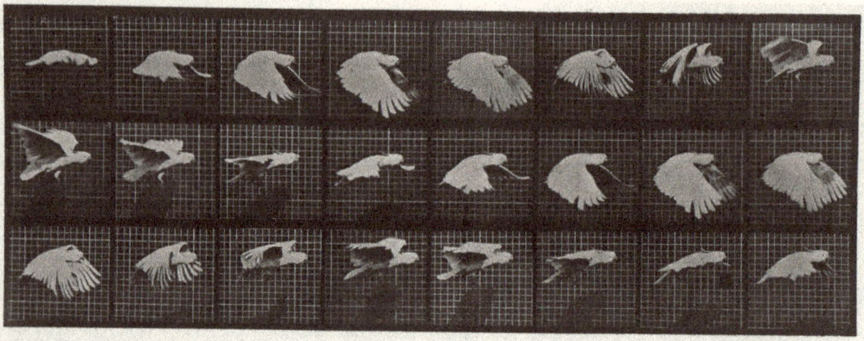

FIGURE 6. Eadweard Muybridge, *Animal Locomotion*, vol. 11, *Wild Animals and Birds*, plate 759, 1887, collotype, Pennsylvania Academy of the Fine Arts, Philadelphia

practice to incorporate contingent atmospherics, mood and tone color, and momentary isolated glances in (and not just on) the world.

Dickinson's "Sets" are groups of loose poems on fascicle stationery—dated at the earliest from 1863—formed by Ralph Franklin and that follow Todd's original organization based on the assumption that each set was meant to be bound together in fascicle form. Franklin organized the sets "by similarity of paper and date."[40] But the composite object of the "set," therefore, is the product of anthologization, not Dickinson's craft. She did not make the sets, just their elements. Socarides speculates that the "misleading designation" may be the result of scholars who "could not abandon the idea of [Dickinson's] methodically-planned and well-orchestrated poetic project [of the fascicles] and therefore continued to read organizing logics where there were none."[41] Yet in poems like "I felt a Cleaving in my Mind -" (F867), now a member of Set 2, the poet explicitly narrates the transition in her working process. But consider first a thematically similar poem from Fascicle 27:

> The Brain, within it's Groove
> Runs evenly - and true -
> But let a Splinter swerve -
> 'Twere easier for you -
>
> To put a Current† back -
> When Floods have slit
> the Hills -

And scooped a Turnpike
for Themselves -
And trodden out† the Mills -

]the Waters
]blotted out - shoved away -

(F563)

Jed Deppman includes "The Brain, within it's Groove" within his category of Dickinson's "trying-to-think" poems, "a lyric subgenre she developed to respond to what most resisted her thought."[42] Such poems tend to reproduce the downward movement characteristic of most of her poems, with the first line establishing a context that is then evacuated, never to return to solid ground.[43] The "Brain" that follows a straight, even path or "Groove" is reminiscent of William James's definition of habit in *The Principles of Psychology*, explained in terms of the nervous system's "mechanical facts." For James, habitual association and action result from a worn path of nervous energy, a "Groove" in the brain where one impulse continually excites another. James even uses the example of a woman knitting or sewing: she can do so perfectly well as she talks because one impulse triggers the next. Dickinson's stitches follow a "Groove" when her sewing process—tied intimately to her glance—becomes automatic and prereflective, temporarily effecting an ampliative relation between her material craft and her speculative metaphysic where the more "details of our daily life we can hand over to the effortless custody of automatism, the more our higher powers of mind will be set free for their own proper work."[44] But this poem then narrates the site (or "Splinter") where the mechanism, as if jolted by a Lucretian atomic "swerve," breaks down.

The "Splinter" is one of Dickinson's small stains or slivers that makes all the difference—like her "Tooth / that nibbles at the soul" (F373) or the "certain Slant of light" (F320)—often sending the poem and the glance off on another track. Deppman calls the speaker of "The Brain, within it's Groove" a "Rortian ironist who struggles between vocabularies and avails herself of tropological redescription . . . adopt[ing] verbs of human industry to describe how thought exceeds itself, the 'turnpikes' and 'hills' recalling the phrenological and anatomical images of brains that Dickinson knew."[45] One might just as well take the "verbs of human industry" literally: the splinter, which recalls the shape of Dickinson's dashes, and, when enlarged, the horizontal white space between her two stanzas, also marks a transition between economic systems, between the "Groove[s]" that mark the binding of the fascicles and the large-scale "scoop[ing]" of a turnpike, another sort of groove dug into the earth. One might then speculate that the swerve Dickinson narrates is from artisanal craft to industry, and manifests an anxious fear of future's shroud over her technical mode. The second stanza also evokes New Testament prophecy—"every valley shall be filled, and every mountain and hill shall be brought low"—in relation to the Hebrew Bible's cosmic position that God created man from earth, dust, and clay and that all things must in time return to that primordial state.[46] The process, Dickinson suggests, is irreversible—one must be God Himself to reverse it—but the poem stops short of imagining an alternative to the deluge, to the inevitable failures of a fascicle project that tries to permanently join lyrics on opposite sides of a swerve (in thought, time, and vision). Both poet and reader traverse a barely discernable but ultimately irreparable gap as they turn the page. The poem simply envisions the negation of the linear groove as principle of thought and poiesis without turning that negation toward the formation of a new poetic object.

Rather than assume the sets are merely the fascicles' remainders or spare parts, one might consider them, as Socarides has, new poetic objects or material supports that generate a more adequate body for Dickinson's ideas as she transitioned out of her binding phase. The perceptual corollary to these new textual bodies, I claim, is animal embodiment. But the way there is beset by many hairpins and cleavages. "I felt a Cleaving in / my Mind -," whose commonly cited first line and stand-in title is actually already split in two, explicitly joins (paradoxically by "Cleaving") the "trying-to-think" thematic of certain late fascicle poems with the practical problem of stitching a sequence together:

I felt a Cleaving in
my Mind -
As if my Brain had
split -
I tried to match it -
Seam by Seam -
But could not make
them fit -

The thought behind, I
strove† to join
Unto the thought before -

But Sequence ravelled
out of Sound† -
Like Balls - upon a
Floor -

]tried
]reach

(F867)

Who could seriously envision this lyric sewn into a fascicle? Or who, at least, would want to? As the concatenation of thoughts fails, as the speaker fails to "make / them fit -," sequence as a governing cognitive principle reaches crisis. The seam is no longer in control, and the poem's spatiotemporal coherence splits as the thought "behind" (in space) cannot harmonize with the thought "before" (in time). Such harmony is a principle of binding poems together in sequence, which assumes that spatial organization follows a corresponding temporal flow.

The last phrase, following the "But," enters the realm of sound, perhaps, because the poem stretches for something beyond the poverty of ordinary sight. But the poem's final variant, which offers a substitution of "reach" for "Sound," marks the poem's transformation from crisis to possibility. The sequence that "ravell[s] / out of Sound -" becomes dissonant noise, but can also be taken as a rolling image, a proleptic vision of purposive scattering and release, a letting-go. A similar trajectory—from growing skepticism and anxiety about the seams that show in crafted sequence to a material unbinding that parallels a poetics of scattering and release—occurs within the subcorpus of Dickinson's animal poems, which more trenchantly foreground the ability of her cleavage in praxis to recast the role of sight in poetic composition.

Dickinson placed a poem shot through with peculiar juxtapositions and mixed animal media in Fascicle 17:

A Bird came down
the Walk -
He did not know I
saw -
He bit an Angleworm
in halves
And ate the fellow, raw,

And then he drank
a Dew
From a Convenient Grass -
And then hopped sidewise
to the Wall
To let a Beetle pass -

He glanced with rapid
eyes
That hurried all around -
They looked like frightened
Beads, I thought -
He stirred his Velvet
Head

Like One in danger, Cautious,
I offered him a Crumb
And he unrolled his
feathers
And rowed him softer
home -

Than Oars divide the
Ocean,
Too silver for a seam -
Or Butterflies, off Banks
of Noon
Leap, plashless as they
swim.

(F359)

Through four stanzas, "A Bird came down the Walk -" is less about the bird than the observer the bird ignores. Anthropomorphisms abound, which is common in her animal poems.[47] From the speaker's initially detached perspective, the bird is a well-mannered diner, cutting his prey in fastidious halves and drinking dew from a grass/glass (an analogy not limited to the fascicle period, as evidenced by the much later "A Saucer holds a Cup" [F1407], which refers to a squirrel's teeth as "His Cutlery"). He takes a postprandial stroll and graciously obeys the natural laws of traffic. In the third stanza the bird glances "with rapid / eyes / That hurried all around -," orbs the speaker reads as "frightened / Beads." But the "I thought," which in adjusted lineation stands out isolated on the page but in manuscript is tucked away in the middle of its stanza, generates a moment of self-reflection that turns on two analogies, the beads and the phrase "Like One in danger," an interpretation that leads to her philanthropic impulse, her two-bit crumb. In the poem's "proper" form, where "I thought" juts out like a headland into the sea or a branch into the air, the speaker's deictic position within the scene is clear, even visible. As reflective observer, her first impulse is, Elisa New says, to take a position of "noblesse oblige" that ultimately "melds her anxiety" with the bird's.[48] Her condescending gift goes unheeded by the bird because it mistakes the function of his glance.

The speaker's error is not anthropomorphism as such, but psychologization. The bird's glance evinces neither anxiety nor fear but preparation. In an unexpected flight through the medium of water, his feathers "rowed him softer / home - // Than Oars divide the / Ocean," with two capitalized Os like a pair of bird's eyes, wide open on the page in contrast with the third stanza's "frightened / Beads." When oars divide the ocean they make the smallest possible "seam" in the aqueous body, a temporary "plash" almost immediately covered back up by infilling water. They make light enough clefts into what Dickinson calls the "syllable-less Sea" (F1689) to heal their own incisions. Here she sonically recodes "Oar" with that glancing conjunction "Or," an act of linguistic attenuation within a single syllable, which folds and sutures the first word even as it expands the verse to take in another analogy.

New calls the poem "an adjustment of perceptual orders, a softening of categories of belonging" in its renewed attention to the bird as he "cuts through an enveloping atmospheric element that closes back over the fissure he carved." The silver seam the wing carves into the world is really no seam at all compared with the poet's red stitch, softer even than the subtle oar of the skilled rower. The final analogy, of the butterfly's "Leap," still compares flying to "plashless" swimming, a figure for any motion "coached on the elements, of pressing an updraft, or of cutting the tide."[49] Dickinson can stitch the joints of her fascicles together but she cannot live seamlessly, at least not until her poetry disavows the stitch entirely, or at least finds one more silvery and supple, one that "closes back over" the fissure it carves. By turning an "Oar" into "Or," suturing in order to connect, she presents while also concealing the glancing perceptual mode that folds back over itself, hiding her stitches without yet throwing them away.

Dickinson's evocative twinning of seam and plash, taken as an image, might remind the American art historian of Eakins's boating pictures. Paintings like *Max Schmitt in a Single Scull* (1871) use the mechanics of rowing to offer a luministic presentation of time and movement on the Schuylkill River.[50] The water's surface is marked by oar strokes, with the passage of the more distant sculler (Eakins himself) traced by segmented parallel lines that turn the river segment into a clock with man-made, discrete intervals traversed by the "hands" of each oar. These marks, though the product of mechanical movement—of the hands of a clock, of the beat of the oars—serve to measure time as a sequence of spatial locations. Schmitt's track, in the foreground, is different. He has just dropped his oars. Set to steep in the river like long wooden teabags, they drag with the course of the scull's inertia as Schmitt rests and looks back toward the picture plane. The oars have made continuous plashlines on the river's surface, not yet filled back in by the overlapping water. Instead of discrete intervals of time marking the speed of the boat's progression, these lines are indexes of pure duration (in Henri Bergson's terminology, which refers back to the Heraclitean inconstancy of flowing water), impossible to measure beyond registration of the body's slowing. Its temporal existence is simply the fact of its enduring, and

FIGURE 7. Thomas Eakins, *Max Schmitt in a Single Scull*, 1871, oil on canvas, 82.6 cm × 117.5 cm, Metropolitan Museum of Art, New York

to endure is to be a "qualitative multiplicity, with no likeness to number; an organic evolution which is not yet an increasing quantity; a pure heterogeneity within which there are no distinct qualities," where "the moments of inner duration are not external to one another."[51]

Taken in its entirety, the painting shows the mechanical beat of trained speed and the counterexperience of drag. It does so with both mathematical precision and Luminist dilation, the difference occurring in the contrast between the Eakins and Schmitt figures (one at work, the other coming to rest), as well as the difference between the hard, spare flora and its reflection at the edges of the composition (on the left, turning the appearance of bare trees into a plenitudinous projection of healthy bloom). The opposing but nonetheless interdependent relationship between the discrete pockets of water and the continuous wash marks Nelson Goodman's distinction between "articulated" and "dense" visual syntax—or discontinuous versus indivisible—that differentiates economies of description and depiction.[52] The former can be turned into a symbol (one can get from the intervals of each plash to the structure of a conventional clock), while the latter remains an index, little more than a record that the oars were there, once. The remainders of the Eakins figure's movement form a *description* of time made through an abstraction of the body's continuous and indivisible kinesthetic motions (which is exactly what chronophotographic motion studies do, as we will see), while the line left by Schmitt—which is also a line left by Eakins the painter, whose body works just as continuously as Eakins the rower—is only a dense *depiction* of movement. It leaves the observer mute, forced to make analogies like Dickinson's in the face of the bird's soft, indivisible rowing.

Even as the subject matter of Eakins's boating pictures (of which *Max Schmitt* is but one example) is the human body in trained motion, it informs readings of other paintings that explicitly position the relation between man and animal. It does so by creating a workable contrast in the temporal experience of vision—between indivisible continuity and abstracted measure—that translates into an internal distinction between manifest human experience and latent animal activity. Eakins's hunting pictures were contemporaneous companions to his boating tableaux. Eakins, unlike resolute Naturalists like his precursor John James Audubon, is always concerned first and foremost with the kinesthetics of the human body at work, and there is no reedbird to be found in the frame of *The Artist and His Father Hunting Reed-Birds* (1874). But the absence of the animal quarry in the painting produces a notable contrast with the boating pictures that immediately preceded this work: the bird is associated, through transference, with the more fluid two-beat activity of the boaters also outside the frame (in those paintings a viewer would have, at one time, seen exhibited with the hunters). Here, the paddle boat's forward movement is arrested in the marsh grass, its gondolier—the artist himself, in notable contrast with his lithe figure in *Max Schmitt*—straining to navigate the vessel through its swampy impasse. The birds are not in immediate danger, and the father's lowered rifle sits at inattention. They row themselves "softer / home -." In view of Eakins's picture, Dickinson's comparative makes new sense: softer than them, her, *us*.

Dickinson anticipates a rich (and still growing) conversation on animal ontology that took off with Jakob von Uexküll's biosemiotic conceptualization of the *Umwelt* in 1909. Uexküll described how all animals, down to the tick and the jellyfish, comported themselves within an encompassing, semiotically rich, and signifying environment-world.[53] By positing and explaining animal life's experiential complexity, Uexküll cut the ribbon to a new kind of science fair. Instead of homely shoebox dioramas, he wrote of the spheres or bubbles (*Seifenblase*) that transcribe animal life: "The space peculiar to each animal, wherever the animal may be, can be compared to a soap bubble which completely surrounds the creature at a greater or less distance. The extended soap bubble constitutes the limit of what is finite for the animal, and therewith the limit of its world; what lies behind that is hidden in infinity."[54]

From the *Seifenblase* came Heidegger's "disinhibiting ring," every animal's (including the human animal's) circle of efficacy or sphere of instinct and influence that circumscribes its behaviors. "Disinhibiting" stands for the fact that the ring "prescribes what can affect or occasion [the animals'] behavior"; the ring "opens up a sphere within which whatever disinhibits can do so in this or that manner." The disinhibiting ring is not a construct of repeated behaviors or patterns of life, but, Heidegger says, "belongs to the innermost organization of the animal and its fundamental morphological structure." Although Heidegger writes that the distance between the human and the animal is "abyssal"—*Dasein* is constituted in its comportment and being-in-the-world while the animal is characterized by behavior and is "poor in world"—as if yielding to the influence of Uexküll he also suggests a more fluid continuum of experience structured by a law of inverse proportionality.[55] The narrowest semiotic circles correspond to the sharpest senses and the strongest drives to art—think of the bee at work in its hive versus the human and its endless field of sensory distractions. The circumscription of animal behavior is tied both to the character of the animal's immediate surroundings and to the form of its body, its sense organs, and its evolved manner of cognition. Animal life is compressed life, lively in its minimalist vibrations that carry worldliness in the minutest gesture. In the direction of compression—the direction Dickinson's poetry often moves—any organism's visual attention thickens as it holds less in its lens.[56]

Much of the difference posited between human and animal cognition, according to twentieth-century Heideggerians, Pittsburgh Hegelians, and evolutionary psychologists, has to do with "online" versus "offline" thinking, or the level of mediation with which objects are regarded or conceptualized (a distinction most radically apparent between sensuous immediacy and linguistic mediation). John McDowell, following Heidegger, conceives this distinction in terms of "world": "My experience [as a human] might disclose to me that an opening in a wall is big enough for me to go through [and a] cat might see that an opening in a wall is big enough for it to go through, [but] my experience would be world-disclosing and so conceptual in form... [whereas] the cat's perceptual intake would not be world-disclosing and so, in the relevant sense, not conceptual in form." McDowell's cat sees the same thing as a human observer, but not in the same way. Only the human being's visual experience is conceptual enough to be "world-disclosing," where "any aspect of its content is present in a form in which it is suitable to constitute the content of a conceptual capacity."[57] McDowell defines concepts as ways of (human) seeing, as created structures that transcend immersion in the sensuous manifold and that are useful as reasons for action outside of any single experience. Concepts, on this picture, would also figure into a definition of poiesis, since the latter relies on repeatable activity and the manipulation of sensuous experience in and through language.

In other words, on the Heidegger-McDowellian picture, there can be no animal poiesis because there is no animal reflexivity and thus no metaphor. Merleau-Ponty seems to suggest as much in a wholly practical example from *The Structure of Behavior*: "If an ape picks up a tree branch in order to reach a goal it is because it's able to confer a functional value on an object of nature. But... having become a stick for the ape, the tree branch is eliminated as such—which is the equivalent of saying that it's never possessed as an instrument in the full sense of the word. For man, on the contrary, the tree branch which has become a stick will remain precisely a tree-branch-which-has-become-a-stick, the same *thing* in two different functions and visible *for him* under a plurality of aspects."[58] The example of the ape is supposed to show how human perceptual cognition is parasitic on a capacity to bracket the immediate practical standpoint in order to determine commonalities among multiple points of view. The animal cannot do that, always remaining "online" in its cognition. But whereas for Heidegger this indeed disqualifies the animal from poetic activity (see his critique of Rilke, who unlike Hölderlin included animals in his "Open"), Merleau-Ponty goes in the opposite direction.

From Uexküll, Merleau-Ponty borrows the notion of an "animal melody," a tune played at the intersection of organism and environment through their rhythmic coordination: "Here the coordinated elements are not only coupled with each other, they constitute each other, by their very union, a whole which has its proper law . . . just as the first notes of a melody assign a certain mode of resolution to the whole."[59] The animal's melody is its drive to art, its poiesis, its mode of rhythmic connection to the world. Metric cohesion occurs through motion, in the rhythm of poiesis and techne that connects the human laborer with the animal, at least in its supplest swings. Merleau-Ponty echoes Dickinson's "too silver for a seam" in his own account of avian movement and its "pure transitions": "The bird which flies across my garden is, during the time that it is moving, merely a grayish power of flight and, generally speaking, we shall see that things are defined primarily in terms of their 'behavior' and not in terms of their static 'properties.' It is not I who recognize, in each of its points and instants passed through, the same bird defined by explicit characteristics, it is the bird in flight which constitutes the unity of its movement, which changes its place, it is this flurry of plumage still here, which is already there in a kind of ubiquity, like the comet with its tail."[60] The bird in flight is a unity of movement, holding itself together through time as a plashless seam in nature's manifold. When it comes to vision, the rhythmic connection that grounds the animal's expressive art occurs through the seeing body rather than through any abstracted gaze, at the site of "a cohesion without concept, which is of the same type as the cohesion of the parts of my body, or the cohesion of my body with the world."[61]

As our most adaptive form of vision, the glance joins us to animal life, even as it is honed in ways specific to human cognitive capabilities. In his evolutionary analysis of motor skills, neuroanthropologist Merlin Donald claims that the difference separating development on the hominid line from other mammals is the human's learned ability to engage in "rehearsal loops." Relating Donald's insight to musicality, Gary Tomlinson stresses that these loops involve "self-initiated performance of an action, observation of the results, remembrance of these, and renewed performance of the action with one or more of its aspects modified."[62] Glances drive the iterative and sequential aspects of rehearsal, pulling us out into the world and back to our bodies, generating subtle differences of attunement. But the glance is trained to erase itself productively, to dissolve its activity back into the locality it helps to manipulate. Casey calls the glance "the vanguard of attention" because it always "scout[s] out the situation that calls for attention," has always already dropped its attachments and leaped ahead of itself.[63]

The glance is fickle, but thankfully so, for in order to engage vision in the "rehearsal loops" necessary for human microindustry we must be able to forget our attachments—an operation Nietzsche links to the glories of animal life—so that we can refocus our drive to art. Indeed, the glance bridges the temporal difference Eakins discovered on his canvases and that for Heidegger separated the human from the animal: the elusiveness or evanescence of the glance, plashless as it covers over the seam it traces in the world by stitching back over itself, picking up and dropping attachments according to the body's rhythm. Theo Davis's reading of Dickinson's "ornamental form" attends beautifully to the way her poetry picks up and drops attachments in equal measure, proposing images and withdrawing them, attending to the "temporariness of noticing: something leaps into view, only to be whisked aside."[64] To me, Davis's emphasis on the artful waxing and waning of attention also describes Dickinson's animalian plashlessness as a term of poiesis. And the subsemiotic elements of visual art, indexical graphic marks necessary for producing meaning but uninterpretable as meaningful units themselves—brushstrokes, lines, light—recur as analogies to Dickinson's plashlessness, evidence that she was likely thinking of painting in concordance with her silvery seams.[65] She also pairs wing and oar in "I've known a Heaven, like a Tent" (F257), where a "Bird's far Navigation / Discloses just a Hue," an avian brushstroke in the air figured as a plash almost immediately "swallowed up" from view.

The basic indivisible movement and energy contained by an uninterrupted brushstroke on canvas or in the air is what "plashless" attempts to name but in so naming cannot achieve. Her dashes, better conceived as marks when handwritten and otherwise ungrammatical, index such nameless energy. Colleen Glenney Boggs is right to call the constructed fragility and poverty of Dickinson's poetic world—becoming, in Heidegger's language, "poor in world"—"a mode of deeper engagement and a means of forging complex subjectivities."[66] In the late scrap poems considered below, her singularly unique material supports—*this* envelope, *this* advertisement, *this* recipe—become subsemiotic (or in Goodman's terms "replete"[67]), taken partially out of a world of human meaning and made into a marked (and intensely relational) surface. In these poems mark and surface are held together, each shedding their ontological distinctness as text and object as the poet's scrawl loops into the corners and crevices of the found material. On the one hand protomodernist in their formal inventiveness, her late object poetics were also atavistic, constructing a rapport between human and animal life akin to and in concert with the most primitively adaptive elements of the glance.[68]

I turn to Dickinson's late scrap poems in this section to show how she metabolizes animal poiesis through a process or activity of distribution, scattering her art and even her self throughout her environmental niche—the household. In showing how Dickinson's work gets there, undoing beyond repair all her sequential stitching, I argue that her late poetics creates an archive in worldly space, performing rather than simply representing her ideal of plashlessness by imitating, or at least asymptotically approaching, animalian gathering and scattering. She achieves a radical practice of embedding and even dissolving her hand and her glance with/in the material circuit of human domestic life, pointing beneath its linguistic, communicational surfaces and built spaces toward the impossible silence of seamless animal seeing and being.

"By my Window have I for Scenery" (F849), a late fascicle poem, puts the poet before an Albertian window, looking out from her room onto a pine tree set for the variable uses of local animals. The tree is a "Port" for the jays in flight and a "Peninsula" for the squirrels who leap onto a branch, though it is just a "Stem" in a "Sea" for her. Later in the poem, she abstracts from the local scene to the system of global "Commerce," echoing her initial seafaring metaphors. Though Dickinson would never stop anthropomorphizing animals, this poem broaches her self-awareness about the limits of clinical vision—turning the (animal) world into a picture or virtual tableaux from which the spectator is removed—alongside its growing celebration in the scientific community. It is very likely that she read some of Louis Agassiz's "Methods of Study in Natural History"—published in the same 1862 *Atlantic Monthly* issue as Higginson's "Letter to a Young Contributor," a central text in Dickinson's poetic life—which emphasizes the epistemic importance of detached observation of nature (in the vein of Lorraine Daston and Peter Galison's "mechanical objectivity").[69] Referring to animal taxonomy, Agassiz attacked anthropomorphism and metaphor as veils occluding a species' "precise and definite plan."[70] Accurate empirical vision requires attaining a perspective neither human nor animal (or whatever the investigation's object) but of a neutral eye, the triangulating aperture of a mechanical apparatus.

As the scientific community rejected anthropomorphism in favor of dispassionate observation, it privileged the clinical gaze (which ironically involves "offline" seeing specific to the human sensorium) over the lively glance (which we share with animals as we negotiate our circumambient environs).[71] Dickinson went in the other direction, immersing herself and her poiesis more thoroughly than ever before in her *Umwelt*, stitching her poems into her local environment in radical form. Her late scrap poems are not about the glance, and no more about animals than the rest of her output; they are glances, and they are animalian.

Werner, who has elsewhere contributed as much as anyone to the gaze's widespread application in Dickinson scholarship, nevertheless associates her late fragments with glancing touches or blows: "Linked to what is in transit, disappearing, they resemble fingerprints, the light touches of the artist who, having submitted fully to the process of writing and constantly reaching new decisions, no longer thinks of finishing any particular text."[72] She writes at an oblique angle or slant through the world instead of through representation's frontal-parallel mode. Dickinson's scraps skim material off the world's surface; they collect material from the skin of the commercial world, the life of private correspondence, and mass print culture and repurpose them through acts of writing-over that do not cancel their place in the layout of an *Umwelt*. Dickinson does not sublate: she makes the manifold complex of paper in a household, in a town, in a region gleam with the quickening attention of a bird recycling a scrap for her nest.[73]

Melanie Hubbard is right to argue that Dickinson's scraps "do their own theoretical work": "poems and prose meditations composed on advertising flyers, newspaper ads, guarantees, commercial stationery, bits of magazines, book and medicine show circulars, a flyleaf, envelope flaps, penmanship practice slips, and shopping lists both embed the motive circumstance for thought at the material level and think about the materiality of that circumstance." Dickinson's poetry is always attuned to the material circumstances of poiesis, but these poems subsist "in such special relation to the paper upon which they appear that they are quite literally unprintable—they simply object."[74] This is one type of critical stance taken by Dickinson critics participating in the material turn: the object-poems cannot be abstracted into print without being mutilated. One cannot take them out of the relevant domain of material praxis without imposing the abstract container ["lyric"], turning the anomalous object into something forevermore overheard. Instead, the object that *objects* becomes the relevant container, as in "Had we our senses" (F1310), where Dickinson's writing bends to fit the shape of the envelope flap. Without seeing the inimitable shape of the poem, one cannot see how its visual speculation really works. A poem that backhandedly praises blindness, or vision filtered by the "Head," for allowing us to "look opon the / Earth - World / So Utterly / Unmoved -," also takes on the envelope's material structure, the concrete distinction between inside and out along a crease or fold. The eyes conceived "within our Head" traverse the crease, "within" sitting on the inside of the flap that, when folded over, leaves the "eyes" alone on the outside of the envelope, the "Head" beheaded as the tip of the triangle takes off its H. By opening and flattening the envelope, Dickinson was able to write the poem entire, joining interior and exterior while nonetheless revealing the conventional mechanisms—the literal sealing of a letter—whereby the world is shut off or separated out by private correspondence. Dickinson's

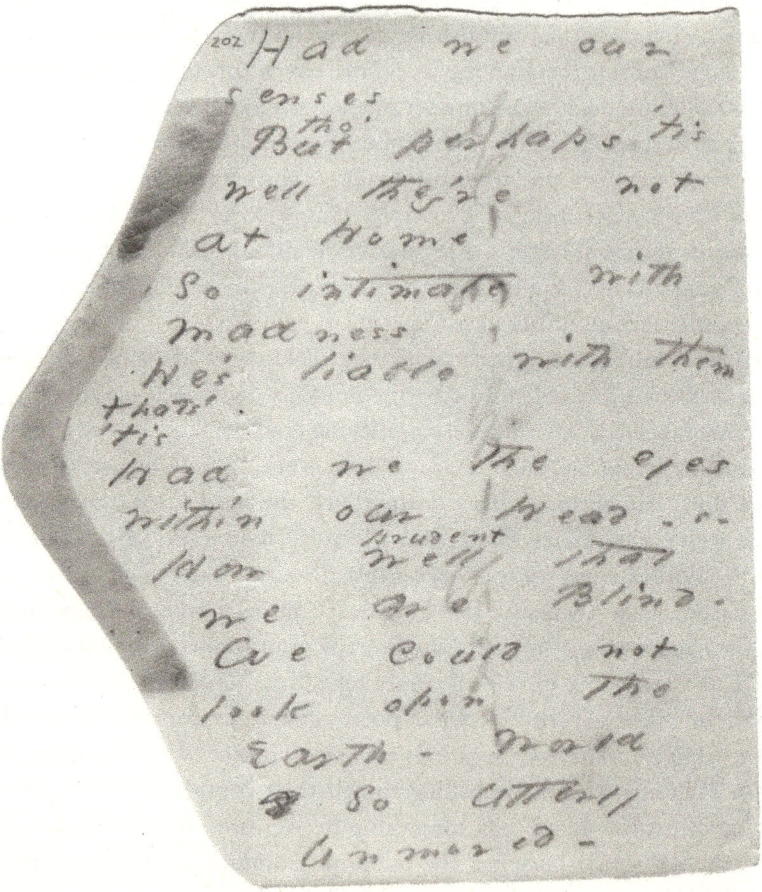
202 Had we our
senses
tho'
But perhaps 'tis
well they're not
at Home
So intimate with
Madness
He's liable with them
tho'
'tis
Had we the eyes
within our Head —
prudent
How well that
we are Blind —
We could not
look opon the
Earth - World
So Utterly
Unmoved -

FIGURE 8. Emily Dickinson, "Had we our senses," Amherst Manuscript #202, Amherst College, Amherst

poetic aim, I believe, is to "move" our eyes along the object-surface so that the object-world in turn "moves" us and brings our senses back "Home" after a swerve, no longer trapped in the head or sealed through the fold of interior subjectivity but *un*folded back into its surrounds.

It is no wonder, then, that Dickinson's late praxis continued her perennial reconsideration of home. Scattering her scraps, not unlike her lifelong epistolary circulation of poems in lieu of publication, seemed to make up for her increasing late-life alienation and developing habit of hiding her face from visitors, becoming what Todd's daughter called "the invisible voice, the phantom in the enchanted corridor." As her already limited sphere of movement shrank, her poems broke out of their locked boxes, lithely taking on the adaptive transformations of the animal in its habitat. Fuss calls Dickinson's relationship to domestic space "eccentric," a way of "lyricising space, recreating in the domestic interior the very condition of poetic address and response."[75] Her found objects broke her stanzas (Italian for "room") for her, absolving Dickinson of any need to enter the drawing rooms containing unwanted family guests. But such "address and response" becomes less obviously social and more fundamentally physiological, as Werner notes in her consideration of Dickinson's "process tense" through which many of the fragments "reveal the kinesthetics of writing-as-dictation, the inscription of *energeia*, in which the hand that has begun to move across the page is seized and directed by an unknown agency, an other who, as Dickinson wrote, 'comes' and 'over takes the mind.'"[76]

I think that by the time she made "In this short Life" (F1292), one of the smallest of envelope scrap poems, Dickinson had metabolized the energeia she associated with perceptive animal being. This poem, just a single triangular envelope flap, presents Dickinson's linguistic compression down to its ultimate point. The flap is shaped like the upper half of an hourglass, each word a grain in the short "hour" of a "Life" spilling toward the small space below "power"—the word itself angled slightly upward to heed the rough adhesive remainder on the paper's bottom edge—that quickly disappears into nothingness. When the poem ends, we have moved beyond language to a power that speaks for itself, through the absent bottom half that, knowing Dickinson, could signify eternity. But the flap and its single point of compression and power beyond words is also the head of an arrow pointing outside itself, outside language and even objecthood altogether. That outside is pure silence, an evanescence or plashless, seamless point the poet/poem can gesture toward but never fully achieve except in death, in the end of life's short hour. That point, implied but materially absent, is where weakness turns into

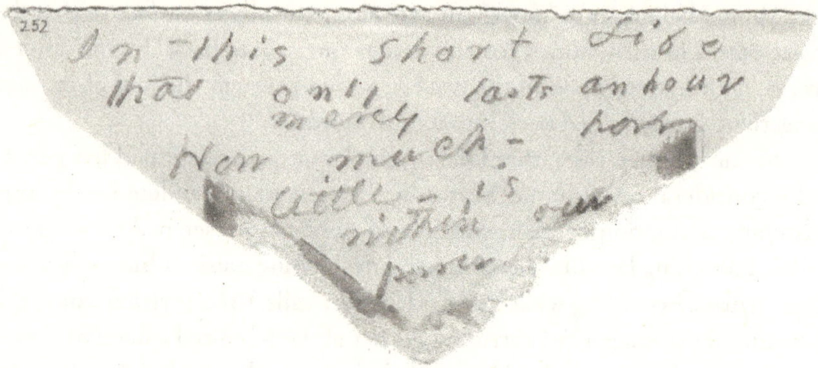

FIGURE 9. Emily Dickinson, "In this short Life," Amherst Manuscript #252, Amherst College, Amherst

strength, smallness into the encompassing, where yielding becomes a force of untold power.[77] The poem is not about the animal (does not *represent* the animal) because here Dickinson comes as close as any human artist can to the beautiful impossibility nonhuman organic life occupies in her pursuit of power through poetic relinquishment.

To relinquish or yield her art to the absence of will or reflexive perception in the animal's way of being—or in her idealization of it—Dickinson chooses to tear pieces off the circuit of human communication and representation: envelopes, advertisements, packaging. The sheer variety of material Dickinson fashioned into poetry is astounding, and supports the notion that she scattered herself through her fragments, transferring the rhythms of both thought and physiological life to her everyday milieu. We find rhythms of immediate inspiration that disappear in the poems' print copies, as in "A Drunkard cannot meet a Cork" (F1630), whose last line is written upside down on the back of a single leaf of lined stationery, the possible result of turning the page over quickly from the bottom to finish her draft. Her proclivity for torn or mutilated paper media whose shapes affect her line breaks and the placement of variants—more and more concentrated in final stanzas or lines—also feeds into a late-life propensity to dwell on endings, or lacks thereof. The late fragments, especially the torn and flattened envelopes, are glances immediately transcribed, their open-endedness markings of distributed consciousness that bleed out through the joints of a box with a broken lock: Dickinson's dark, interior self.

Indeed, when Andy Clark and David Chalmers first articulated "extended cognition" for the philosophy of mind, they could have used Dickinson as their primary example. They came quite close with the fictional Otto, a memory-impaired subject who scribbles in a small portable notebook that "plays the role usually played by biological memory."[78] He scribbles the Museum of Modern Art's address down where he knows he can easily find it, filing it in a paper hard drive rather than his brain. Clark would go on to extrapolate from this example—and several more in *Supersizing the Mind*—that under certain circumstances, cognitive processes are realized in the interaction between brain, body, and environment. Dickinson, like Otto, writes on and into her environment, changing the primary model of her poetic archive from the privately sealed book to a topology of worldly space, from sequential collection to scattered network.[79] Her work had always scattered, of course, with many fascicle poems sent into the world in various forms as correspondence. But only here does poetry as a mode of extended mind become her primary system of poiesis, an embodied practice where thought and writing occurs at the meeting place of self and world—on envelopes, on pinned scraps, on the backs of recipes, on advertisements and fliers. Dickinson's stitching glance, with the brute material world warp to her pencil's weft, finally supplants her glancing stitch. Her quickened attention follows the gaps and spaces inherent in the given figures of found materials, foregrounding in her adaptive lines what and how those materials offer room for artful intervention.

Dickinson's use of a stained candy wrapper, on which she wrote "To her derided Home" (F1617) and which forced her writing to the margins of its backside to avoid the stain's stickiness, shows how resourcefulness in scavenging (I am thinking of a raccoon here, perhaps) was ampliative in terms of formal invention. Dickinson's line placement, transcribed with the grain of the objects themselves, Socarides writes, "allows the poem to multiply and intensify its inclination to include variants . . . the constraints presented by the material itself [forcing her] to renegotiate the relationships of space and text, urging her to press against and play off its multiple boundaries."[80] In the case of the wrapper, fields open up in the stain-marked dead center of the paper; on advertising fliers variations in font size produce playful interregna; on envelopes the drift of her handwriting as it seeks the curved and crooked edges shape her lines into the paradox of a ready-made concrete poem, shaded in by variants. Dickinson shows that working with the grain of the object goes hand in hand with deconstructive impulses, with renewed attention to the limits of a fully present interior self, with the immanence of materialist ontologies, and with the dissociative character of the glance.

Dickinson praised the art of the spider in "The Spider as an Artist" (F1373)—"his / surpassing Merit / Is freely certified // By every / Broom and / Bridget," by the same domestic tools tasked with snuffing out his ubiquitous art. Written on one of her last pages of formal stationery, the poem marks a definitive passage in 1875 to a more spidery art, her construction of a delicate linguistic web across the many nooks of her Amherst household. Walter Benjamin's description of nineteenth-century domestic interiority applies to Dickinson's arachnid poetics in nearly every sense but one: "To live in these interiors was to have woven a dense fabric about oneself, to have secluded oneself within a spider's web, in whose toils world events hang loosely suspended like so many insect bodies sucked dry. From this cavern, one does not like to stir."[81] There is nothing dry about Dickinson's object-poems; they stir within the cavern, giving breath and projecting miniature worlds in the dusty sepulchral air of the bourgeois chamber.[82]

The spider is a significant figure for Dickinson and post-Puritanical American literature more generally, with Jonathan Edwards's "Spider Letter" always in the background. The future Northampton revivalist describes the spider's "whole manner of working" at the "mysteries of these their amazing works."[83] New names the mystery of the Edwardsean spider "a mystery of origins, intention, or simply, will, since the spider's web, medium of the arachnid's most brilliant definition, is also the vehicle of its demise and death. The spider's knitting is an unraveling of its very being."[84] Edwards's flying spiders stitch their way seaward, where "their webs grow damp and moist and lose their levity and their wings fail them, and let them down into the water." They fly that way "for nothing but their own ease and comfort, they suffer themselves to go that way that they can go with the greatest ease, and so where the wind pleases."[85] The spider works with what it has, stitching its world along its axes, sending its filaments forth and merging its body with any available support. It moves along the path of least resistance as it composes its art, just as Dickinson's glancing stitch would forgo the resistance of all book forms by making her poetry an activity bound to an everyday lifeworld with its wealth of tiny interstices beckoning for nimble commentary, penetrating because so slight. Like the spider, too, she worked this way until her death.

Considered ecologically, Dickinson's art became a space-time event, though of a different order than Muybridge's temporal arrays. His locomotive studies atomize the temporality of visual perception as finely as possible, then stitch it back together in units bound by conventionalized white space or grid cells, creating an object of knowledge, an abstracted diagram of visual sequence.[86] Dickinson's abstraction in her late poetics is the result of the opposite impulse, closer to the initially inscrutable object left behind by an animal at work, not easily sublated into a larger world construction we carry with us on our diagrammatic way. In other words, the late fragments are abstract because so concrete, *décollage* rather than collage, acts of unsticking objects from their symbolic relations in order to re-emplace them back into the world with an illuminating difference. The scraps are apparently fragmentary when isolated and gazed at because they are wholly immanent to life, resistant to automatic synthesis by the reader's innocent eye. Her permanent techne decisions were made in the name of impermanence, like her move from pen to pencil in 1879, which Werner puts down to "Dickinson's increasingly acute sense of transience. For, unlike the pen, which produces a permanent memory trace, the lines drawn by the lead point of the stylus are easily erased or retraced so that each act of copying constitutes a new performance—improvisation or extension of a thought-event."[87] Her hand sought her eye as her craft sought the *here* to which glancing returns are always made, a poetic springboard for further writing and looking.

Muybridge undoes the worldly spatial layout within which glances move, gathering images in order to posit a transcendental spatial plan organized by white space. His glances are neither animal nor human, neither horse-like nor approximations of an observer on the sidelines but turned by his mechanism into self-sufficient monadic units of a perceptual code. If the white space between his sequence's cells accords structurally with Dickinson's fascicle stitches, her late work tends to undo the method of substitution, to alter her code in order to more immanently distribute her poetic objects in space and time.[88] She soothes without denying the world's dimensional goonishness, its relentless designs on spatiotemporal distension. Unlike Muybridge, Étienne-Jules Marey, and even Eakins in his own motion studies, Dickinson's goal was not to overcome human vision's limitations but to accept them unconditionally as productive membranes of interaction with other views—including those of the animals surrounding her home—as they see and work within their own bodily limitations, in their forms of life rather than their sculptural deaths, suffered with each shutter snap.

Muybridge's work, which opened up all manner of conceptual possibility for the photographic medium, also accorded with analytic measurements of the (animal and human) body, coinciding with late nineteenth-century advances toward maximizing the efficiency of Taylorist work systems. In service to railroad magnate Leland Stanford, they were a part of contemporary advances in the spatialization of time (most evident in the time of the train schedule), what Bergson diagnosed as a reduction of temporality to number and extensive magnitude, to the mechanical divisibility of fluid movement and gesture. These motion studies posited the body as an enclosed mechanical system that could be implanted into workspaces. Marey and Eakins present more complicated cases by preferring single-frame presentations constructed through "reciprocal operation[s] of decomposition and reunification," preserving "a vector of spatial and temporal coherence" instead of Muybridge's "blunt dismantling of the apparent continuities of movement and time."[89] But the final images still capture prominent bodily positions in the midst of a motion, visual grist for an industrial mill hellbent on regulating physiological reflexes (including the eye's) into the most efficient, repeatable patterns.

As conceptual objects, Muybridge's arrays were limited by the objective qualities of the printed page, thereby falling short of the final translation to cinema they seemed to predict (and that many have retrospectively posited). So were poems, one would have thought, though Dickinson's scraps escape the page's gravitational field. They let the world into the work, not through metaphorical texture alone but through real acts of gathering, literalizing the equally constructive and deconstructive properties of the glance. And as we glance from one scrap to another, variably restitching the whole that has been sundered, Dickinson's household is revealed as not just an ideological abstraction but a free space where conventional art forms—forms as medium-sized, packaged dry goods—can be unmade in order to be remade as integrated parts of the artist's *Umwelt*. These fragments become an exploration in dynamic relations, iteratively collected, scattered, pinned, detached, and reattached. Jen Bervin notes the evidence of Dickinson's ritualistic unmaking of her "gorgeous nothings," asking, "Where do those cuts fall and what shape do they prefigure when the space is opened out? . . . At Amherst College Library, Margaret Dakin has acquired what is believed to be Emily Dickinson's lap desk; its painted wooden surface is positively riddled with myriad fine cuts."[90] I would be opening out a new field were I to repeat the common (and commonly contested) observation that Dickinson was a protomodernist. I agree with Werner that it was Dickinson who opened the field: "Slit open, [an envelope] functions not as a soothing bandage, but, rather, as . . . a site of rupture," a concrete site of deformation that precedes poetic daybreak.[91] "It is as if she wanted her poems to be shaped by objects that were themselves on the way out of form," Arsić speculates, "unfolding into surrounding objects, connected to them by the cuts she inflicted simultaneously on the envelope and the desk."[92] It is as if she wanted her poems, against the synthesizing analytic culture of her time, to finally achieve the status of the plashless glance, inscribing the tiniest of marks on the world before folding again on the way back out of form. She unmade her world in order to live in it more nimbly.

Portraits and Portability

James's Glancing Impression

From June 9 through September 10, 2017, the Morgan Library and Museum in New York exhibited *Henry James and American Painting*, curated by Colm Tóibín and Declan Kiely. The show gathered paintings, watercolors, drawings, photographs, sculptures, letters, and manuscripts in order to trace the varied and often intimate relationships between the Master and visual artists he knew, sat for, corresponded with, learned from, and influenced. In the exhibition catalogue, Tóibín writes that his "connection to the visual arts would nourish James's fiction in different ways, providing him with a social and intellectual hinterland he otherwise lacked, allowing the gallery and studio space, the expatriate dilettante and the collector, a privileged place in his work but also offering the scene—a single, significant moment in the narrative, captured as though by a painter—a central pillar in his house of fiction." Tóibín also notes, en passant, that in James's fiction "the glance, the glimpse, the gaze are essential tools in creating drama."[1]

If James's great dichotomy is American-European, not far down the list might sit gazes versus glances.[2] And like the former, it is a distinction that shifts like dunes in the wind throughout his life. Near the beginning of his career as a novelist—though after he had published several pieces of art criticism in venues like *Atlantic Monthly*, *The Nation*, and *Galaxy*—James superimposed his lifelong concerns with how we see and how we socialize. *The American* (originally serialized in the *Atlantic* in 1876–77) follows wealthy industrialist Christopher Newman as he attempts to navigate Parisian society and capture its treasure, the beautiful Claire de Cintré. From the beginning, where we encounter him on his first visit to the Louvre, "It was our friend's eye that chiefly told his story; an eye in which innocence and experience were singularly blended." His eye, we are told, is "frigid yet friendly, frank yet cautious, shrewd yet credulous, positive yet skeptical, confident yet shy, extremely intelligent and extremely good-humoured, there was something vaguely defiant in his concessions, and something profoundly reassuring in its reserve." His eye is "full of contradictory suggestions," as if caught free-floating without any assurance of what it is seeing, suspended in limbo between the experience of Newman's New World success and his ignorance of Old World art and custom. Indeed, the "Raphael and Titian and Rubens" he encounters there "were a new kind of arithmetic, and they inspired our friend, for the first time in his life, with a vague self-mistrust."[3] The paintings make a swarm of Charons, carrying our friend from the land of naive self-made horizons to the European underworld of stifling social decorum and perceptual subtlety. They also let us in on a secret in advance of any narrative anagnorisis: just as there is nothing obviously "self-made" about these paintings, and just as the American relies fruitlessly on his "little red guide-book" to unlock the mysteries of European treasures, his strained attention and dizzy frustration with art en masse reveals a false promise of self-sufficiency that will snare Newman in a world where the power of social arrangements dominates brute individual wills to interpretation. There is no Baedeker to help him see what he will need to see. So his progress as protagonist stalls like a wet engine.

Newman's eye—and the eyes of his patrician interlocutors, centered in the intimidating force of Madame de Bellegarde and her imperious eldest, Urbain—truly does tell his story, one of missed cues and furtive glances, which is also a story of his creator's literary career and the dense social textures he observed and represented in fiction. From his earliest novels and stories to *The Portrait of a Lady*, *What Maisie Knew*, *The Sacred Fount*, and his late masterpieces, James's dramas turn on looks that underlie the intricacies of his language and dialogue, his increasingly baroque style. The glance takes on a social function in James, albeit one that often contains contradictions and projections of the unspeakable in James's world: impersonality, sexual desire, flight or escape, as well as propriety, restraint, secretiveness.[4] Glances are where social connections are made or severed, but they are also tenuous tethers connecting James's craft to the world he sought to evade: visual culture, photography, Impressionism, Post-Impressionism, illustration, and theater (the site of his greatest artistic failure) just as much as the stately portraiture he preferred.

Hawthorne's influence on James has been addressed at length by his critics. But both writers thought through the implications of new visual forms and technologies on aesthetic culture more widely, progressively implicating their own art, despite personal skepticisms and even hostility, in wider orbits of art making. And though an unimpeachable prose stylist of augmentation, allergic to linguistic compression on the sentence level, James follows both Harper and Dickinson as a writer for whom close attention to the mechanics of glancing revealed its advantages as well as its risks. Like Harper, James saw the glance as a mode of possible social misrecognition, but also as an opening to new generic forms and, eventually, liberatory abstractions.

Like any of his great novels, this story is too intricate to relate in its entirety. The trick is to heed where we are heading with James and his art: in constructing *The Portrait of a Lady* by integrating (and narrativizing) techniques of visual movement and formal collision concurrently developed in painting by the Impressionists, he took major steps toward accommodating the new century's turn toward optical and mechanical portability (even in traditional novel and book forms). James was more polemical than any of the writers I have considered about the comparative value of visual art forms, as we will see. For that reason I proceed a bit more biographically in this chapter, and following a close look at *Portrait* and its incisive use of glances as narrative events, I track James's redeployment of Impressionist style toward a late-career modernist, intermedial, and even impersonal aesthetic that takes the psychological novel he mastered to the brink of its fusion with an emerging cultural regime of portability.

James describes the artist as a man with "eyes greatly open," who responds to the "mystic solicitation, the urgent appeal, on the part of everything to be interpreted," one "addicted to seeing 'through'—one thing through another, accordingly, and still other things through *that*."[5] Contained in this famous statement on both art and life is a curious distinction, perhaps between the young Henry, who, according to Viola Hopkins Winner, was given to "habitual gazing and gaping and his need to find order and coherence in inchoate impressions,"[6] and the mature Henry of the *New York Edition* (1907–9), whose prefaces consider the unmystical processes of revision, composed sequence, everyday seeing, and the pan-semiotic truth that "everything refers." As a matter of representation, James would depict figures with "eyes greatly open" and unfortunately closed, eyes stuck on one thing and eyes glancing between several. The postures of seer and seen are the bases on which his stories get told, since the central "events" of his novels and stories are presented as visual-perceptual acts. His much-discussed narratorial "point of view" principle means that what cannot be presented as seen through some character's eyes is usually not presented at all. As vehicles of vision, characters are either perceptive or blind at various moments, and the drivers of James's plots are the ones who can, when necessary, step outside its frame.[7]

Winner traces James's "interest in pictures" back to his first memory, a view through a moving carriage window of Paris's Place and the Colonne Vendôme. According to Winner, the "infant impressed by the view through the window was to become James the observer-artist, passionately involved yet objective and detached."[8] In part because of the wealth of biographical material supplied by James—including in *A Small Boy and Others* (1913), from which the above quote is gleaned, and *Notes of a Son and Brother* (1914)—critics have been quick to trace the author's artistry to childhood experiences, visions, attachments, and anxieties. His most comprehensive biographer, Leon Edel, stresses his juvenile reticence to act in the shadow of his more gregarious older brother William, preferring to observe life from the sidelines. Such connections, while compelling, remain loosely speculative as the ground of his entire career.

Or maybe not. Maryanne Wolf argues that the foundation of emerging literacy in a child is in emotional-physical contact, in the "association between hearing written language and feeling loved,"[9] a developmental extension of Wittgenstein's understanding of literacy and context in the *Philosophical Investigations*. Ben Morgan's study of embodied cognition in the bildungsroman (a form more or less repeated in traditional biography, though not one James would readily use in his fiction) links Wolf's research to Leila Berg's on "the emotional and physical environment from which an immersive engagement with books emerges"—as well as to Colwyn Trevarthan's findings on cultural meaning acquisition through imitative triangulation between stories and other human beings—in order to claim that the somatic effects of reading, storytelling, and aesthetic engagement "are shaped and supported by the early sensuous and communicative interactions from which the habits of literacy develop."[10] James famously writes that we "must grant the artist his subject, his idea, what the French call his *donnée*; our criticism is applied only to what he makes of it."[11] One can stretch that truism too far into one encompassing an examination of the artist Henry James: more important than the subject matter of his works are the social interactions that produced them and that shine through them. It is up to others to judge how "formative" the solitary habits of his early years truly were.

But it is up to the critic, as it was up to James qua self-critic, to understand and evaluate the formative elements of the author's practice. How can an artist's view of social worlds in which they are not a knowing part turn into something that captures a truth? In "The Art of Fiction" (1884), James recalls

> an English novelist, a woman of genius, telling me that she was much commended for the impression she had managed to give in one of her tales of the nature and way of life of the French Protestant youth. She had been asked where she learned so much about this recondite being. . . . Once, in Paris, as she ascended a staircase, [she] passed an open door where, in the household of a *pasteur*, some of the young Protestants were seated at table round a finished meal. The glimpse made a picture; it lasted only a moment, but that moment was experience. She had got her impression, and she evolved her type. . . . Above all, however, she was blessed with the faculty which when you give it an inch takes an ell, and which for the artist is a much greater source of strength than any accident of residence or of place in the social scale. The power to guess the unseen from the seen, to trace the implication of things, to judge the whole piece by the pattern, the condition of feeling life, in general, so completely that you are well on your way to knowing any particular corner of it—this cluster of gifts may almost be said to constitute experience.[12]

Glimpses, or what James will go on to call "impressions," make a picture in which an inch becomes an ell, a single image turns into a textured world. Or at least some power or gift of "experience" gives the impression scale and dimension so that it can become whole cloth, as if rewinding the process of patterning a garment. In the language of color, an impression is like a bit of dye shot through a drab fabric.

Some of James's critics have tried to think through visual impressions as moments where piece temporarily wins out over whole cloth. Leo Bersani calls these moments "visual shocks which constitute crucial turning points for [James's] heroes and heroines"; Colin Meissner calls them "sudden anomal[ies]."[13] Like wax on the wings of perception, the impression must be played out and dissolved through narrative, in tension with the entire plan or social structure James's observers try to navigate. Daniel Hannah, in response to Bersani and Meissner, warns against missing the significance, in James's narrative patterns, of "act[s] of exposure," moments when characters are thrown perceptually across thresholds guarding private and public spheres. For Hannah, Jamesian glimpses are indeed moments of narrative and subjective instability—flashes of lightning that make readings and interpretations taken for granted stumble and flail—but they also reveal worldly instability, the touch-and-go character of public life undergoing transformation. The impression produces "a state of vulnerability and imaginative vitality through which individuals can attempt to contain, and constructively respond to, perceived erosion of the borders between these once-stable understandings of public and private."[14]

No doubt Impressionism as a painterly movement evolved alongside and in intense dialogue with rapid upheavals in the arrangement of social space, most notably the Haussmannization of Paris. T. J. Clark's *The Painting of Modern Life* may still be the best account of the dialectical relationships between the impression, the Impression, and the destabilization of public and private life.[15] The territory charted by Édouard Manet, for instance—the ball, the picnic social, the barroom, the brothel, the café, the concert—"all seem to be places laid on for display but also for equivocation; places where people are hard to make out, their gestures and expressions unconvincing, their purposes obscure; and it is hereabouts that the city can be seen most sharply."[16] But as much as Impressionistic seeing might coincide with what we've come to call Jamesian point of view—as John House notes, these painted scenes "involved, and implicated, the viewer in unfamiliar ways, by collapsing the barrier between the viewers' space and the action within the picture"[17]—we move too quickly if we throw James right into the deep end of Paris's burgeoning café society. His initial interests lay elsewhere. Like James, we will come around to the Impressionists eventually.[18]

James reached his first apex as an art critic in the five or so years before the serialization of *The Portrait of a Lady* (1880–81).[19] In 1875 he revealed, in one of several reviews of American painting for *The Nation*, his preference for portraiture over all other genres.[20] It is no wonder, then, that he constructed a "portrait" of his own shortly thereafter, though James's critics have never exactly agreed on what kind of portrait he made for his heroine Isabel Archer, or whether he was able to make one at all. It is not too simple a point to stress that James had no interest in painting, commissioning an illustration, or producing a photograph of his protagonist (Alvin Langdon Coburn's frontispiece to the novel in the *New York Edition* would be a mansion, not a woman). And James's description of Isabel throughout the novel is nondescript, beginning with her cousin Ralph Touchett's first glance: "The person in question was a young lady . . . a tall girl in a black dress, who at first sight looked pretty." While Viola Hopkins Winner, Michael Gorra, and Miciah Hussey, among others, discuss recurring scenes of Isabel's objectification—taken as the engine of her fate at the hands of Gilbert Osmond and Madame

Merle—one might as easily stress her reduction to visual cliché. After her marriage, Ned Rosier beholds her "dressed in black velvet. . . . Framed in the gilded doorway, she struck our young man as the picture of a gracious lady." Ralph, even more strikingly, compares her to a "Titian, [received] by the post, to hang on my wall—a Greek bas-relief to stick over my chimneypiece."[21] To domesticate, both as woman and image.[22]

But if she is an object-image to be possessed like Rosier's bibelots, Isabel does not seem to know it, and her competing visions come closer to the open landscape form than the closed, claustrophobic portrait: "She spent half her time in thinking of beauty and bravery and magnanimity; she had a fixed determination to regard the world as a place of brightness, of free expansions, of irresistible action." Early in the novel, Isabel's glimpse of infinite vistas is countered by caricature, as in Ralph's opinion that her free impulse is frightfully American. Indeed, he makes a drawing of her "in which she was represented as a pretty young woman dressed, on the lines of the prevailing fashion, in the folds of the national banner."[23] Already the narrative's pulse and counterpulse, which is also gaze and countergaze, is revealed by James to a reader who is not confined to either but can glance between Isabel and her interlocutors in a rhythm that measures her perceptions against the others'. That his heroine is never fully described prevents us from ever sitting and staying comfortably with her caricatures.[24]

But before James could introduce Isabel to the European snake pit where she would be gazed at, framed, possessed, and commodified—in ways James would prefer us not to—he had to envision her. In the preface he recalls her origin as an item "in the dusky, crowded, heterogeneous back-shop of the mind," tended to by an author-figure less a portraitist than a "wary dealer in precious odds and ends."[25] There she waits, conserved, protected, and enjoyed by the keeper alone in a backroom purgatory, not yet on the shelf for general consumption.[26] And yet James also begins with an intimation of Isabel in motion:

> My dim first move toward "The Portrait," which was exactly my grasp of a single character—an acquisition I had made, moreover, after a fashion not here to be retraced. Enough that I was, as seemed to me, in complete possession of it, that I had been so for a long time, that this had made it familiar and yet had not blurred its charm, and that, all urgently, all tormentingly, I saw it in motion and, so to speak, in transit. This amounts to saying that I saw it as bent upon its fate—some fate or other; *which*, among the possibilities, being precisely the question.[27]

How then do we reconcile these competing accounts of Isabel's figure as a founding impression, as both an object stashed away in the author-portraitist's cluttered studio and the trace of an image fleeing that very same person, forever "in transit"?

We should not simply ascribe this contradiction to James's ambivalences as a writer; one can say more forcefully that he was hitting on a tension at the very heart of portraiture itself. Catherine Soussloff writes of "the functional dialectic of portrait representation," where the exteriority, objectivity, and materiality of the portrayed figure coexists "in the genre" with a claim to the very same figure's interiority, subjectivity, and spirituality. One side of the dialectic, reliant on indexicality and recognition of a historical individual, has from the fifteenth century through the nineteenth "reassert[ed] the social relations between individual, spouse, family, the institution of marriage, and class." Soussloff's ultimate antiquarian example, well before Van Eyck's *Arnolfini Portrait*, the decorative drawing room paintings of the nineteenth-century bourgeois, and the photographic cartes de visite, is the death mask, which "ensured the continuation through the generations of an emphasis on kinship in portraiture."[28] Thus the dark possibility, in James's retelling, that Isabel would always remain, even when imprinted on the page and circulated through copies of the *Atlantic* and *Macmillan's*, a dusky memento mori of a doomed woman type in the curiosity shop of James's (and his age's) mind. But then James also admits, as he looks to insert this seeming ready-made into narrative flow, into the right place in the novel's formal mechanism so that her "destiny" will come about as if of sheer necessity, that she is "still at large, not confined by the conditions, not engaged in the tangle, to which we look for much of the impress that constitutes an identity."[29] Her fate is not analogous to the painter's last brushstroke that completes the work. The other side of the portrait's "dialectic," an excessive feature of the object—a consciousness, a soul, a personality, an evanescent point of identity irreducible to static markings—comes to be associated with movement, the forward motion of a character in a narrative fiction.[30]

Madame Merle makes her "very metaphysical" case to Isabel about the self nearly in direct contradistinction to Jacob Burckhardt's ideal of the subject in portraiture, where the history of the form declined from Renaissance representations of a "free subject," "expressed visually in paintings that exhibit no elaboration of context, nor an obvious social engagement" into decorative, costumed figures whose material draperies express only their social station.[31] Merle tells Isabel,

> When you've lived as long as I you'll see that every human being has his shell and that you must take the shell into account. By the shell I mean the whole envelope of circumstances. There's no such thing as an isolated man or woman; we're each of us made up of some cluster of appurtenances. What shall we call our "self"? Where does It begin? where does it end? It overflows into everything that belongs to us—and then it flows back again. I know a large part of myself is in the clothes I choose to wear. I've a great respect for *things*! One's self—for other people—is one's expression of one's self; and one's house, one's furniture, one's garments, the books one reads, the company one keeps—these things are all expressive.[32]

Merle could be seen here, despite James's association, as the heroic forerunner to a twentieth-century, anti-metaphysical critical materialism or poststructuralist Bourdieuvianism, if not for the fact that her doctrine—resisted initially by Isabel, who holds on to a sense of the deep(er) self ("My clothes express the dressmaker, but they don't express me. To begin with it's not my own choice that I wear them; they're imposed upon me by society")—prepares the way for her victim's entrapment. Jonathan Freedman reads Merle's partner-in-crime Osmond as an incorrigible art collector or dealer, regarding his wife Isabel "as he views everyone in his narrow world, as an objet d'art, a potential 'figure in his collection of choice objects.'" While James eventually came to accept "with increasing confidence and self-assurance the *entire* burden of the [British] aesthetic movement—internalizing and deploying not merely its praise for a highly pitched and mobile consciousness, but also its ambivalent acceptance of the commodification of consciousness,"[33] in *Portrait* he still critically opposes Osmond's material aestheticism to the promise of (a feminized) immaterial consciousness subject to but ontologically distinct from the contagion of the former.[34] Bill Brown, taking the material-immaterial distinction back to the things themselves, refers to a Jamesian uncanny, "an indeterminate ontology" or an "inability to distinguish between the animate and the inanimate" extending to consciousness "as a great thing in excess of things, as it were, which can hardly be measured by any logic of possession or possessive individualism."[35] Maybe it is not right to call consciousness a "thing" in the first place (to do so risks succumbing to the very aestheticist impulse such formulations are meant to combat). But while the Merle-Osmond nexus views Isabel as a thing among things—a beautiful object amid the furniture, valuable because she might make little Pansy one too—James's narration resists succumbing to her complete reification. It does not even reveal the color of her eyes.[36]

The Isabel who bursts onto the scene has a curiosity tuned toward the visible: "She had a great desire for knowledge, but she really preferred almost any source of information to the printed page; she had an immense curiosity about life and was constantly staring and wondering. She carried within herself a great fund of life, and her deepest enjoyment was to feel the continuity between the movements of her own soul and the agitations of the world." So James invests her with "a great fund of life"—and an imagination "by habit ridiculously active; when the door was not open it jumped out of the window"[37]—an endowment vague enough to generate Romantic associations or promises of transcendence whose wings the novel will unceremoniously clip. When the early portions of *Portrait* were appearing in the *Atlantic*, James wrote in his notebook (echoing a line of Ralph's) that the "success of the whole story greatly depends upon this [upcoming] portion," the five installments following Isabel's marriage, where "the poor girl, who has dreamed of freedom and nobleness, who has done, as she believes, a generous, natural, clear-sighted thing, finds herself in reality ground in the very mill of the conventional." And so Isabel's recognition of her error must involve clear-sightedness where it was once only assumed, a visual concentration that James echoes formally when he describes these later chapters as "crowded," a rather "good defect in consideration of the perhaps too great diffuseness of the earlier portion."[38] Her marriage to the reptilian Osmond flattens Isabel's perspective on the world and marks the major contraction of the novel's diffuseness (and the flights of Isabel's fancy in expansive metaphors): "The desire for unlimited expansion had been succeeded in her soul by the sense that life was vacant without some private duty that might gather one's energies to a point. She had told Ralph she had 'seen life' in a year or two and that she was already tired, not of the act of living, but of that of observing."[39] But is the recognition that Osmond objectified her, narrowed her life, and sapped her energy sufficient for understanding why Isabel grows tired not of living, but "of the act . . . of observing"?

A clue comes in a passage that analogously links Osmond's presence to Isabel's visual acuity. It comes in the climactic chapter 42, Isabel's "vigil of searching criticism" by the fire, a scene James describes as having "all the vivacity of incident and all the economy of picture."[40] James calls it a "representation simply of her motionlessly *seeing*," which is not to say that Isabel is "observing" anything. Osmond has just revealed his expectation that Isabel will use Lord Warburton's desire for her to marry off Pansy. Prior to their conversation, Isabel "received an impression" while coming upon the threshold of the drawing room she "herself usually occupied."[41] It is the subtlest sort of in flagrante moment. She stumbles upon a scene she "had often seen" before, but she now "notice[s]" that Osmond and Madame Merle's

> colloquy had for the moment converted itself into a sort of familiar silence, from which she instantly perceived that her entrance would startle them. Madame Merle was standing on the rug, a little way from the fire; Osmond was in a deep chair, leaning back and looking at her. Her head was erect, as usual, but her eyes were bent on his. What struck Isabel first was that he was sitting while Madame Merle stood; there was an anomaly in this that arrested her. Then she perceived that they had arrived at a desultory pause in their exchange of ideas and were musing, face to face, with the freedom of old friends who sometimes exchange ideas without uttering them. There was nothing to shock in this; they were old friends in fact. But the thing made an image, lasting only a moment, like a sudden flicker of light. Their relative positions, their absorbed mutual gaze, struck her as something detected. But it was all over by the time she had fairly seen it.[42]

The difference between seeing and noticing in this scene comes close to Casey's distinction between "glancing around" and "concerted glancing." Isabel had seen Osmond and Merle together many times before, even in situations where they felt themselves to be alone. But her attention was "on idle . . . not turned off to the point of oblivion but not directed to any particular item either." The difference is in the detail, in the nontrivial distinction between glancing "on idle" and glancing as a way of directing one's attention to singularities, as if "casting a psychical lasso around them and pulling them into the net of [one's] active mind, there to be illuminated."[43]

In this case, the detail is one of visual reciprocity, or Isabel's careful attention to Madame Merle's eyes, to Merle's glance, which locks with Osmond's into an "absorbed mutual gaze" that temporarily turns Isabel into an unseen observer.[44] James's prose becomes about as paratactic as it ever gets, turning Osmond and Merle into grammatical near-equals, balancing each other and their intimate looks in a chiasmus miniaturized by the clause "face to face." Perhaps as a symptom of Isabel's conventionalized representation as a static portrait of a lady, she had heretofore only regarded Merle as a static form of her own, hence the recognition of her "usual" erect posture. Her renewed attention to Merle's eyes, bent on Osmond, allows Isabel to follow the look to the relation between the two, to the anomalous composition of their positions in her visual frame. This is not a transition from glance to gaze for the image lasts "only a moment" to Isabel, "like a sudden flicker of light." Rather, James identifies a distinction within the economy of the glance, between the idle, empty seeing in which Isabel had been previously engaged and the very sort of lithe but directed glancing she needs to re-illuminate her awareness. It's like catching a momentary glimpse of the zipper on the back of a monster's costume.

Isabel retrospectively pieces together Osmond and Merle's plot. Meditating on the "darken[ing]" of her world, Isabel thinks of her marriage's progress "as if Osmond deliberately, almost malignantly, had put the lights out one by one." She convinces herself that the "shadows" creeping in around her "were not an emanation from her own mind" but "were a part, they were a kind of creation and consequence, of her husband's very presence." The "impression" of the two in the drawing room becomes the central image around which her thoughts circulate, and Isabel "wonder[s] it had never come before."[45] The reemergence of Isabel's consciousness in such a pivotal moment engenders both a narrative and gendered transgression, restoring her as a subject able to construct the truth of her social world through the concerted glance, through the surface details technically available but theretofore missed or unretained. And once the floodgates open, there is no closing them. That's the power of the Jamesian "impression": its stickiness.

How does Isabel's impression relate to what was happening in the arts at the time of James's composition? Consider Manet's 1879 *In the Conservatory*, on its surface an Impressionist compromise to critics like James who complained about the school's propensity to "send detail to the dogs."[46] Indeed, Jules-Antoine Castagnary noted in his review of the 1879 Salon that here Manet presents "faces and hands . . . more carefully drawn than usual," one of several to note the painter's uncharacteristically conservative approach to natural form.[47] Michael Fried agrees with the critics, calling the painting "almost excessively 'finished,'"[48] a judgment Crary (to my mind) accurately revises: "It is in this sense of an *excessive*, overcompensating finish that I see the work as an anxious attempt to reconsolidate a cohesive visual field, in whose disassembly Manet had already prominently participated."[49] Manet engaged in an act of "reassemblage," an attempt to hold fast the spinning, spectacular world in a moment of self-reflexive intimacy, piecing back together the shards of a reality principle just as Isabel does in her vigil.

Isabel by the fire "leaned back in her chair and closed her eyes; and for a long time, far into the night and still further, she sat in the still drawing-room, given up to her meditation."[50] Manet's woman in the garden appears equally absorbed, though with her eyes open. She strikes a slightly recumbent, casual pose, her stillness partly a function of her corseted and tightly belted dress. Crary remarks on the proliferation of binding and constraint in

FIGURE 10. Édouard Manet, *In the Conservatory* (*Dans la serre*), 1879, oil on canvas, 115 cm × 150 cm, Alte Nationalgalerie, Berlin

Manet's mise-en-scène, "necessary for the construction of an organized and inhibited corporeality": the flowerpots and vases as "instruments of domestication," the bench's vertical posts "echoes of the cinched figure of the woman," the entire image "as holding action, a forcing back of expansive or floating components into a semblance of fixed pictorial and social organization."[51] And yet the face of the woman does not meet the gaze of her male companion behind the bench. She is in one sense the perfect portrait of a Victorian lady, but her trancelike countenance marks the otherwise closed composition's singular site of openness and escape. Her reverie, like Isabel's, looks outside the social frame. It is, as Rei Terada would put it, an act of looking away.[52]

James's Isabel and Manet's woman in the garden—his modern Eve—both dramatize the abyssal element of the subject that strains against its objecthood and the social object-world (Merle's curated collection of "things"). Their visionary capacities, in Isabel's case a renewed or regained capacity after conjugal atrophy, evade possession without repossessing the possessor in turn; Manet's woman explicitly turns away from the man who appears to be begging for attention. This is not gaze and countergaze but something far more subtle, uncaptured by the social jiujitsu of domination, propriety, and restraint that populates their worlds. We might call it, after Erving Goffman, "civil inattention," the woman's look a prereflective signal establishing a limit to public intimacy while in some sense acknowledging its presence.[53] It is, in Manet's corpus more generally, a look common to women for sale, as in the famous examples of the courtesan in *Olympia* and the barmaid in *A Bar at the Folies-Bergère*. Fried reads those looks as the height of an art historical critique of the gaze, a critique meant to be beheld, and a means of actually subverting absorption.[54]

William James, as if sharing a moment with Manet, began writing *Principles of Psychology* (eventually published in 1890), in which he writes of a "curious state of inhibition [that] can at least for a few moments be produced at will by fixing the eye on vacancy." When the eyes are "fixed on vacancy," he writes, "the attention becomes dispersed so that the whole body is felt, as it were, at once, and the foreground of consciousness if filled, if by anything, by a sort of solemn sense of surrender to the empty passing of time. In the dim background of our mind we know what we ought to be doing: getting up, dressing ourselves, answering the person who has spoken to us. . . . But somehow we cannot start."[55] Henry would put it slightly differently than his brother, whose work shares many psychological affinities despite occasional key deviations:[56] time for the novelist never passes emptily (though many of his readers have begged to differ). After all, as he writes in the novel's preface, Isabel's vigil "throws the action further forward than twenty 'incidents' might have done."[57] But the movement of the interior monologue advances by occasionally retreating. As Dorrit Cohn shows in a short but intricate reading of the chapter's verb tenses, shifts and lapses between simple past, pluperfect, and the conditional mood gives the vigil a "Chinese-box effect" of "a narrated fantasy within a narrated memory," a complex temporal situation where certain memories of Isabel's past with Osmond are recognized as "past illusions about the future: a future that, at the moment of her retrospection, already lies in her disillusioned past."[58] Isabel's vacant look pierces each temporal layer the Chinese box accumulates, levels of narration associated for her with stratified forms of imposed and self-imposed entrapment.

William's "sense of surrender" and its is/ought opposition to acting within proscribed social and sartorial milieus nicely describes the concentrated drama of Manet's painting and his brother's keystone scene. It describes, on the one hand, the dialectic of portraiture, its figures always staring off into empty space, its "asymmetry of intensity between external and [hypothetically] internal fact perceptions" offering the inkling "of a shocking gulf between the sensible and the supersensible."[59] The phrase also, taken phenomenologically and through the guise of reverie, describes the "empty" glance as a line of flight, a looking away from social interpellation, a refusal to give one's master the counterlook that confirms one's allotted place as socialized object ("Get up! Dress yourself! Answer me!").

When Henry James writes, in the preface, of his "dim first move" toward constructing his novel—his "grasp of a single character," his "acquisition"—he narrates a writerly process whereby an individual "under favour of occasion" comes to take on "a constituted, animated figure or form." The imagination initially "preserves, protects, enjoys" the figure in the "back-shop of the mind," but the character cannot stay there for long. James does not identify the artist with the dealer who is "resigned to keeping the precious object locked up indefinitely rather than commit it, at no matter what price, to vulgar hands."[60] That dealer, we find, has more in common with Osmond than the author. James thus foregrounds a particular social problem, a problem of translation inhering in the visible and possessable body of the Victorian-era female. It is not simply that Isabel becomes the passive object of the male gaze. As I have already mentioned, she receives "an impression" of Osmond and Merle on the threshold of their drawing room, "an image, lasting only a moment, like a sudden flicker of light," a glance from out of the very frame James repeatedly uses to contain her figure. As if triggered by the scene's decisive moment, standing outside the "absorbed mutual gaze" locking Madame Merle and Isabel's husband together in a scheming visual embrace, she begins to see her surroundings "illumined by lurid flashes." It is as if her flattened, painted world comes to take on the characteristics of the moving pictures: "The effect was strange, for Madame Merle was already so present to her vision that her appearance in the flesh was like suddenly, and rather awfully, seeing a painted picture move. Isabel had been thinking all day of her falsity, her audacity, her ability, her probable suffering; and these dark things seemed to flash with a sudden light as she entered the room."[61] One cannot grasp the narrative significance of this moment if one stays in the interpretive frame of the traditional portrait. Here, time frames and modalities collide, Madame Merle appearing "in the flesh" just as Isabel was thinking more abstractly of her "falsity." The collision, where concept and perception meet, is the site of the glance (the "flash"), where the "painted picture" suddenly moves.[62]

While there is little obviously Impressionistic about *Portrait* (certainly less so, for instance, than a later novel like *The Ambassadors*[63]), in these moments of formal collision one finds a resolutely literary example of a "broader attempt to reconfigure human identity by means of representational innovation, at times working within, at times transforming, and at times subverting this time-honoured and seemingly unproblematic, indeed self-explanatory, pictorial genre [of the portrait]," as Linda Nochlin says of Impressionism more generally.[64] James does not treat Isabel as his sitter, though he does have her recline in front of the fire like Manet's woman in the garden, in contradistinction to the fronto-parallel orientation of the typical painted likeness. But this is exactly, as in Manet, where consciousness wriggles free, where the look darts off in another direction. Her glance finally activated again, Isabel sees outside the frame of her carefully curated experience, and thereby sees *through* a single static image of Osmond and Merle to a sequence of events, transformed from the objet d'art into the artist herself, glimpsing "one thing through another . . . and still other things through *that*." James's description of aesthetic vision, active in Isabel's breaking through Osmond's "charm," parallels Crary's analysis of visual "gesture" in *In the Conservatory*, producing centrifugal glances through the woman's off-frame look, through the man's pointing finger and the woman's pointing umbrella, confirming "the impossibility of a direct perception, of an attention that was an immediate possession of its object," an entire "system of deflection, in which vision is bound up in a relational field within which every point of fixation is a deferral and relay to another one."[65] Breaking presentational convention, deictic deflections point away from focal centers rather than toward them. James and Manet, through different media forms, allow us to see for ourselves the possibility of new perceptions, of lines of flight past the bounds of propriety, outside of the narrow attentional bands proscribed by the unhappy marriage of male gaze and female countergaze.

If the glance has the capability of breaking the cage of propriety, it is because of the nimble way it relates "acts of perceptual attention and those of mental attention."[66] In chapter 42, Isabel plays with the glances that had fooled her as well as the new one that revealed a stark complicity to make a final leap toward an irreversible revelation: "The real offence [according to Osmond], as she ultimately perceived, was her having a mind of her own at all." The delayed playback of the events of Isabel's capture allows the reader to recognize that James has been swerving this way all along, the visual material of reflection having already been provided to the mind by glances of the eye. Returning to the opening paragraph of the novel, one finds again, as it were, a scene straight out of the Impressionist toolkit, afternoon tea at Gardencourt precious for its liminal atmospheric quality, when "the flood of summer light had begun to ebb, the air had grown mellow, the shadows were long upon the smooth, dense turf." James calls his description a "peculiarly English picture I have attempted to sketch."[67] Laurence Holland writes of all "posed in a state of suspension within which the novel begins to unfold arcs of widening, deepening recognition," arcs of vision already "infused with the scheme or plot—the taking up and taking hold, the giving—which has been projected in creating them."[68] These "arcs of vision," one then notices upon rereading the sketch as a sketch, as the lineament or schematic of a narrative to be progressively filled until chockablock with incidents, are glances: one initially anonymous figure "looked with a certain attention at the elder man, who, unconscious of observation, rested his eyes upon the rich red front of his dwelling." With Isabel's entrance, Ralph's eyes are led by his terrier—a convenient sightline—to the girl in the doorway who "at first sight looked pretty." Isabel in turn surveys the scene "with an eye denoting clear perception."[69]

As Holland and Carolyn Porter, among others, have argued, there is in *Portrait* and in James in general (once again, a later theme in *The Ambassadors*) "an antithesis between *seeing* and the full partaking of experience."[70] But James makes you careful to distinguish the modes of seeing his dramas turn on. From the beginning of the novel Isabel's ability "'to see for [her]self'" is associated with a determination to look "all around her [in] a comprehensiveness of observation," to take in a scene of life as a whole, as a complex rather than a mute thing. In her later envy at Ralph's dying condition, her desire to "cease utterly, to give it all up and not know anything more" like those valuable art pieces that "only grow in value, while their owners lose inch by inch youth, happiness, beauty," we do not find the reification of the heroine James's working metaphor of the objet d'art suggests. Instead, we meet the constitutive distance of consciousness from the state of the thing-in-itself, a recognition that Isabel's felt "absence of purpose," characterized by eyes that "gazed vaguely before her," is not the same sort of beautiful, tranquil absence at the heart of the art object. Even as she has been flattened and objectified by Osmond and Merle, James does not pump the breaks on the reconstructive facility of Isabel's glance. Among the ruins in Rome, Isabel rests "her weariness upon things that had crumbled for centuries and yet were still upright," deposits her "secret sadness into the silence of lonely places." Seeing the remains of human history once again as they really are—the "starved churches, where the marble columns, transferred from pagan ruins, seemed to offer her companionship in endurance"—activates a mourning process through environmental reintegration, where "in a world of ruins the ruin of her happiness seemed a less unnatural catastrophe."[71] Isabel is thus able to reconstitute an affective community with Pansy and the Countess Gemini, fellow victim and witness to the forces of dissolution that turn delicate objects and arrangements to ruin.

James's narrative logic involves dissociation, emptying Isabel's gaze in reverie and transforming her interior energies into a scene of moving pictures that *she* controls, followed by her reinsertion into things with a difference: not back into the flattened, gilded portrait but into the rhythm of the world we all share, into the ruin whose decay does not threaten life but indexes its ceaselessness. There are chinks in the house of fiction, some of James's million windows "pierced . . . by the need of the individual vision and by the pressure of the individual will," by the pressure of conscious self-reflexive vision that brings us to the brink of the novel's own architectural ruin. But Isabel's experiential path doubles back on itself, never staying within the domain of dissociation, always eventually recovering a sense of the founding site of literary and aesthetic creation:

> As for the origin of one's wind-blown germs themselves, who shall say, as you ask, where *they* come from? We have to go too far back, too far behind, to say. Isn't it all we can say that they come from every quarter of heaven, that they are *there* at almost any turn of the road? They accumulate, and we are always picking them over, selecting among them. They are the breath of life—by which I mean that life, in its own way, breathes them upon us. They are so, in a manner prescribed and imposed—floated into our minds by the current of life.

James's empiricism, which is a glancing accumulation of sensations (germs) then reconstructed, selected, and combined, becomes his heroine's living experience, her reclamation of visual power coming in the delayed playback and in assent to the "current of life." This is something we must learn how to do again, to learn to see and travel in that "straight path" Isabel takes after her final revelatory interview with Caspar Goodwood, which we know is not geometrically straight but has the character of a clear sightline, a unity of seeing and being that is the active condition of any art, available to us in the bleakest of circumstances.[72]

We are left not knowing the why of her straight path back, impressed only by the how. Isabel finally keeps something, some reason for acting and being, all to herself. Once again, as if returning to the novel's beginning through the gauntlet of arduous experience, we want to see what and how she sees.

As I have already mentioned, in his preface to *The Portrait of a Lady*, James compares the novel form to a house with a million windows, "at each of [which] stands a figure with a pair of eyes, or at least with a field-glass." The novelist is on this account primarily a "watcher," attached to the "human scene" through a series of apertures "of dissimilar shape and size" rather than via "hinged doors opening straight upon life."[73] This passage comes up again and again throughout the critical history of James's style and method, which has been dominated by a preoccupation with "point of view" as a means of access to the psychology of an individual seeing subject or observer, what Carolyn Porter calls his "exploitation of the third-person center of consciousness . . . designed to maintain the visionary seer's contemplative stance despite the fact that this stance removes the 'lucid reflector' from the world in which she or he performs a host of nonvisual acts."[74] Porter traces James's maturity in the "narrative miracles" he works on the late novels, casting away the troubled first-person experience of *The Sacred Fount* where either seeing or being constantly obscured the other (one cannot do both, the unnamed narrator finds, as a condition of finite subjectivity). That is, James's principle of "point of view" narration—a load-bearing concept in his house of fiction—is built and maintained on the foundation of a hero's or heroine's attaining the stance of a third-person narrator (the most exceptional cases being Lambert Strether and Maggie Verver), adopting a new and more adequate vantage outside their previously inhabited social world.[75]

Sharon Cameron acutely argues, however, that such metavisual dramatic renderings can obscure the extent to which (for James) consciousness is "reconceived as extrinsic, made to take shape—indeed, to become social—as an *inter*subjective phenomenon . . . separated from the confines of a self."[76] James's stylistic experiments, up to and including his so-called late style, act as moves in a social field taken over by late Victorian mass visual culture, aggressive or defensive ones depending on what angle one takes on them. *Portrait*, a story about among other things an eclipse of innocence, still partakes in an innocence of its own insofar as James sticks to painterly tropes and keeps the world of new representational technologies at bay. I have suggested that, beneath the competing visual registers of Isabel's increasing reification that are consummated in her marriage to Osmond, was a growing optical-technological culture of the spectacle, one that James himself was uneasy about as a potentially unassailable competitor to his writing's ponderous density and representational depth. I will argue now that, as a further stage in James's desire to create visually attentive art that assents to carriage along the "current of life," he forced himself to grapple with a new social and aesthetic regime of portability.

One might reasonably call James's life a portable one, his childhood split between Albany, Washington Square, Paris, rural England, Geneva, Newport, and Boston-Cambridge, and his adult life situated on the edge of several cultures and nations. He would never completely come to terms with his abandonment of America and his split life between metropolis and countryside. His letters suggest a man often desiring to be elsewhere, rarely content in the refuge of a "Great Good Place" otherwise important for the working artist (even in his favorite home in Rye, his thoughts often wandered back to London or the Italian cities). Coincident with his reflections on the role of habitation, place, and travel in the novelist's worldview were anxieties about the necessity of producing a portable, movable literature as an impatient, inattentive, and rapid modernity creeped into his world. In the age of the Kodak and the snapshot, he would wonder, how can one write a big, serious, *and* successful book? When his relationship to photography came to a head around the turn of the twentieth century, his novels and prefaces became, among other things, guides to portable seeing and thinking. As he came to see, think, and write *diagrammatically*, he was able to envision (if not fully achieve) a bridge between the initially immobile bourgeois subjects that populate his stories and the velocity of an increasingly alien world.

In the 1882 story "The Real Thing," James returns to the site of portraiture to make a case against the naive realism that attends to the cult of the model (one that would be finally eclipsed for a time by modernist Pictorialism, by the Cubists at first and by the Abstract Expressionists more completely).[77] Although a story about a painter, one cannot help but locate photography as the extreme instance of the narrator's problem, which is that his overbearing and overdetermining models, Mr. and Mrs. Monarch, are too much like the "real thing" he wishes to transform into art. As Edel writes, for James, "the 'real thing' was simply itself, photographic," while "Art transfigured reality."[78] His portraitist refers to an "innate preference for the represented subject over the real one. . . . [He] liked things that appeared; then one was sure. Whether they *were* or not was a subordinate and almost always a profitless question." He even refers, notable given James's longtime disregard for accompanying imagery, to the woman as "like a bad illustration," too much given over to a single, obvious look that refers his drawing back to the indexical, biographical subject that exists prior to the initial sketch. He prefers another model who, "being so little in herself . . . should yet be so much in others," a blank, plastic slate perpetually open to "the alchemy of art."[79]

Recall that, in his working notes for *Portrait,* he described the idea of Isabel (but no actual living person) as a model-object, a barely visualizable form that only needed to be placed into the right scene for her fate to unfold dramatically. The narrative progressively fills in her being even as James resists overdescription, describing Isabel only as she is *seen* rather than as she *is*. Isabel is not a Monarch. Alexandra Wettlaufer describes a shift in the work of Diderot, Baudelaire, and Ruskin in which "visual prose" solicits the reader's imaginative capacities of visualization, just as the painter's sketch (rather than the finished product) produces a desire for completeness in the viewer.[80] The vicissitudes of this desire as a visual and aesthetic principle—for an imaginative visual *activity* that makes of the world something other than it is, that completes an impoverished visual field by seeing "one thing through another . . . and still other things through *that*"—haunt James's writings of this period, not only in "The Real Thing" but in "The Aspern Papers" (1888), "The Figure in the Carpet" (1896), *The Spoils of Poynton* (1896), *What Maisie Knew* (1897), and *The Sacred Fount* (1901). What the first makes clear in the others is, paradoxically, the lack of visual clarity haunting the artist at the time; "the challenge facing the late-nineteenth-century artist was, as James saw it, to learn to see in the dark," or perhaps more accurately, to learn how to see in the blinding light, when everything is *too much* on display.[81]

James's writings in the 1890s often trouble the means by which writers typically affect visual display. *The Spoils of Poynton*, in the most superficial sense, is a story about a collection of pretty things whose visual profiles are never described. Brown calls *Spoils* a "Balzacian novel in excess of Balzac," testing realism's limits by "evacuating the genre of . . . its material possessions."[82] The conflagration that, at the end of the novel, destroys all Mrs. Gereth's precious objects is from this perspective set and ignited by James himself, casting all the Balzacian trinkets—which always signify something about their possessor's moral status, an error played out to great effect in James's novel—into a purifying blaze. The more radically realist (Flaubertian) object-description as pure "reality-effect" was anathema to James, who saw in the plodding minutiae only the crease in Mr. Monarch's trousers that stunts his artist's progress (recall the distinction between James's nondescriptions of Isabel and his villains' attempts to reduce her to the things she wears).[83] Significantly, the point of view of his child heroine Maisie, who quickly followed Fleda Vetch and Mrs. Gereth into print, could not lead James's narration that way because of her age and inexperience as a seer; on her own, she would have been denied admittance into Balzac's Maison Vauquer.

More so even than in Isabel's vigil, Maisie's cognitive experience throughout the novel is vision dramatized, all the action in her scanning eye's search for sensuous knowledge (James even calls her, in the *New York Edition* preface, a "register of impressions").[84] Spiegel defines James's "late manner" visually, as if the formal result of the conflagration that ended *The Spoils of Poynton*: "Seen objects are dematerialized by the detached and considered appropriations of a critical intellect. . . . James translates the object into a function of analytic discourse and speculation." His "analytic" comes to seem much like the visual-syntactic discourse of the cinema. In James's earlier "scenographic" visualizations, objects are solid, time-continuous wholes, like props on the theatrical stage.[85] Now, in several key scenes, he engages the object-profiles in Maisie's visual field obliquely as the narration traces her eye's sensuous vector, exploring and piecing together the fabric of her surrounding world.[86] Indeed, "fabric" is more than a metaphor: in one scene, Maisie stitches up the appearance of her mother's dress by glancing. She first sees a "fair high drapery," which prompts her eye to follow its "stiff sheen—up and from the ground, where it had stopped," until the sudden cut of a "fixed face . . . surmounting it . . . offer[ed] the climax of the dressed condition."[87] The intrusion of dashes and short subordinate clauses (elided in my presentation by ellipses) effect a linguistic version of cinematographic syntax, the isolation of close-up shots through the grammar of montage editing. Scenes like this one are constructed as if from a storyboard translated into semifocused cinematic shots—or, alternatively, *snapshots*—resulting from the tracks and pans of a narrative lens sutured into the eye(s) of little Maisie. Conscious discovery occurs at the climaxes of visual series. James slows Maisie's eye and thereby accentuates the singularities and opacities of the visual field, consonant with the tentative and erratic explorations of an inexperienced child and, more generally, any mind in the process of perceptively mediating an obscure mystery.[88] The knowledge the novel pursues is of how Maisie can know herself, her own mind and her own desires. As any James novel ensures, one only achieves self-knowledge and self-oriented action by playing social games, with eyes open to the concealments and deceptions of other people.

James's choice of the inexperienced Maisie, like Edmund Husserl in his famous transcendental reduction, strips "the epistemology of the Jamesian reflective centre" down to its barest coordinates, to a scanning eye-pole.[89] That is the formal origin of Maisie's mind as it develops confidence in its own interpretive skills. James writes that his design was "to make and to keep [Maisie's] so limited consciousness the very field of [his] picture."[90] In his *Notebooks*, he writes, as if to remind himself, "EVERYTHING TAKES PLACE BEFORE MAISIE."[91] James continues, in the preface, to express just how much careful reflection and technique goes into the paradoxical creation of an innocent yet accessible eye:

> My first view of this neat possibility was as the attaching problem of the picture restricted (while yet achieving, as I say, completeness and coherency) to what the child might have been conceived to have *understood*—to have been able to interpret and appreciate. Further reflexion and experiment showed me my subject strangled in that extreme of rigour. The infant mind would at the best leave great gaps and voids; so that with a systematic surface possibly beyond reproach we would nevertheless fail of clearness of sense. I should have to stretch the matter to what my wondering witness materially and inevitably *saw*; a great deal of which she either wouldn't understand at all or would quite misunderstand—and on those lines, only on those, my task would be prettily cut out.[92]

The author's task, to "prettily cut out" what "TAKES PLACE BEFORE MAISIE," is to record in language the visual material that would be inevitably recorded by a largely impersonal eye when placed in a situation initially beyond formal understanding. The child, as a Jamesian focal standpoint, allows the story and discourse to meet on the terrain of information processing, revealing the visual-perceptual truth of novelistic discourse as such: that it can produce internal points of view only by filtering out tons of descriptive data. After distilling and recording that data, the author then must take on the role of a curator or proto–film editor (with an emphasis on the "cut") to arrange that material in a pleasing and minimally coherent way for an audience at second-degree removal from the primal scene of the glance. In this two-step editing operation, even in the linguistically mediated discourse of the novel, concepts guiding the formal development of contemporaneous visual media meet early phenomenological methodology, then being constructed by Franz Brentano, Wilhelm Dilthey, and Ernst Mach.[93]

James's new camera model, The Maisie 1897, was a tool for sociocultural critique as well as narrative development. The novel's opening announces a recurring visual trope, equally literary-poetic and literal-technological, of the phantasmagoria: "She was taken into the confidence of passions on which she fixed just the stare she might have had for images bounding across the wall in the slide of a magic-lantern. Her little world was phantasmagoric—strange shadows dancing on a sheet. It was as if the whole performance had been given for her—a mite of a half-scared infant in a dim theatre."[94] Magic lantern projection, reproduced in the style of James's narration, antagonizes the novel's psychological realism from the inside. By association, phantasmagoria and its medial counterparts depend on and produce solipsism, dimness, infantility—all obstacles to the well-developed, mature, socially astute realism James hopes to achieve again in *Maisie*. Referencing James's most famous metaphor for visual perspective, Christine Britzolakis writes that his "shift from the field-glass, or binocular telescope, to the magic lantern, announces a redefinition of the realist project. Whereas the 'field-glass' represents an aspiration to verisimilitude, the magic lantern is associated with theatrical performance and illusion, substituting a reflected image for a direct one."[95]

One might think here of Marx's use of visual technology as a metaphor for ideology, wherein "men and their circumstances appear upside-down as in a *camera obscura*."[96] Maisie, we discover, after the money runs out on her French classes "with all the smart little girls . . . was to feel henceforth as if she were flattening her nose upon the hard window-pane of the sweetshop of knowledge," a flattened screen onto which commodities and the lifestyles of the London rich dance in their own phantasmagoric procession.[97] The image of the city as a display window stocked with attractive articles of consumption is mapped onto Maisie's consciousness through the conduit of her *impressionable* eye. She is the zero level vessel through which James clarifies what Andrew Miller calls a "penetrating anxiety" on the part of Victorian intellectuals "that their social and moral world was being reduced to a warehouse of goods and commodities, a display window in which people, their actions, and their convictions were exhibited for the economic appetites of others."[98] By exposing a near tabula rasa to the sort of dangerously intricate narrative conflicts his readers were used to, James proposes (without endorsing) "a new fictional optic" beyond psychological realism—an ideal which defines Jamesian fiction to its end, and which *Maisie* securely holds fast to as its heroine matures into social aptitude—to begin the process of reconciling a "perceived crisis of cultural authority," an imbrication of art, entertainment, vision, urbanity, and the commodity form.[99]

James perhaps felt this crisis most acutely when faced with the photographic camera's growing portability and user-friendliness in the 1880s and 1890s. The Eastman Kodak blew up as if someone popped the tab on a shaken soda. It became rival to the sort of books James was writing—long, dense, difficult, multivolumed, and physically heavy when in bound form.[100] As already mentioned, the period of the Kodak's ascendence corresponded in his career with his biggest disappointment, the failure of his play *Guy Domville* at St. James's Theatre, a rather violent sign—given the uproar and comic rebuff from the galleries—that his style and approach would never attain mass popularity.[101] He despaired at the sign of the times that exceeded the narrower boundaries of literary culture: "The terms of contemporary journalism more and more impose themselves, announce themselves as, increasingly, irresistibly, the universal, the only terms, and exactly by the same law as that by which so many other modern conveniences have become indispensable, by which new machinery supersedes old, the kodak displaces the camera. They represent the portable, and the portable now is everything."[102]

Though he eventually acknowledged, sadly, that he would (or could) never write a bestseller, and that he was never to fully feel at home as the new century dawned (referring on January 1, 1900, to "this dreadful gruesome New Year, so monstrously numbered"),[103] he would admit his desire to somehow combine his ambition with the ascendant portable visual regime: "I want to see all of all this I can, to miss no possible impression—that is the very basis; but I can't knock off pages of prose like a war-correspondent writing on his knee or his hat, & I want to do a really artistic and valuable book."[104] Indeed, when he took to dictating his writing—initially to hired stenographer William McAlpine in 1897—he found that the leash on his mobility was shortening, with the heavy typewriter standing in the way of the travel that had always accompanied his work. He had already been dealing with the contradictions of wide-ranging transatlantic reception, as Michael Anesko relates in great detail, since short editorial deadlines coupled with the slowness of international transit "often made it logistically impossible for proof sheets to reach James—and be returned with his corrections—before the presses had to roll"[105] out their serial editions, the leash on his capacities for complete and timely revision shortening as demand for his fictions increased.[106] If James could not write like a war correspondent, he would have to open his work up even more to the contemporary world, reconceiving his writing in "transmedial" terms. Jordan Brower calls a writer's capacity to imagine the afterlives of their prose works at the moment of composition fiction's "transmedial possibility." This capacity Brower sees developing in the decade after James's *New York Edition* (focusing on Fitzgerald's *Gatsby*), when the extension of copyright protection to literary film adaptations produced an "acute awareness" of how one might prepare fiction for adaptation.[107] For James this meant revis(it)ing his long-held aversion to visual illustration, developing an awareness of the diagrammatic relationship between word and image inescapable for writers in the Kodak era.[108]

James resisted, for most of his career, any accompanying illustration to his writing. He preferred serializing his fiction in the *Atlantic Monthly* over *Century Magazine*, in part because the latter included illustrations and the former did not: "as a writer one hates 'em," he complained, according to biographer Leon Edel, "and how their being as good as they are makes one hate 'em more! What one writes suffers essentially, as literature, from going with them, and the two things ought to stand alone."[109] Such was his sentiment in the mid-1890s. By "stand[ing] alone," James sought to fight the mobility of word and image, and perhaps—given the mass market appeal of illustrated serials in magazines like *Collier's*, where "Turn of the Screw" was published and which Edel compares to James's childhood favorite, *Frank Leslie's New York Journal* "of Romance, General Literature, Science, and Art"[110]—police the class boundaries inherent within the most common premodernist media crossings. But the slight change of heart (or mind) that led to his collaboration with photographer A. L. Coburn, who took the frontispieces for the *New York Edition*, accorded with an intuition he'd had for a longer time on the visual arts writ large.

Though always a sharp-eyed lover of painting, James could not conceal his general agitation after attending an 1876 Durand-Ruel exhibition in Paris, claiming that the Impressionists on display were "absolute foes to arrangement, embellishment, selection, to the artist's allowing himself . . . to be preoccupied with the idea of the beautiful." I mentioned his criticism of Impressionism earlier, as the public position a young James took despite slowly (and quietly) integrating compositional insights of contemporaries like Manet. He also recognized that their system reconfigured conventional perspective by inventing a role for the mobility and subjectivity of the artist, their attentiveness to the fugitive moment: "the painter's proper field is simply the actual, and to give a vivid impression of how a thing happens to look, at a particular moment, is the essence of his mission."[111] This was a gamble for James, and long odds justify second thoughts: "To render the impression of an object may be a very fruitful effort, but it is not necessarily so; that will depend upon what, I won't say the object, but the impression, may have been."[112] Or, as Winner writes, "To James's way of thinking, the painter who records a quick visual impression of a scene runs the risk of being shallow if his perceptions are limited. To achieve the highest result, the painter must take time to see deeply into his subject."[113] It is as if James celebrated or at least recognized the power of the quickened impression while nevertheless castigating the process by which the Impressionist achieved it. Indeed, French critics writing on the first three group exhibitions were clearer on this point than James was. Emile Blémont writes that the Impressionists succeeded in extracting from the landscape the multiple lines and colors that, "in one glance, the eye perceives before a scene." Descubes relates the supposed intention of the painters to give "the impression of the first glance, of the first shock, so to speak, in order to fix the fleeting vision of a . . . landscape as if seen through a window suddenly thrown open." He adds that they capture "a fugitive form, which disappears as soon as it is glimpsed." And Théodore Duret, using a similar term in "fugitive impressions," writes in 1883 of the Impressionist method as an "impulsive" coup d'oeil, "a glance cast upon the natural scene."[114] James appears to have objected not to the fugitivity or the shock of the Impressionist glances but rather to the impulsiveness; for James, impressions are valuable resources for the artist and writer alike, but sometimes their glitter turns out to be pyritic. They must be mediated, something the rhetoric of the "innocent eye" or "blind sight"—promoted in this circle by Charles Baudelaire's writing on Constantin Guys and in English by John Ruskin—takes us away from by making the fresh vision a matter of achieved epistemic ignorance rather than technique, of passivity rather than selectivity, of imposition rather than composition.

For Wendy Graham, James's engagement with Coburn and modernist visual culture "helps us puzzle out the obvious paradoxes in James's attitude towards Impressionism."[115] Writing about John Singer Sargent, he praises "the artist who sees deep into his subject, undergoes it, absorbs it, discovers in it new things that were not on the surface, becomes patient with it, and almost reverent."[116] James struggled to "reconcile this fundamental requirement with the art of painting quickly" (not to mention writing or kodaking quickly).[117] The impression—which initially seemed all surface to James—presents one end of the transformation, through the nineteenth century, of Albertian constructions of linear perspective into strategies of selective description. The pictorial world expanded beyond the purview of the studio artist who had previously unhinged the formal-visual pyramid from his body's concrete confines to wield at large in pursuit of his subject, staging a stable scenic geometry within which that subject matter would be emplaced. Plein air Impressionism, mobilized through technical advances like tin tubes that kept oil paint fresh and portable, could capture immediate and ephemeral atmospheric properties otherwise unavailable to large-format cameras with inefficient exposure times. Eventually, when cameras attained a sufficient level of portability, artists could dispense with the first procedure of linear perspective—establishing the visual pyramid as an abstract container—because they carried around with them a program for translating any site into perspectival form. Whereas the Baudelairean ideal of the innocent eye dispenses with all forms of optical program as so much habitual and academic deadweight, the camera reminds us that there is always a controlling schema at work in the coordination of image-world and body, even if impersonal and preconscious.

Indeed, control is a significant concept for James, and it leaks out into his metatextual writing in several ways. It is a critical commonplace that, despite discussions in the prefaces of the reader's role in his work's reception, he in fact erects barriers to the reinterpretation of his oeuvre by ultimately making the supreme seer, author, and reader the same person: Henry James. In order to grant himself the authority he desires as a rereader of his own work—the purpose of the late-career *New York Edition*'s prefaces in the first place—James is forced to acknowledge the contribution "the reader" makes to the meaning of the text, if only to foreclose all the bad readings already circulating. On this view, James commandeers all the available critical territory in a deliberate act of intellectual imperialism (or managerial control) that supplements his original act of creation both by retelling the tale and by interpreting it again from a later position. One of the more charitable deconstructive versions of this argument is Paul Armstrong's reference to "doubled acts of attention" in the prefaces, where we encounter a "future reading or rereading through James's reflections on the past": "James's repeated recollections about the origins of a work or his aims in writing it claim to give definitive guidance about how it should be taken, and a large part of the authority that the prefaces have accrued as magisterial documents of James's artistic intentions is a recognition of this ambition. But when critics turn to the prefaces to resolve an interpretive dispute, they typically find that James is silent or ambiguous on crucial matters."[118] Whereof one cannot speak, thereof one must be silent, perhaps, or maybe James's desire to foreclose new interpretations is just too prodigious a task. Either way, his prefaces chase their own tails.

Of all the prefaces, *The Golden Bowl*'s (one of the last written) focuses at most length on revision: "What has the affair [of revision] been at worst," James asks, "but an earnest invitation to the reader to dream again in my company and in the interest of his own larger absorption of my sense?" By this time, he seemed to think too that new visual media provided a channel for the "larger absorption of his [literary] sense." There were pangs of jealousy and anxiety for James: he refers to the great number of "plastic" possibilities in the staging of his work, and wonders whether literature can be "pictorial enough" by itself to generate the visceral images relished by the modern reader. He had long given the cold shoulder to photography as an art form; still James hired Coburn to provide the frontispieces to the *New York Edition*, even wandering the streets with him to look for "optical echoes" of and "connexions" to his works.[119]

With the concurrent rises of the avant-garde Photo-Secession movement and mainstream snapshot culture, photography at the turn of the century provided the most literal access to the "renewed visions" James speaks about in his preface.[120] Perhaps soon his readers could find his stories' sites in London, or Paris, or Venice; giving in to the budding connection between new visual media and literature could be another way to forestall bad fan photographs (certainly James admired Coburn, ever since he sat for him in 1905, above almost all other practitioners and amateurs who could have sought and captured the storefront they put at the front of the novel). He did tell Coburn to avoid the "pompous and obvious things that one everywhere sees photos of."[121] But we also know that James admired his heroine Maggie Verver's ability to reenvision her world from outside of her experience's frame, and the Master was more open than ever about doing so himself. As David McWhirter notes, he too was seeking images outside their original frames: "The photographs, typically of houses, streets, or landscapes, unpeopled scenes or images that indirectly evoke settings from James's narratives, are striking in their radical break with long-prevalent practices in illustrating fiction, which dictated the representation of specific dramatic scenes from a narrative in drawings, and the use of accompanying captions quoted directly from the illustrated text."[122] James's prefaces and photographs, "sister foyers for his fictions," Anna Kornbluh posits in her architecturally minded analysis, "powerfully articulate the work of the novel chez James: myriad productions of unindexable social space." The illustrations were meant to unfix the novels' social scenes for the reader's eye, just as "the prefaces' discussions of settings emphatically dislocate his works from recognizable geography."[123] Before his death, James acceded to the possibility of ampliative transmedial rapport as a form of revision and adaptation, as a productive and portable echo of word in image and image in word.

John Bender and Michael Marrinan use "rapport" to describe the portable, combinatorial relationality that characterizes a diagram's use value. Their "culture of the diagram"—whose Enlightenment origin they locate in Diderot's and d'Alembert's *Encyclopédie,* constructed to promote epistemological relays between images and activities, profiles and tableaux—is a culture of portability, in which images become user-friendly objects in the world rather than its distanced reflections. The virtual space interfacing correlated elements in the *Encyclopédie* "provides support for the composite play of imagery and cognition that is the motor-energy of the diagram."[124] The useful diagram—or the difference between a diagram and a mere image—augments or enhances the user's ability to make worldly connections, to move forward with a task by transporting its visual lineaments beyond the page and into the world. Thus a diagram is never merely illustrative; it is not secondary to a written text nor designed to replace it. Diagrams integrate. They solve the problem of representing relation, impossible to achieve in a single image, as James acknowledges in his preface to *The Awkward Age*: "Though the relations of a human figure or a social occurrence are what make such objects interesting, they also make them difficult to isolate, to surround with the sharp black line, to frame in the square, the circle, the charming oval that helps any arrangement of objects to become a picture." James's preface to *The Golden Bowl* complains of images with their "'picture-book' quality that contemporary English and American prose appears more and more destined, by conditions of publication, to consent, however grudgingly, to see imputed to it." As he bemoans illustration's supplementary logic, he leaves room for a good kind of portability, one that would not "graft or 'grow' . . . a picture by another hand onto my own picture—this being always, to my sense, a lawless incident."[125] James hoped to discover, by contrast, a lawful relation between linguistic and pictorial imagery, which would also be a law of portable seeing, heightening a reader's ability to move from one visual register to the next in seamless sequence.

Kendall Johnson writes that Coburn's frontispieces "coordinate the pictures and text to avoid any unrestrained promiscuity."[126] Yet there was a certain sort of promiscuity in the writing on their process: as James and Coburn wandered the streets of London together, their "pleasure of exploration" turned the metropolis into "a field yielding a ripe harvest of treasure."[127] Johnson elsewhere claims that James sought to protect the aura of the traditional work of art—in Walter Benjamin's sense, from "The Work of Art in the Age of Mechanical Reproduction"—which is "not predicated on the original art object per se, but rather on a visual economy of representation and reproduction whose underlying network of social relations, courtesies and hierarchies in status and taste James glances backward to appreciate."[128] But he was looking forward when wandering with Coburn, their visual "treasure" a glint from the future, not the past. I prefer to avoid getting distracted by Benjamin's reference to the lost "aura" of the artwork, as James's visual modernism captures the ambivalence underlying the appeal. Benjamin first conceives of the camera as epitome of the destructive, consumptive political economy of capitalism, dispelling the aura of things by reproducing them in an automatic, rationalized, portable form: "That which withers in the age of mechanical reproduction is the aura of the work of art. . . . To pry an object from its shell, to destroy its aura, is the mark of a perception whose 'sense of the universal equality of things' has increased to such a degree that it extracts it even from a unique object by means of reproduction." Yet photography is also a potential agent for dialectical inversion, "the first truly revolutionary means of production," a medium that was invented simultaneously with the rise of socialism, capable of revolutionizing the whole function of art and the human sensorium.[129]

James held such a desire for his art—revolutionizing the human sensorium—at least since "The Art of Fiction." He aims at least to spur the sensorium, "not only to *show* things to the reader but to *act upon* him," enjoining him to negotiate the intersecting imaginations and idealizations of a shared world.[130] Like his older brother, he champions writing from "experience," which "is never limited and is never complete," like a "kind of huge spider-web, of the finest silken threads, suspended in the chamber of consciousness and catching every air-borne particle in its tissue."[131] James's sense of worldly visual rapport in his late work, the seeds of which can already be found in "The Art of Fiction," was among other things a response to growing feelings—and even contemporary theories, sciences, and technologies—of irreversible perceptual mobility.[132] His fiction, too, did its own theorizing on portability, often grounding James's deepest perceptual (and formal) concerns in object representations, circulating in the midst of whirlwind commodity exchange and a general economy of advancing reification.[133]

Even if the advance of capital, consumerism, urbanization, and industrialization is best considered on a continuity rather than rupture model of history and temporality, a sea change occurred in James's rhetoric as the new century dawned. How did the Master, who always seemed to possess, as his friend John La Farge claimed, "a painter's eye"[134] and who disdained photography as a dumb link to the "real thing" in its grayest countenance, take on a late style more photographic and cinematic than painterly? How did he not only allow Coburn's work to enter the *New York Edition* but come to actively pursue that work alongside a coconspirator he would once have given his gouty toe a hundred times to avoid? Ralph Bogardus notes the turn in his language in a letter to William Dean Howells in 1896, James's positive use of "images" and "impressions" together, and phrases that "suggest photographs and photographic vision": "impressed with a view, framed by the clear window," "saved intensity," "individual *vivid* image," "experience consists of impressions."[135]

Walking the streets of the European metropolis with Coburn, James was on the one hand doing something he had always done, and that had always been attached to his art, beginning with the childhood walks that, "with an obsession of their own, constantly abetted our daubing."[136] He explained the impetus of *The Princess Casamassima* (1886) in his "habit and interest in walking the streets" during "the first year of a long residence in London. . . . One walked of course with one's eyes greatly open. . . . Possible stories, presentable figures, rise from the thick jungle as the observer moves, fluttering up like startled game."[137] With Coburn an experiential ecology, a walking technique of the bodily eye in motion, came to be presented through the glancing rapport between word and photograph. The photographer would later pointedly remark, "Henry James must have had sensitive plates in his brain on which to record his impressions."[138]

It is as if James, at the end of his career, worked out the contradiction Charles Baudelaire could not: between a devotion to modish flânerie and a hatred of photography on epistemological grounds. "If photography is allowed to supplement art in some of its functions," the French Symbolist wrote in 1859, "it will soon have supplanted or corrupted it altogether, thanks to the stupidity of the multitude which is its natural ally."[139] In his vitriolic critique of photography as an aesthetic practice, Baudelaire retreats to the primacy of the inner eye's gaze, as in Constantin Guys's example, wherein "all good and true draughtsmen draw from the image imprinted on their brains, and not from nature . . . [so that] finally ideal execution may become as unconscious and spontaneous as is digestion for a healthy man." The relation here established between imaginative seeing and digestion turns vision into a Nietzschean will to power (shot through with masticatory metaphors), wholly on the side of the gaze that thoroughly digests its object. And yet Baudelaire's analogy relies on Guys's particular working method, the way he sketches his scene after the fact of viewing rather than *en plein air*, a distinction clarified by the former's use of "glance" as a thing the artist transcends:

> Bending over his table, darting on to a sheet of paper the same glance that a moment ago he was directing towards external things, skirmishing with his pencil, his pen, his brush . . . in a ferment of violent activity, as though afraid that the image might escape him . . . the external world is reborn upon his paper, natural and more than natural, beautiful and more than beautiful, strange and endowed with an impulsive life. . . . All the raw materials with which the memory has loaded itself are put in order, arranged and harmonized, and undergo that forced idealization which is the result of a childlike perceptiveness—that is to say, a perceptiveness acute and magical by reason of its innocence![140]

Baudelaire's celebratory description of Guys at work partakes in classic empiricist representationalism, the artist merely an arranger of a "forced idealization" from the scraps of daily life collected by the glance, which is guilty rather than innocent because it is a habitual form of seeing shared with everyone else on the street. It is peculiar, then, that a poet whose most famous lyric turns on a glance in the street, "À une passante," and who along with Poe brought the twentieth century its celebrated figure of the flaneur, would associate the base form of photography with the multitude while making the true artist (and his innocent eye) a priestly figure, presiding over the natural world's rebirth once back in his chamber, with a hunched, ritualistic stoop over his altar.

For such purposes one must entrap a child's eye, which actually wanders too much rather than too little, in a vice or a restrictive metaphor. In the 1880s one might think of the tachistoscope, a new device that turned glance into gaze, immobilizing the patient's eye and body so that the former cannot shift its point of focus during a rapid exposure (its shutter moving faster than the eye's muscular capabilities). As Paul Virilio argues, faster mechanical shutter speeds, from "Niépce's thirty minutes in 1829 to roughly twenty seconds with Nadar" to the approach of instantaneity at the end of the century, produce bodies more firmly situated in place, for now "seeing the world becomes not only a matter of spatial distance but also of the *time-distance* to be eliminated," a gathering of the dynamic worldly surround into atemporal near-immediacy.[141] As attention deficit became a problem of overstimulation—a common refrain for theorists of urbanization like Georg Simmel and Walter Benjamin—the seeing subject was conceptualized as the immobile center of an increasingly mobile lifeworld. The Baudelairean artist's "forced idealization" is the result of a tachistoscopic operation, his vision turned wholly to the page, his pen or brush fervently registering and organizing images at a speed now in excess of his previous glances, the speed of his hand keeping the rest of his stooped figure still all the while.

By comparison, James strikes the unlikely figure of a flaneur—we know how much he liked to walk, both in the city and from his country house at Rye. His walking tour collaboration with Coburn collected glances in the street that, instead of serving as heightened, transfigured representations of scenes from his stories, embody the impersonal origins of dramatic action and emotional discovery. For all the Baudelairean and Ruskinian celebration of childlike seeing in painterly originality, James gives us a child (Maisie) with a camera eye as if to mark the birth of photographic portability as the ocular regime on which all art must now stake its visual truth claims. Coburn's depeopled glances, of storefronts and housefronts and equipages and doorways, suggest modern anomie, modernist depersonalization, and the "wind-blown germs" one finds at "almost any turn of the road," images as spores that settle on the mind unbidden. They are sites to be found, used, and traversed, as Coburn's diagonals suggest, offering landmarks along an open path rather than static monuments that dominate the mind. Coburn and James, setting in motion a relay or rapport between isolated images and literary worlds, resituate the site of aesthetic inspiration outside interior mental space, along the "current of life" canalized on the boulevard, its velocity matched by the speedy shutter. When James writes that the image-germs "accumulate, and we are always picking them over, selecting among them," he identifies the two-sided aspect of the modern artist's vocation: a rapid accumulation of (photographic) sensations and a second-order construction that is equally rapid on another ontological level, the analytic arrangement of a stable and coherent world of action out of the materials offered by an unstable and incoherent environment and mediated by a physiological apparatus no less slippery and unsettled.

Photographing urban cityscapes became much easier with the introduction of high-speed emulsions, a technology consonant with the chronophotographic revolution of Eadweard Muybridge and Étienne-Jules Marey. City and country, already marked with rhetorical differences in nineteenth-century literature, demanded different things of the photographic apparatus, with the slow speed of rural life already perfectly amenable to the far less portable collodion wet plate process. The photographer's access to the urban lifeworld as a function of camera technology thus mirrored the awkward transition many felt between country and city life, literalizing the analogy between human and machine vision that had also been developing in contemporary optical science. Meanwhile, among the Impressionist painters one finds many scenes of Parisians out for a stroll in which compositional form has moved away from a stable center, seen obviously in the negative space of Edgar Degas's *Place de la Concorde* (1879). The scene's network of visual relay contributes to the centrifugal character of the figural placement, the Vicomte Lepic and his daughters looking off frame in three different directions, their dog and a horse-drawn carriage turned along alternate vectors of movement. James and Coburn's urban frontispieces, taken no doubt in a Post-Impressionist world, can be seen to radicalize the visual rapport activated in a dynamic tableau like Degas's, with each photograph a node in an urban network made up of all the other pictures. One should, I suggest, read them as a series of their own, as a sequence of rapid exposures to city life as much as a collection of isolated image-text relations, and thus as much an anticipation of the twentieth-century photobook as a modernist residue of Victorian serial illustrations. In writing, this proleptic impulse appears at the time the *New York Edition* was being collected, in *The American Scene* (1907), where James's return to his native land (and, in four out of fourteen chapters, his native New York City) is managed by a series of verbal snapshots, which taken together "seemed not at all to speak of different things—by so quick a process does any one aspect, in the United States . . . connect itself with all the rest."[142]

What I am barely hesitating to call the "Jamesian moment" at the turn of the twentieth century Thierry de Duve baptized the "Cézannean moment," characterized by two "inseparable" questions: "What is the world, if my very vision, modeled by that of my artistic predecessors, is no longer certain of its own reality? And who am I, if my image in the mirror vacillates, unsure of its own objectivity?"[143] Paul Cézanne died mere months before James's *New York Edition* was published, prior to which he wrote a striking letter to his son:

> Finally I must tell you that as a painter I am becoming more clear-sighted in front of nature, but that with me the realization of my sensations is always very difficult. I cannot attain the intensity that is unfolded before my senses. I have not the magnificent richness of coloring that animates nature. Here on the edge of the river the motifs are very plentiful, the same subject seen from a different angle gives a subject for study of the highest interest and so varied that I think I could be occupied for months without changing my place, simply bending my head a little more to the right or left.[144]

For Cézanne, visual intensity is premised on proprioceptive mobility, a feature of his work that many art historians have classified as Proto-Cubist and commensurate with the phenomenological moment on the horizon. An unlikely bedfellow, Cézanne's Post-Impressionist work shares with James's a desire to become a "recording machine," or what Crary calls a "grave attentiveness," a sensorial attunement that is "simultaneously a piercing social estrangement and a mode of unprecedented invention which imagined the radiant dissolution of the monadic confines of the self."[145] The monad already cracked in *The Portrait of a Lady*, but it is thrown wide open on the way to James's late style, arriving in the integration of Coburn's impersonal pictures with a protocinematic syntax, sentences wandering like the author's stuttering gait, images of bridges and doorways and windows just barely askew as if one simply bent one's head a little to the side before continuing down the way.

Coda

Slicing the Eyeball

> Surgeons must be very careful
> When they take the knife!
> Underneath their fine incisions
> Stirs the Culprit - *Life!*
>
> EMILY DICKINSON, F156

> Content . . . is a glimpse of something, an encounter, you know, like a flash. It's very tiny—very tiny, content.
>
> WILLEM DE KOONING

> Got me a movie
> I want you to know
> Slicing up eyeballs
> I want you to know . . .
>
> THE PIXIES

Louis Lumière's *Boat Leaving the Port* (*Barque sortant du port,* 1895) captures a simple sequence. A small boat, rowed by two men and steered by a third at the back, enters the frame from the right foreground and makes its way diagonally toward the back left. The tip of a jetty peeks out in the right middle ground, on which stand two women and two children. There is a breeze, though not a gale, as registered by the fabric of the most prominent woman's dress. For about twenty seconds the boat handles the swell easily, until the wake turns it broadside to the wind. A larger wave lifts the boat sideways. The camera cuts and the film ends.

There is nothing spectacular about Lumière films except the fields they open up. What could be more banal than workers leaving a factory after a long day, a train pulling into a station, men paddling out from a harbor? Indeed, early cinema's achievement, at least on the realist side (trick films present a different challenge), can be measured against its routine pro-filmic matter, in many Lumière films the mere fulfillment of a time schedule. Which is why I should be clearer: there is something about *Boat Leaving the Port* that suggests other possibilities. As Dai Vaughan recognizes, in contrast with the short film that started it all, *Workers Leaving the Lumière Factory* (1895), here the "unpredictable has not only emerged from the background to occupy the greater portion of the frame; it has also taken sway over the principals." Those principals are not simply following an institutionally pre-prescribed path out of the workplace but reacting spontaneously to an uncontrolled element, the waves, which draw human self-representation "into the contingency of events."[1]

Lumière's framing leaves space and time open for contingencies to develop, the camera set up to allow a scene to unfold whichever way it will. Noël Burch writes of a "quasi-scientific attitude" in his practice, his camera like a microscope set to allow something to "happen" under its purview, albeit at a human scale.[2] Lumière eventually described his work to Georges Sadoul as "endeavors of technological research" without "what they call 'direction.'"[3] We are back to what Lorraine Daston and Peter Galison call "mechanical objectivity," a residual fin de siècle need for an "objective view" marked by an ability to see "without interference [or] interpretation," or in the realist filmmaker's vein, without the theatrical manipulations of that unabashed magician-trickster Georges Méliès.[4] Whereas Méliès largely rejected linear perspective in favor of the flat tableau vivant, built on set according to the structure of the theatrical proscenium, Lumière's seemingly undirected mise-en-scène (a contradiction in terms recognized as such by many subsequent film critics and theorists) won out in the new century only to be sliced up by new techniques in film editing, perhaps most obviously in the chase films that progressively stitched temporal sequences along axes of continuity while taking fuller advantage of the depth of the frame's perspective box.

There is no single path to the institutional mode of representation, no neat linear sequence of developments from the single-shot (non)narrative film to D. W. Griffith's continuity system of film editing and beyond to Hollywood's golden age. What one finds, digging through the messy and woefully incomplete archive of early cinematic genres, is a plethora of experiments in possible continuity techniques constructing synthetic diegetic geographies in piecemeal fashion: through eyeline matching and countershots, sequential and parallel cuts, alternating shot scales, and oblique camera angles that reinforce the positionality of objects. One also finds a silent cinema that wasn't so silent, not only because of accompanying organs and orchestras but also thanks to "lecturers" who served several functions at the site of projection—narrator, showman, barker—before soundtracks made them largely obsolete. "No period was ever more noisy than that of the silent movies," as Christian Metz puts it.[5]

Lecturers played a key role in exhibiting films that were neither self-evident single-shot shorts nor near-seamless narratives edited into sufficient coherence. André Gaudreault writes that around 1902, with the explosion of multishot films, transparent cinematic meaning "came under threat," for "every camera hiatus could cause spatial or temporal hiatuses, knock a hole in the narrative thread and leave room for interpretation—or incomprehension."[6] In 1908, the year Griffith's career as a filmmaker began, Van C. Lee claimed in *Moving Picture World* that "not more than one out of every fifty feature films is properly understood by the audience to whom it is shown" unless some explanation is given prior to or during the viewing.[7] Intertitles were an option, but they were costly and visually cumbersome, an obstacle to the viewer's fantasy of cinematic absorption. Live lecturers accompanying the film, standing in an ambiguous space both inside and outside of it ("out there" with the spectators while acting as a necessary supplement to the film's structural breaks, gaps, and lacks), commonly operated as extra-diegetic narrators until an adequate narrator function immanent to the film itself could be institutionalized. They corralled and directed audience attention to the film's most important details; they told viewers what they "should" be looking at when the text failed to do so clearly.

No wonder Ezra Pound had mostly negative things to say about cinema at the beginning, even as Susan McCabe suggests that Imagism's "ideographic roots anticipated Eisenstein's theory of montage as 'copulation (perhaps we had better say, combination) of two hieroglyphs.'"[8] She may have Hugh Kenner's surprising definition of the movement in mind, where (as if in anticipation of Charles Olson's poetic theories) "perception succeeds perception like the frames of a film."[9] But just as with the era's intrepid filmmakers, how the Imagists got there is as telling as their polished products. Pound formulated his Imagist doctrine at the very time visual presentation in cinema was sundered by the overlapping of two lacks—of sound and of adequate editorial principles—that had to be filled in with prosaic language and deictic direction from the outside. Amy Lowell writes, as her final "rule" of Imagist doctrine, that "most of us believe that concentration is of the very essence of poetry," that good poetry directs the attention, which is also to say that it needs no supplement. It admits no vagary, no blurred outlines characteristic of Decadent art and of a cinema whose primitive montage effects are not visually or semiotically transparent. Imagism, which in another context could be (mis)taken to mean "cinematicism," does share something with celebrations of the artistic freedom film opens up in the new century, particularly in Lowell's allowance of "absolute freedom in the choice of subject," acceptance of "the artistic value of modern life," and call to "create new rhythms."[10] But as filmmakers and operators struggled to find the visual grammar that would guide the eye in interpreting soundless narrative sequence, Pound, H.D., and Richard Aldington agreed on their own principle of semiotic transparency: the poet must "use absolutely no word that does not contribute to the presentation" of the poetic object.[11]

So no lecturer need apply, nor any writer of intertitles; the poet already has the semicolon. Take perhaps the most famous example of an Imagist poem:

> In a Station of the Metro
>
> The apparition of these faces in the crowd;
> Petals on a wet, black bough.[12]

Pound gives his two lines (cut down from an initial thirty-six) a title straight out of Lumière. Much is demanded of that semicolon. If it stands in for a "like," it does so in much the same way a cut in one of Eisenstein's dialectical montages stands in for an "and" or a "but." If Soviet-style montage seeks to form an experience of dialectical correspondence out of visual singularities, then film syntax must be designed to accommodate multishot linkages without any outside source giving away the sequence's internal logic. Pound's semicolon, likewise, caresses and eases the line's jamb, like a cross-dissolve. As in montage, simile is implied rather than asserted, neither vehicle nor tenor subsuming its other; each insists or pulls like a tide on its partner image across the porous membrane fashioned by the line break.

There is, of course, little movement in Pound's finished fragment except what that semicolon contains. And if there is any one thing that distinguishes cinema from the other arts that ground its technics, it is movement. The sheer number of frames even the most rudimentary films squeeze into a small segment of clock time explodes the meandering rhythm of the magic lantern shows, generating the tantalizing possibility of visual narration without monstration. In the early twentieth century, visual comprehension was being learned again at the screenings of not yet continuous films, and modernist poets asked themselves a question that paralleled filmmakers' then experimenting with visual syntax: how can we organize language, taken as opaque and material rather than transparent or immediately representational, to better direct our newly fickle and fragile attention? Later on, in *The Cantos* (most dramatically in its *Rock-Drill* section), Pound would include Chinese characters in vertical arrangements alongside horizontal English lines, producing what Brian Reed calls "a wandering, wondering perusal of a poem, in which the eye moves as readily backward, upward, or diagonally as well as down or to the right."[13] Pound's graphic experimentation opens the reader's visual sensorium, meeting cinematic montage halfway in its groping feel for the human eye's capabilities and limits, preying on and playing with the way it collects figures out of informational flow and gleans meaningful patterns.

William Carlos Williams writes that the "new" poetics requires a formidable understanding of the "physiology of the nervous system" as it relates to "the larger processes of the imagination."[14] Poets fight alongside filmmakers in a battle over spectators' attention, but poets have already lost the war to modernity if they do not wedge down into the body with their art. Béla Balázs helped inaugurate film theory by arguing that cinema revives the body by feeding it again after its aggressive commercial print diet, the "dematerialized, abstract, and over-intellectualized" culture of words making way for a "new language of gestures . . . aris[ing] from our yearning for the *embodied human* being who has fallen silent, who has been forgotten and has become invisible."[15] Balázs's vision for cinema is remarkably similar to Williams's poetic program, which takes arms against any writing "designed to keep up the barrier between sense and the vaporous fringe which distracts attention from its agonized approaches to the moment."[16] Language, in its densest materiality, is a thick frontier through which we direct our senses in/through the world: "But can you not see, can you not taste, can you not smell, can you not hear, can you not touch—words? . . . Words roll, spin, flare up, rumble, trickle, foam—."[17] For Williams, poetry is a muscular feeling for words, and the poem must have movement in space, the form of a motion, if it is to pull the "agonized" tensions of a moment together in feeling. We organize ourselves to give the mind its stay, he says, but the self is in the poem as much as it is in the film for an artist like Griffith. To give the mind its stay, to settle it down, one must inhabit the cuts through which motion, sequence, and sums are built.

In *The Great American Novel*, published in 1923 along with *Spring and All*, Williams writes that "America is a mass of pulp, a jelly, a sensitive plate ready to take whatever print you want to put on it. . . . We have only mass movement like the sea."[18] Dr. Paterson, on his walk in the late long poem, would refer to the public he encounters as "the 'great beast' come to sun himself."[19] But here, photographic technology figures prominently: if the American mass is a "sensitive plate," naturalized like the endlessly mutable formal canvas of the sea, all the poetry fit to "print" will cut into the mass in order to select the elements that, taken back together, form new objects. Williams specifically disparages the realist metaphor of the "mirror up to nature" not for being too photographic but because poetry rarely stays, despite popular misconception, within the boundaries of the single frame. In *Spring and All*'s first poem, "One by one objects are defined— / It quickens: clarity, outline of leaf"; the eye accelerates toward the edge of things, where Williams's famous line breaks make incisions not simply to dismember but also to suture.[20] The poet's sense of internal edge suggests Cubist compositions of figures cut and reanimated as if viewed from all sides at once, capturing on still canvas the viewer's feel for sensorimotor movement around real objects.

Poem VII cuts a prose passage on Juan Gris off at midsentence, continuing to snip the tradition's rose to give it back its edge: "The edge / cuts without cutting."[21] The edge is where the action is, and Williams's heteroclite line breaks are where his poetry's tension resides. As in collage, Bonnie Costello writes, objects in his poems "retain the memory of their tearing."[22] And each snip gives a word its thickness back, even the littlest one, though it reaches out onto the page for the next word that will reconnect it to a network of sense. "It is at the edge of the / petal that love waits," and the waiting is the hardest part (as in the sharpest point, the nonsite across which the eye must relearn to track change according to new rhythms). The poems of *Spring and All* emphasize absence and fragmentation. Williams does not "dissolve" one image into another, and his rose is not Mallarmé's ideal flower "absent from all bouquets": "to engage roses / becomes a geometry— // Sharper, neater, more cutting," so that at the end (of an object, a line, a frame) "the start is begun."[23] The overdetermination of a single image or metaphor is dislodged / new permutations can commence / the field is open / the age of montage is upon us.

In Poem XI, which begins with "In passing with my mind," Williams's moving car—a recurring motif—pulls the eye past a scene as it glances backward. The poet launches the "art of driving a car," as opposed to Baudelaire's "art of taking a walk," McCabe thinks, as "a means of observing the 'seeing eye' in flux and disarrayed."[24] That eye is only able to make out a couplet's worth of detail in discrete units, as if the unfolding poem is structured by a sequence of saccadic jerks. In what may be the first lyric to address the twentieth century's newest form of (non)seeing, so-called highway hypnosis, the driver's mind passes "on nothing in the world / but the right of way." But the absorbed directness granted the driver "by / virtue of the law" gives way to a "spinning" relay of glances: "I saw // an elderly man who / smiled and looked away // to the north past a house"; "a woman in blue // who was laughing and / leaning forward to look up // into the man's half / averted face"; "a boy of eight who was / looking at the middle of // the man's belly." Each look traverses the gap produced on the page by the white space in between the couplets, the directed glance split from its direct object. The double strokes I have produced above replicate Williams's doubled cuts, jumps made not only in the gap between eye and object but also between the speaker-driver-viewer's (meta)eye and *its* double object, the permutations of which make up "the inevitable flux of the seeing eye toward measuring itself by the world it inhabits." The poem asks how the eye can master scenic continuity once it has been set in motion, and ends with a literalization of enjambment, with a vision of "a girl with one leg / over the rail of a balcony," a close-up amputation of the female body (a Lillian Gish turned upside down) in a hanging "jambe."[25]

If we are right to imagine a Dr. Williams wielding his scalpel, how far he nevertheless takes us from the serene dissection of the cow's eye in Descartes's *Dioptrics*! Discussing the "fixed categories into which life is divided," Williams emphasizes that they exist only insofar as they are *not* "dead dissections." What he goes on to call "cleavage" is the effect of the imagination, not of "anatomitization."[26] For Williams, to watch one's own cleaved/cleaving eye—to watch oneself watching, to strain after an impossible maneuver—is to "[witness] the larger processes of the imagination," an embodied faculty that does not cut one off from the world but rather cuts and folds oneself into it. As Hillis Miller writes, the imagination for Williams is not a vehicle of "indirection or transposition" but of a "paradoxical movement both toward and away from the object."[27] The eye splits because it works both ways, its glance a two-beat oscillation: out and back. As in Luis Buñuel's and Salvador Dalí's *Un Chien Andalou* (1929), a slit or cut in the eye becomes a "self-reflecting comment on the very process of making metaphors."[28]

Buñuel writes in his notes, in a negative formulation straight out of a modernist poetic manifesto, "NOTHING in the film SYMBOLIZES ANYTHING."[29] Instead, so his initial story goes (as related by Georges Bataille), Dalí devised the famous shot of a man slicing a woman's eyeball with a razor after seeing "a narrow and long cloud cutting across the lunar surface."[30] And that is precisely what's shown in the preceding shot, as if the master anti-ocular metaphor of Surrealist art is cut out of a situated vision in/of the natural world and a sense of the embodied eye's perspectival limitation. Martin Jay notes the Surrealists' "rich ocular iconography," a preoccupation with "enucleated, blinded, mutilated, or transfigured" eyeballs (common in the work of de Chirico, Ernst, Man Ray, and Magritte as well).[31] Bataille's novella *Story of the Eye*, written just a year before Buñuel's film, performs an even more grotesque ophthalmology: torturing the organ, dissecting the dissector, turning it against itself into a figure of glutinous excess. But Buñuel argued against relegating his violent imagery and jarring sequential juxtapositions to an unconscious, oneiric manifold often taken as the movement's ground zero: "The plot is the result of a CONSCIOUS psychic automatism and, to that extent, it does not attempt to recount a dream, although it profits by a mechanism analogous to that of dreams."[32] This mechanism, with Freud as the main source, is metaphor (condensation), but here it is born not out of unconscious pressure but conscious "automatism," or in visual terms: the glance. The filmic cut, made self-reflexively thematic by the opening of *Un chien* (not to mention gendered so pertinently at the same time, a point film theorists would eventually jump on), marks the institutionalization of the glance as the structuring unit of visual art in the twentieth century.

In the wake of Williams (and the new art form that would be the twentieth century's aesthetic and commercial obsession), how poets and visual artists used or misused cuts and jambs became the key question of measure. Later in his career, Williams developed the variable foot—most famously in his triadic line—as if to forcefully reclaim an experiential freedom from the regularity of so many frames per second. Hugh Kenner posits, in a letter to Mike Weaver, that Williams's triadic line originated in an inability, following his late-life strokes, to scan *with his eyes* (demonstrating, with this hypothesis, the intimate triadic relationship between the eye, ear, and poetic meter): "His eyes could follow a line but not jump back and locate accurately the beginning of the next line. . . . I'm convinced that the 3-ply typography of his late verse was originally a set of helps (with the tab stops) for just such line-finding in rereading."[33] Whether this is true or not, the step-down line served to reintegrate the sensorimotor body of the poem, to put the body back into action when arts like the cinema threatened to do the opposite, to isolate and even disable (to slice and therefore fragment) the passive, spectatorial eye. The glance, as the acts of driving and cinematic viewing made readily apparent, can be taken away from the coordinated capacities of the body. The poet, through the integration of the body in action, can also take back the constructive qualities of the glance. In *Paterson* (completed in 1958), Williams does just that, using his variable foot to "catch something of the walking world's measure,"[34] to reclaim the shifting space-time intersections of the stroll that "leaves the path, finds hard going / across-field, stubble and matted brambles":

> The descent beckons
>   as the ascent beckoned
>   Memory is a kind
> of accomplishment
>   a sort of renewal
>   even
> an initiation, since the spaces it opens are new
> places
>   inhabited by hordes
>   heretofore unrealized,
> of new kinds—
>   since their movements
>   are towards new objectives[35]

To walk is to quicken and lengthen one's step as needed, just as to glance is to accelerate and decelerate one's look as needed. And the tether between body and image is in memory as "a kind / of accomplishment" or "a sort of renewal," not as a metaphysical transport but as a slight lengthening of the thought to complete a movement. Memory inheres in thought's variation and in the body's (and the eye's) directedness, in its movements "towards new objectives." As the eye steps down in a dilating and contracting rhythm corresponding with the body's walking movement, it also moves out and back across the field of the page, returning to the margin from which it endlessly projects itself.

As we move and see and write, we collect, as long poems like Whitman's *Song of Myself*, Williams's *Paterson*, and A. R. Ammons's *Sphere* do, "rolling / up the sum" of concrete particulars as doggedly (if also as futilely, from the perspective of some impossible democratic ideal) as Whitman's Sisyphean dung beetle.[36] When the final volume of Williams's most famous poem was published, Robert Frank's photobook *The Americans* was prepping for its United States release. At a time when the *Life* photo essay was most Americans' chief exposure to serious photography—a form where pictures follow each other according to a written narrative logic independent of the visual series—Frank (in the mode of predecessors like Walker Evans) tantalized with the possibility of visual narration without monstration, the very engine of early cinema's development. "I wanted to create some kind of rhythm," Frank said of his masterwork.[37] Or many kinds of rhythms. His photographs depict presence and absence in oscillation, open and closed forms, acts of looking and things looked at, movement and stillness, power and impotence. As in Williams's poetry, meaning inheres in the jambs where investigation happens and connections are made and remade—in Frank's case, in the cut of his frames, often made in unorthodox compositional locations, that maintains the tension between inside and outside, a self and an other.

All a writer (and teacher) can do, most of the time, is cut off a sliver of those innumerable connections. Sometimes it's enough just to show or tell someone where to look, knowing full well that one's worldview is far from exhaustive and always will be. That's the thing about the glance: it doesn't come to a full stop and it's never fully satisfied. But I take only one of Frank's photographs here, because I really must insist on coming to a full stop. And because one of his photographs, smartly replicated on the cover of *The Americans*, provides a user's key for the kind of relational looking Frank's series demands. In *Trolley—New Orleans*, white and Black passengers look out

FIGURE 11. Robert Frank, *Trolley—New Orleans*, 1955, gelatin silver print, Metropolitan Museum of Art, New York

toward the picture plane, separated by the stanchions that cut them up into cells, as if caught in their own film negatives. A white boy and Black man, the two figures whose attentions are most directly oriented toward the camera, reach outside of their frames. Near opposites, they both break out of their delineated portraits at the juncture where the segregated trolley turns from white to Black. And above each "cell," closed upper windows reflect while abstracting the unseen side of the picture, the site of the photographer's position. These reflections form a surface where the visible meets the invisible, a positive meets a negative, the seen meets the unseen, the scene meets the unscene.

Frank shot this photograph in 1955, only weeks before Rosa Parks refused to give up her seat on a Montgomery bus. Glancing horizontally and vertically along the picture's complementary axes, one submits to a visual syntax no less social for being intricately formal, and no less bewitching for being ethically and politically urgent. The appearance of classical symmetry is there, with the children's window square the central element, but it is the off-center jamb between them and the Black man to the camera's right that holds the picture together—the dark backdrop on the right half of his square creating the effect of his face dissolving into or out of a void, which places the white skin of the children against the stooped figure behind them into further relief. How far we are here from the avowedly Edenic pro-filmic world Lumière's camera gives us, but also how close we are to the power of the cut in *Boat Leaving the Port*, where at the edge of the composition we're thrown into the contingencies of a world we didn't make but that we nevertheless hope to shape. At the edge of the civil rights era, or at the edge of our own precarious future (but what future isn't precarious?), we look for the jamb on which we can hang the right relation, to make something that will last. When we make a world through our glance, we are that jamb, our eyes the cut that precedes the picture.

NOTES

Introduction

Epigraph: Friedrich Nietzsche, *Thus Spoke Zarathustra*, in *The Portable Nietzsche*, ed. Walter Kaufmann (New York: Viking Penguin, 1976), 389.

1. Walt Whitman, "A Glimpse," in *Complete Poetry and Collected Prose* (New York: Library of America, 1982), 283.

2. Whitman, "Song of Myself," in *Complete Poetry and Collected Prose*, 76.

3. Whitman, "Not Heaving from My Ribb'd Breast Only," in *Complete Poetry and Collected Prose*, 274.

4. Lorraine Daston, "The Coup d'Oeil: On a Mode of Understanding," *Critical Inquiry* 45, no. 2 (Winter 2019): 309, 312–13 (Jean-Charles Folard quotation, 313).

5. Dennis Berthold, "Charles Brockden Brown, *Edgar Huntly*, and the Origins of the American Picturesque," *William and Mary Quarterly* 41, no. 1 (January 1984): 62.

6. Jennifer J. Baker, "Hawthorne's Picturesque at Home and Abroad," *Studies in Romanticism* 55, no. 3 (Fall 2016): 424.

7. On the proleptics of the American picturesque and Manifest Destiny politics, see Kris Fresonke, *West of Emerson: The Design of Manifest Destiny* (Berkeley: University of California Press, 2003); Kendall Johnson, "'Rising from the stain on a painter's palette': George Catlin's Picturesque and the Legibility of Seminole Removal," *Nineteenth-Century Prose* 29, no. 2 (Fall 2002): 69–93; Rochelle L. Johnson, *Passions for Nature: Nineteenth-Century America's Aesthetics of Alienation* (Athens: University of Georgia Press, 2009); and Bryan Jay Wolf, *Romantic Re-Vision: Culture and Consciousness in Nineteenth-Century American Painting and Literature* (Chicago: University of Chicago Press, 1982).

8. Angela Miller, *The Empire of the Eye: Landscape Representation and American Cultural Politics, 1825–1875* (Ithaca, NY: Cornell University Press, 1993), 84. Alternatively, see Cindy Weinstein, *Time, Tense, and American Literature: When Is Now?* (Cambridge: Cambridge University Press, 2015), for a study of time and tense in American literature that presents novels that lose their hold on ordered sequence. But Weinstein still relates her objects' grammatical and temporal wobbles with contemporaneous political forms, like constitutional ratification and abolition.

9. Albert Boime, *The Magisterial Gaze: Manifest Destiny and American Landscape Painting, c. 1830–1865* (Washington: Smithsonian, 1991), 1.

10. Anne Baker, "Word, Image, and National Geography: Panorama Pamphlets and Manifest Destiny," in *American Literary Geographies*, ed. Hsuan Hsu and Martin Brückner (Newark: University of Delaware Press, 2007), 94.

11. David Miller, *Dark Eden: The Swamp in Nineteenth-Century American Culture* (Cambridge: Cambridge University Press, 2010). The visual semiosis of America as an imagined community does become more complicated once familiar icons and texts are analytically exposed to transnational histories. See, for example, Brooke Blower and Mark Philip Bradley, eds., *The Familiar Made Strange: American Icons and Artifacts after the Transnational Turn* (Ithaca, NY: Cornell University Press, 2015).

12. Foundational literary accounts of the possessive American eye (in addition to those discussed later in this chapter) include Sacvan Bercovitch, *The American Jeremiad* (Madison: University of Wisconsin Press, 1978); Christopher Collins, *The Uses of Observation: A Study of Correspondential Vision in the Writings of Emerson, Thoreau, and Whitman* (The Hague: Mouton, 1971); Michael T. Gilmore, *Surface and Depth: The Quest for Legibility in American Culture* (Oxford: Oxford University Press, 2003); Annette Kolodny, *The Lay of the Land: Metaphor as Experience and History in American Life and Letters* (Chapel Hill: University of North Carolina Press, 1984); Perry Miller, *Nature's Nation* (Cambridge, MA: Harvard University Press, 1967); Richard Slotkin, *Regeneration through Violence: The Mythology of the American Frontier, 1600–1860* (Middletown, CT: Wesleyan University Press, 1973); and Hyatt H. Waggoner, *American Visionary Poetry* (Baton Rouge: Louisiana University Press, 1982).

13. Elisa New, *The Line's Eye: Poetic Experience, American Sight* (Cambridge, MA: Harvard University Press, 1998), 2, 7.

14. Myra Jehlen, *American Incarnation: The Individual, the Nation, and the Continent* (Cambridge, MA: Harvard University Press, 1986), 3.

15. See Donald Pease, *Visionary Compacts: American Renaissance Writings in Cultural Context* (Madison: University of Wisconsin Press, 1987). For an example of a study that takes the American difference to be something less rhetorically grand, see Ezra Tawil, *Literature, American Style: The Originality of Imitation in the Early Republic* (Philadelphia: University of Pennsylvania Press, 2018). Looking primarily at literature of the early republic, Tawil argues that the very notion of American literary originality depended on European traditions of novelty and were mostly legible through stylistic deviation.

16. Sacvan Bercovitch, "The Image of America: From Hermeneutic to Symbolism," in *Early American Literature: A Collection of Critical Essays*, ed. Michael T. Gilmore (Englewood Cliffs, NJ: Prentice-Hall, 1980), 158. Sometimes the type/antitype hermeneutic extends further beyond the theological while maintaining its temporal form. Jonathan Arac bases his account of the emergence of American national literary narratives on the constitutive gap between republican myths and present realities, and the resolution of that distinction in proleptic projections of a free nation (with George Bancroft a primary example). See Jonathan Arac, *The Emergence of American Literary Narrative, 1820–1860* (Cambridge, MA: Harvard University Press, 2005).

17. Sacvan Bercovitch, *The Puritan Origins of the American Self* (New Haven, CT: Yale University Press, 1975), 28. "Like Christ, the Bible could be rightly perceived only by one who had transformed himself in His image. . . . Interpreter and text confirmed one another in their mutual *imitatio*. . . . The calculated result was a one-sided mode of confirmation: 'Let *Israel* be . . . our glass to view our faces in.' . . . Nothing more clearly attests to the Puritans' subjectivism than does [the] conjunction of *sola fides* and *sola scriptura*; and nothing more clearly demonstrates their regimentation of selfhood" (28).

18. The mid-1990s was a fecund critical moment for revisiting the totality of American literature and the nation form while also turning critique of all allegorical Americas onto

the discipline of American studies itself. Much of this work set the tone for where American studies remains today, in the shadow of but not overdetermined by arguments like Bercovitch's. Many of these studies retain the sweeping, panoptic vantage of the metadiscourse of America even while putting America itself in conceptual quotation marks and marking the historical exclusions that shape its discursive form. See, for example, all published within a span of a few years, Jack P. Greene, *The Intellectual Construction of America: Exceptionalism and Identity from 1492 to 1800* (Chapel Hill: University of North Carolina Press, 1993); Frederick M. Dolan, *Allegories of America: Narratives, Metaphysics, Politics* (Ithaca, NY: Cornell University Press, 1994); David R. Shumway, *Creating American Civilization: A Genealogy of American Literature as an Academic Discipline* (Minneapolis: University of Minnesota Press, 1994); and Priscilla Wald, *Constituting Americans: Cultural Anxiety and Narrative Form* (Durham, NC: Duke University Press, 1995). Lauren Berlant's impressive career-long analysis of the American national imaginary got off the ground earlier with her book on Hawthorne, *The Anatomy of National Fantasy: Hawthorne, Utopia, and Everyday Life* (Chicago: University of Chicago Press, 1991). Later studies focusing on nineteenth-century American literature and nationhood continue to map its disjunctions in the face of discursive hegemony, including Thomas M. Allen, *A Republic in Time: Temporality and Social Imagination in Nineteenth-Century America* (Chapel Hill: University of North Carolina Press, 2008), and Robert S. Levine, *Dislocating Race and Nation: Episodes in Nineteenth-Century American Literary Nationalism* (Chapel Hill: University of North Carolina Press, 2008). Another American literary historical study, Christian P. Haines's *A Desire Called America: Biopolitics, Utopia, and the Literary Commons* (New York: Fordham University Press, 2019), articulates a tradition that maintains a sense of American (utopian) uniqueness and exemplarity without typically corresponding capitalistic, nationalistic, and individualistic exceptionalisms.

19. For a comprehensive, pluralist, and transatlantic history of Puritanism, see David D. Hall, *The Puritans: A Transatlantic History* (Princeton, NJ: Princeton University Press, 2019).

20. On the critique of ocularcentrism in twentieth-century philosophy and critical theory, centered on the French, see Martin Jay's comprehensive study *Downcast Eyes: The Denigration of Vision in Twentieth-Century French Thought* (Berkeley: University of California Press, 1993).

21. Cartographic representations of the American continent have long provided other fruitful avenues for deconstructing sedimented geometries. For a study of the cultural-ideological impact of mapping in early America, see Martin Brückner, *The Social Life of Maps in America, 1750–1860* (Chapel Hill: University of North Carolina Press, 2017).

22. René Descartes, *The Philosophical Writings*, vol. 1, trans. John Cottingham, Robert Stoothoff, and Dugald Murdoch (Cambridge: Cambridge University Press, 1985), 153.

23. Laura Mulvey, "Visual Pleasure and Narrative Cinema," *Screen* 16, no. 3 (October 1975): 7, 11 (italics in the original).

24. Mulvey, "Visual Pleasure and Narrative Cinema," 9.

25. Todd McGowan provides a thorough discussion of these differences among nominally Lacanian gaze theories in *The Real Gaze: Film Theory after Lacan* (Albany: State University of New York Press, 2007).

26. Jacques Lacan, "The Mirror Stage as Formative of the *I* Function, as Revealed in Psychoanalytic Experience," in *Écrits: A Selection*, trans. Bruce Fink (New York: Norton, 2002), 5.

27. Christian Metz, *The Imaginary Signifier: Psychoanalysis and Cinema*, trans. Celia Britton, Annwyl Williams, Ben Brewster, and Alfred Guzzetti (Bloomington: Indiana University Press, 1982), 54 (italics in the original), 3.

28. T. J. Clark, *The Painting of Modern Life: Paris in the Art of Manet and His Followers* (New York: A. A. Knopf, 1985), 8.

29. One major thread moves through Stanley Cavell's influence on pragmatist readings of Emerson. See Stanley Cavell, "What's the Use of Calling Emerson a Pragmatist?," in *The Revival of Pragmatism*, ed. Morris Dickstein (Durham, NC: Duke University Press, 1998), 72–80. For a reading in this vein fully committed to Emerson as a democratic radical, see Michael Magee, *Emancipating Pragmatism* (Tuscaloosa: University of Alabama Press, 2004). For consideration of the tension between nascent pragmatism and idealism in Emerson, see Kristen Case, *American Pragmatism and Poetic Practice* (New York: Camden House, 2011).

30. Ralph Waldo Emerson, *Essays and Lectures*, ed. Joel Porte (New York: Library of America, 1983), 14, 48, 24.

31. Emerson, *Essays and Lectures*, 32.

32. Carolyn Porter, *Seeing and Being: The Plight of the Participant Observer in Emerson, James, Adams, and Faulkner* (Middletown, CT: Wesleyan University Press, 1981), 97.

33. Emerson, *Essays and Lectures*, 10; Porter, *Seeing and Being*, 106.

34. See Peter John Brownlee's *The Commerce of Vision: Optical Culture and Perception in Antebellum America* (Philadelphia: University of Pennsylvania Press, 2018) for a cultural and material history of antebellum optics that begins with Emerson's 1837 claim "Our Age is Ocular" and that enumerates the objects and practices that made, unmade, and commodified American commercial visual culture throughout his lifetime.

35. Georg Lukács, *History and Class Consciousness: Studies in Marxist Dialectics*, trans. Rodney Livingstone (Cambridge, MA: MIT Press, 1971), 130.

36. Emerson, *Essays and Lectures*, 47.

37. Emerson, *Essays and Lectures*, 487, 478.

38. New, *Line's Eye*, 2, 3.

39. Emerson, *Essays and Lectures*, 459. See also David Jacobson's *Emerson's Pragmatic Vision: The Dance of the Eye* (University Park: Pennsylvania State University Press, 1993) for an account of Emerson's transition between visual theories, where nature is eventually seen to interpose opacities for the eye, withholding full view of itself as a constitutive rather than merely empirical contradiction.

40. Michelle Kohler, *Miles of Stare: Transcendentalism and the Problem of Literary Vision in Nineteenth-Century America* (Tuscaloosa: University of Alabama Press, 2014), 3, 12–13 (italics in the original), 10, 17.

41. Other impressive studies that precede mine in shifting the focus of American literature's perceptual infrastructure include Theo Davis's work on the ornamental poetics of impermanent attention in *Ornamental Aesthetics: The Poetry of Attending in Thoreau, Dickinson, and Whitman* (Oxford: Oxford University Press, 2016) and Jennifer L. Leader's account of the tradition of typological seeing and epistemology in *Knowing, Seeing, Being: Jonathan Edwards, Emily Dickinson, Marianne Moore, and the American Typological Tradition* (Amherst: University of Massachusetts Press, 2016). Both consider the subject of my fourth chapter, Emily Dickinson, as part of an alternative tradition of perceptual knowledge in American literature.

42. Sometimes the gaze determines our literary-historical analysis in hypersubtle ways.

For instance, while Shelly Jarenski and I share an interest in writerly experimentation through contact with visual art and technology, she describes this contact as an aesthetic power "nineteenth-century writers captured in their emergent literary techniques." Shelly Jarenski, *Immersive Words: Mass Media, Visuality, and American Literature, 1839–1893* (Tuscaloosa: University of Alabama Press, 2015), 4. *Capturing* a form or process is too possessive an analogy for my purposes. I prefer to think of writers *borrowing*—taking and renouncing in equal measure—as they glance between their work and visual media. For an alternative yet equally phenomenological take on antebellum possession, ownership, and property focusing on embodiment in literature, see Chad Luck, *The Body of Property: Antebellum American Fiction and the Phenomenology of Possession* (New York: Fordham University Press, 2014).

43. Johann Wolfgang von Goethe, *Theory of Colours*, trans. Charles Eastlake (Cambridge, MA: MIT Press, 1970), xl.

44. Edward Casey, *The World at a Glance* (Bloomington: Indiana University Press, 2007), 139.

45. Elizabeth Grosz, *Volatile Bodies: Toward a Corporeal Feminism* (Bloomington: Indiana University Press, 1994), 128.

46. My use of "concern" here intentionally calls up Martin Heidegger's *Sorge*. Husserlian phenomenology presumes that perceptual objects are encountered primarily in a series of one-sided perspectives. Heidegger's major break with his teacher was over this point: for Heidegger, our primary mode of being-in-the-world is engagement with objects-as-gear (*zuhanden*, ready-to-hand) rather than distanced intentional presentations of objects in their one-sided perspectives (*vorhanden*, present-at-hand). We comport ourselves originarily as concerned beings, not alienated, distanced, or even theoretical subjects.

47. Robert Smithson, "A Sedimentation of the Mind: Earth Projects," in *Robert Smithson: Collected Writings*, ed. Jack Flam (Berkeley: University of California Press, 1996), 112.

48. James Elkins, *What Painting Is* (New York: Routledge, 1999), 17.

49. Maurice Merleau-Ponty, "Eye and Mind," trans. Carlton Dallery, in *The Primacy of Perception*, ed. James M. Edie (Evanston, IL: Northwestern University Press, 1964), 164–65.

50. Paul Klee quoted in Will Grohmann, *Paul Klee* (Paris: Flinker, 1954), 99, cited in Merleau-Ponty, "Eye and Mind," 188.

51. Jacques Derrida, *Memoirs of the Blind: The Self-Portrait and Other Ruins*, trans. Pascale-Anne Brault and Michael Naas (Chicago: University of Chicago Press, 1993), 54.

52. Merleau-Ponty, "Eye and Mind," 162–63.

53. Alva Noë, *Action in Perception* (Cambridge, MA: MIT Press, 2004), 78.

54. For anthropological studies of skill as ecologically attuned mindedness that includes the body and its form-giving techniques, see Tim Ingold, *The Perception of the Environment* (New York: Routledge, 2000); and Tim Ingold, "Five Questions of Skill," *Cultural Geographies* 25, no. 1 (2018): 159–63.

55. Richard Sennett refers to "the celebrated cook Ting," in the early Taoist text *Chuang-tzu*, famous for his ability to use his cleaver to "find 'the gaps in the joints,' a fine dissection that will ensure that human teeth can get to all the edible meat in an animal." Following such examples of skilled craftsmen in action, Sennett borrows Michael Polanyi's concept of "focal awareness" to describe the temporal rhythm extended by the craftsman to both "the hand and the eye," the "stress on a beat and tempo, the speed of an action" coordinated by the moving glance. Richard Sennett, *The Craftsman* (New Haven, CT: Yale University Press, 2008), 166, 175.

56. Several of Merleau-Ponty's examples on this point suggest normative (rather than simply descriptive) effects of indeterminate visual backgrounds on embodied perceivers. For instance, he argues that as atmospheric lighting conditions affect the perceived color of objects in our visual field, we see how the lighting context must change and/or how we must change our position toward an object in order for us to see the color better (or more clearly against its background). "Lighting and reflection, then, play their part only if they remain in the background as discreet intermediaries, and *lead* our gaze instead of arresting it." Indeterminate (but not wholly absent) elements of a visual field direct our bodily comportment through our environment and its network of affordances. Maurice Merleau-Ponty, *Phenomenology of Perception*, trans. Colin Smith (London: Routledge Classics, 2002), 361.

57. My formulation of the glance as distributive extends the visual logic of Jonathan Kramnick's coinage "paper minds," which are "the formal construal[s] of a world as it shows up for an agent engaged or coping with built or natural environments." Like Kramnick's, my analysis gravitates toward extended cognition of nonrepresentational sorts. As I will show in a following chapter, Emily Dickinson's poetry even literalizes the "paper" in paper minds, and reveals the distributive workings of the glance as it weaves the subject into and through her ecological niche. Jonathan Kramnick, *Paper Minds: Literature and the Ecology of Consciousness* (Chicago: University of Chicago Press, 2018), 2.

58. Charles J. Woodbury, *Talks with Ralph Waldo Emerson* (New York: Baker & Taylor, 1890), 27.

59. Stephen Best and Sharon Marcus, "Surface Reading: An Introduction," *Representations* 108, no. 1 (November 2009).

60. Heather Love, "Close but Not Deep: Literary Ethics and the Descriptive Turn," *New Literary History* 41, no. 2 (Spring 2010), 375.

61. Emerson, *Essays and Lectures*, 473.

62. See Kate Stanley, *Practices of Surprise in American Literature after Emerson* (Cambridge: Cambridge University Press, 2018), for an account of surprise in modernist American literature in the tradition of Emersonian pragmatism.

63. Emerson, *Essays and Lectures*, 434, 433, 434; Branka Arsić, *On Leaving: A Reading in Emerson* (Cambridge, MA: Harvard University Press, 2010), 71.

64. Alexander Gottlieb Baumgarten, *Aesthetica* (Turnhout, Belgium: Brepols, 2010), 7; see Jacques Rancière, *The Politics of Aesthetics: The Distribution of the Sensible*, ed. Gabriel Rockhill (London: Bloomsbury, 2013).

65. Jacques Rancière, *Aisthesis: Scenes from the Aesthetic Regime of Art*, trans. Zakir Paul (London: Verso, 2013), xi.

66. Georg Lukács, *The Ontology of Social Being*, vol. 3, *Labour*, trans. David Fernbach (London: Merlin, 1980), 13, 33.

67. Henry Staten, "The Origin of the Work of Art in Material Practice," *New Literary History* 43, no. 1 (Winter 2012), 53.

68. Whitney Davis, *Replications: Archaeology, Art History, Psychoanalysis* (University Park: Pennsylvania State University Press, 1996), 116.

69. Alva Noë, *Varieties of Presence* (Cambridge, MA: Harvard University Press, 2012), 19–20.

70. Paying more attention to the glance's *smallness* might place my approach in what follows within what Mark Seltzer has termed "the new incrementalism," a turn in criticism characterized by renewed attention to "the minor and the scaled-down." Mark Seltzer, "The Official World," *Critical Inquiry* 37, no. 4 (Summer 2011): 727. Some of the most

well-known examples include Anne-Lise François's account of self-quieting and recessive action in *Open Secrets: The Literature of Uncounted Experience* (Stanford, CA: Stanford University Press, 2008); Heather Love's scholarly project on micropolitics in "Small Change: Realism, Immanence, and the Politics of the Micro," *Modern Language Quarterly* 77, no. 3 (September 2016): 371–91; Anahid Nersessian's pruning of Romanticism's excesses in favor of what she calls "low adjustment utopias" in *Utopia, Limited: Romanticism and Adjustment* (Cambridge, MA: Harvard University Press, 2015); Rei Terada's account of aberrant, fleeting, and nonfactual perceptual experiences in post-Kantian thought in *Looking Away: Phenomenality and Dissatisfaction, Kant to Adorno* (Cambridge, MA: Harvard University Press, 2009); Sianne Ngai's exploration of neglected "minor" affects in *Ugly Feelings* (Cambridge, MA: Harvard University Press, 2005); Elisha Cohn's study of noninstrumental moments of diminished consciousness in the Victorian novel in *Still Life: Suspended Development in the Victorian Novel* (New York: Oxford University Press, 2016); and Alex Woloch's magisterial study of minor characters in *The One vs. the Many: Minor Characters and the Space of the Protagonist in the Novel* (Princeton, NJ: Princeton University Press, 2003). In some of these cases (Woloch's study, for instance), the small or minor is shown to be significant in disproportion to its ostensible size. Others (like François) attempt something closer to the impossible in attending with great depth to phenomena that approach nothingness or fold back over that very critical act. My study, I believe, tends in the former direction while also respecting moments of (near-)evanescence that escape the glance's more constructive qualities.

Chapter 1

1. Nathaniel Hawthorne, *The Centenary Edition of the Works of Nathaniel Hawthorne*, vol. 9, *Twice-told Tales*, ed. William Charvat (Columbus: Ohio State University Press, 1974), 452, 454.

2. Andy Smith, "Sensitive Emulsions: Hawthorne's Proto-Photography," *Nathaniel Hawthorne Review* 35, no. 1 (Spring 2009): 46.

3. Leon Edel, *Henry James: A Life* (New York: Harper & Row, 1985), 121.

4. In addition to her article on Hawthorne and portraiture cited below, see Susan Williams, *Confounding Images: Photography and Portraiture in Antebellum American Fiction* (Philadelphia: University of Pennsylvania Press, 1997), for an exemplary study of the competing markets for literature and visual art in antebellum America. See also Marcy J. Dinius, *The Camera and the Press: American Visual and Print Culture in the Age of the Daguerreotype* (Philadelphia: University of Pennsylvania Press, 2012).

5. From at least Lukács onward, there has been much discussion on the formal, representational, and ideological structures of novelistic realism, including in Amy Kaplan's now-classic *The Social Construction of American Realism* (Chicago: University of Chicago Press, 1988). This tradition includes, beyond American realism specifically, Fredric Jameson's *The Antinomies of Realism* (London: Verso, 2013) and Franco Moretti's *The Way of the World: The Bildungsroman in European Culture* (London: Verso, 1987). For later studies, from two nearly opposite perspectives on Victorian-era realism, see Elaine Freedgood, *Worlds Enough: The Invention of Realism in the Victorian Novel* (Princeton, NJ: Princeton University Press, 2019); and Anna Kornbluh, *The Order of Forms: Realism, Formalism, and Social Space* (Chicago: University of Chicago Press, 2019). This chapter follows Hawthorne himself in focusing on the perceptual dimensions of the real—associated with the critical tradition following from Erich Auerbach's classic *Mimesis: The Representation of Reality in*

Western Literature, trans. Willard R. Trask (Princeton, NJ: Princeton University Press, 1953)—rather than on the novel's relationship to social totality. See Kaplan, *Social Construction*, for a consideration of late nineteenth-century American realism's symbolic intervention into real (urban, class) antagonisms.

6. It is important to note that while Crary's take on the camera obscura as the Enlightenment device par excellence has become nearly commonplace in histories of visual culture, there are compelling dissents. Wendy Bellion argues in her study of early republican Philadelphia that in America, at least, a diversity of viewing instruments and a broad range of public and private spaces in which they were exhibited created a "visual culture in which no single modality of vision prevailed," and in which trompe l'oeil illusions and spectacles like Charles Willson Peale's *Staircase Group* and Samuel Lewis's "Imitations" and "Illusions" challenged both optical and political models of passive reception. But this is not necessarily a critique of Crary, as Bellion intends it to be; postrevolutionary America may have been an avant-garde of sorts for developments only solidified (by optical science as well as artists) in the nineteenth century. Wendy Bellion, *Citizen Spectator: Art, Illusion, and Visual Perception in Early National America* (Chapel Hill: University of North Carolina Press, 2011), 59. See Jonathan Crary, *Techniques of the Observer: On Vision and Modernity in the Nineteenth Century* (Cambridge, MA: MIT Press, 1990).

7. Norman Bryson, *Vision and Painting: The Logic of the Gaze* (New Haven, CT: Yale University Press, 1983), 96, 98, 94–95, 94.

8. Michael Fried, *Absorption and Theatricality: Painting and Beholder in the Age of Diderot* (Berkeley: University of California Press, 1980), 93.

9. Erwin Panofsky, *Perspective as Symbolic Form*, trans. Christopher S. Wood (New York: Zone, 1991), 27, 77n5, 31.

10. G. W. F. Hegel, *Hegel's Aesthetics: Lectures on Fine Art*, trans. T. M. Knox (Oxford: Oxford University Press, 1975), 794–95 (italics in the original).

11. Gregory Schufreider, "Iconoclastic Images," *Yearbook of Comparative Literature* 56 (2010): 29.

12. See also Derrida's analysis of the *parergon* in Kantian aesthetics, on the frame that supplements and threatens the enframed picture's integrity, destabilizing the opposition between work and the work's outside. The frame fixes the picture as a work of art even as it unfixes it and integrates it in its surroundings. Jacques Derrida, *The Truth in Painting*, trans. Geoff Bennington and Ian McLeod (Chicago: University of Chicago Press, 1987).

13. Nathaniel Hawthorne, *The Business of Reflection: Hawthorne in His Notebooks*, ed. Robert Milder and Randall Fuller (Columbus: Ohio State University Press, 2009), 217.

14. Victor I. Stoichita, *A Short History of the Shadow* (London: Reaktion, 1997), 58.

15. I have not found any evidence in his notebooks that he did. Hawthorne's notebooks evince rare excitement for the Italian masters, going as far as saying, "There is something forced, if not feigned, in our tastes for pictures of old Italian schools." Nathaniel Hawthorne, *The Centenary Edition of the Works of Nathaniel Hawthorne*, vol. 14, *The French and Italian Notebooks*, ed. Thomas Woodson (Columbus: Ohio State University Press, 1980) 115.

16. Nathaniel Hawthorne, *The Centenary Edition of the Works of Nathaniel Hawthorne*, vol. 1, *The Scarlet Letter*, ed. William Charvat (Columbus: Ohio State University Press, 1962), 36 (emphasis mine). In this "territory," all the geographical and political valences that come with the term blend into the abstract shapes of imaginative schemas. Jonathan Arac notes that by explaining, in the same preface, "his spiritual dejection by claiming that

'imagination' was incompatible with receiving 'public gold'" he established his "literary authority" by implicitly distancing his practice from extractive narratives associating the imagination with the real spaces of the West. Jonathan Arac, *The Emergence of American Literary Narrative, 1820–1860* (Cambridge, MA: Harvard University Press, 2005), 138–39.

17. Hawthorne, *Centenary Edition*, 1:35, 36.

18. John Locke, *An Essay Concerning Human Understanding*, vol. 1 (New York: Dover, 1959), 211.

19. Richard Rorty, *Philosophy and the Mirror of Nature* (Princeton, NJ: Princeton University Press, 1979), 49, 50, 143–44.

20. Hawthorne, *Centenary Edition*, 1:36.

21. Harry Levin, *The Power of Blackness: Hawthorne, Poe, Melville* (New York: Alfred A. Knopf, 1958), 63, 36.

22. Hawthorne, *Centenary Edition*, 1:35 (emphasis mine), 36, 37.

23. Cennino d'Andrea Cennini, *The Craftsman's Handbook*, trans. Daniel V. Thompson Jr. (New York: Dover, 1954), 5.

24. Stoichita, *History of the Shadow*, 58 (italics in the original).

25. See Samuel Y. Edgerton, *The Mirror, the Window, and the Telescope: How Renaissance Linear Perspective Changed Our View of the Universe* (Ithaca, NY: Cornell University Press, 2009).

26. Schufreider, "Iconoclastic Images," 30n13.

27. Crary, *Techniques of the Observer*, 41, 46.

28. For a compelling take on early American art that considers this general epistemic contract, see Alexander Nemerov's book on Raphaelle Peale, whose still lifes construct an interior space where "reflections—tokens of the outside world—seem to adhere to the objects. The outside comes inside and alights there, becoming part of the object itself—part of a hermetic autonomy it maintains from a street, a sky, a city, a nation whose expansive spaces it yet contains." Alexander Nemerov, *The Body of Raphaelle Peale: Still Life and Selfhood, 1812–1824* (Berkeley: University of California Press, 2001), 7.

29. Shawn Michelle Smith, *American Archives: Gender, Race, and Class in Visual Culture* (Princeton, NJ: Princeton University Press, 1999), 3, 8. Sources range from Matthew Brady's "Gallery of Illustrious Americans," Francis Galton's composite eugenics catalogues, the 1900 Paris Exposition's "American Negro" exhibit, and a variety of family albums. Examining similarities between the promotion of family photographs in women's magazines and Galton's eugenics manuals and albums, for instance, Smith charts how the sentimentalized ritual of the baby picture, the focal point of the family album, became a "racially-inflected act" promulgating and confirming white supremacy. For more on facial types in (early) American literature and visual culture, including raced and classed facial identifications and distinctions as they play into reading practices, see Christopher Lukasik, *Discerning Characters: The Culture of Appearance in Early America* (Philadelphia: University of Pennsylvania Press, 2011).

30. At the center of a long and rich discussion in Hawthorne scholarship, see Michael Colacurcio, *The Province of Piety: Moral History in Hawthorne's Early Tales* (Durham, NC: Duke University Press, 1995), for more on the moral history embedded in Hawthorne's fictions and character types.

31. See Lorraine Daston and Peter Galison, *Objectivity* (Cambridge, MA: MIT Press, 2007).

32. "The Magnetic Daguerreotypes," *Photographic Art-Journal*, June 1852, 355.

33. Smith, *American Archives*, 11.

34. Nathaniel Hawthorne, *The Centenary Edition of the Works of Nathaniel Hawthorne*, vol. 2, *The House of the Seven Gables*, ed. William Charvat (Columbus: Ohio State University Press, 1965), 91.

35. Smith, *American Archives*, 12.

36. David Greven provides a broader consideration of the gendered look in Hawthorne, speculating that "Hawthorne used writing to negotiate anxieties about his own personal appearance and its incitement of the gaze." While I cannot get into the complexities of Greven's Freudian reading of Hawthornian scopophobia, my impulse is to take the fork opposite Greven's and Smith's path and find the routes of visuality that take the writer beyond narcissistic identifications. David Greven, *The Fragility of Manhood: Hawthorne, Freud, and the Politics of Gender* (Columbus: Ohio State University Press, 2012), 94.

37. Dinius, *Camera and the Press*, 6.

38. Smith, *American Archives*, 15.

39. Smith, *American Archives*, 21.

40. Hawthorne, *Centenary Edition*, 2:209, 212.

41. Smith, *American Archives*, 24.

42. Hawthorne, *Centenary Edition*, 2:307, 201.

43. The nineteenth century has been a focal point for historians explaining the rise of domesticity as both an economic and cultural fact. For literary historians, the analysis tends to turn on the domestic sphere's ideological insulation from public life. For more on the complexity of the public-private distinction, see Michael McKeon, *The Secret History of Domesticity: Public, Private, and the Division of Knowledge* (Baltimore: Johns Hopkins University Press, 2005). For an account of the emergence of gendered subjectivities in British novels that rewrite domestic practices, see Nancy Armstrong, *Desire and Domestic Fiction: A Political History of the Novel* (Oxford: Oxford University Press, 1990).

44. Hawthorne, *Centenary Edition*, 2:1, 3.

45. Alan Trachtenberg, "Seeing and Believing: Hawthorne's Reflections on the Daguerreotype in *The House of the Seven Gables*," *American Literary History* 9, no. 3 (October 1997): 461.

46. Photography already affords visual reproduction, which Stuart Burrows claims to be Hawthorne's contribution to realism in *Seven Gables*: "The impact photography has on fiction is to turn every text into a realist one—not in the sense of a concern for verisimilitude but in the sense of a formal redundancy." Stuart Burrows, *A Familiar Strangeness: American Fiction and the Language of Photography, 1839–1945* (Athens: University of Georgia Press, 2010), 32.

47. Trachtenberg, "Seeing and Believing," 462.

48. Aaron Kunin, *Character as Form* (London: Bloomsbury, 2019), 174.

49. Harriet Beecher Stowe, *Sunny Memories of Foreign Lands*, 2 vols. (Boston: Phillips, Sampson, and Co., 1854), 2:161, quoted in Susan Williams, "'The Aspiring Purpose of an Ambitious Demagogue': Portraiture and *The House of the Seven Gables*," *Nineteenth-Century Literature* 49, no. 2 (September 1994): 221.

50. Hawthorne, *Centenary Edition*, 2:105.

51. Hawthorne, *Centenary Edition*, 2:165, 48; Williams, "'Aspiring Purpose,'" 224–25.

52. Gotthold Ephraim Lessing, *Laocoon: An Essay upon the Limits of Painting and Poetry*, trans. Ellen Frothingham (New York: Noonday, 1957), 91.

53. For a discussion of the "fruitful moment" in Lessing in the context of the history of

theories of "the present," see Michael North, *What Is the Present?* (Princeton, NJ: Princeton University Press, 2018), chap. 4.

54. See Edmund Husserl, *On the Phenomenology of the Consciousness of Internal Time (1893–1917)*, trans. John Barnett Brough (Dordrecht: Springer Netherlands, 1991).

55. Ernst Gombrich was one of the first art historians to strongly conceptualize the saltatory aspects of viewing ostensibly static works. For Gombrich, this perceptual truth is the engine of developing schemas of naturalistic techne on the part of artists, not simply a fact about viewing. See E. H. Gombrich, *Art and Illusion: A Study in the Psychology of Pictorial Representation* (New York: Pantheon, 1961).

56. By deemphasizing historical painting and battle scenes, Lessing brings out the sharpest possible contrast between the visual and the textual, a contrast that is really not so sharp, as the Cubists and the Surrealists among many others recognized.

57. Samuel Taylor Coleridge, *Biographia Literaria, or Biographical Sketches of My Literary Life and Opinions*, ed. James Engell and Walter Jackson Bate (London: Routledge & Kegan Paul, 1983), 528–29, 529; Samuel Taylor Coleridge, *The Notebooks of Samuel Taylor Coleridge*, ed. Kathleen Coburn (New York: Pantheon, 1973), 419.

58. W. J. T. Mitchell, *Iconology: Image, Text, Ideology* (Chicago: University of Chicago Press, 1986), 35–36.

59. For more on the image in *Paradise Lost*, see Stephen Dobranski, *Milton's Visual Imagination: Imagery in Paradise Lost* (Cambridge: Cambridge University Press, 2015).

60. See David Greven, "Incest and Intertextuality: Female Desire and Milton's Legacy in *The House of the Seven Gables*," *ESQ* 62, no. 1 (2016): 39–76, on Milton's legacy for Hawthorne, specifically in *The House of the Seven Gables*, with a focus on female desire.

61. Henry James, *Hawthorne* (Ithaca, NY: Cornell University Press, 1997), 99.

62. Hawthorne, *Centenary Edition*, 2:305. Frederick Crews's widely cited analysis, which includes a close but not too close look at this scene, is another example of Hawthorne criticism's allergy to the literal. Crews argues that Holgrave's relation to Jaffrey in this scene, and the anxious and perverse feelings accompanying his discovery, is mediated by a metaphorical Oedipal conflict. See Frederick Crews, *The Sins of the Fathers: Hawthorne's Psychological Themes* (Oxford: Oxford University Press, 1966).

63. Phoebe anticipates Roland Barthes's famous reflection here, in which the photograph "represents the very subtle moment when, to tell the truth, I am neither subject nor object but a subject who feels he is becoming an object: I then experience a micro-version of death (of parenthesis): I am truly becoming a specter." Both Phoebe and Barthes, though, express common enough sentiments for subjects of early photography. Roland Barthes, *Camera Lucida: Reflections on Photography*, trans. Richard Howard (New York: Farrar, Straus, and Giroux, 2010), 14.

64. Hawthorne, *Centenary Edition*, 2:91.

65. Hawthorne, *Centenary Edition*, 2:156, 177.

66. Hawthorne, *Centenary Edition*, 2:261.

67. Hawthorne, *Centenary Edition*, 2:276.

68. Dinius, *Camera and the Press*, 55.

69. Maurice Merleau-Ponty, *Phenomenology of Perception*, trans. Colin Smith (London: Routledge, 2002), 352.

70. Michelle Kohler, *Miles of Stare: Transcendentalism and the Problem of Literary Vision in Nineteenth-Century America* (Tuscaloosa: University of Alabama Press, 2014), 86.

71. Edward Casey, *The World at a Glance* (Bloomington: Indiana University Press, 2007), 143; Hawthorne, *Centenary Edition*, 2:2.

72. Frank Kermode, "Hawthorne's Modernity," *Partisan Review* 41 (1974): 429.

73. Peter Betjemann, *Talking Shop: The Language of Craft in an Age of Consumption* (Charlottesville: University of Virginia Press, 2011), 11–12, 32, 59–60, 87, 103. The following discussion was first presented in an essay Alex McCauley and I wrote on Hawthorne's craft in light of large-scale concerns about environmental exhaustion and decay. See Alex McCauley and Zachary Tavlin, "The Art of Extraction and Preservation: Hawthorne's 'Dirty Nature,'" *Nathaniel Hawthorne Review* 43, no. 2 (Fall 2017): 19–34, esp. 25–32.

74. For a classic study addressing Hawthorne among others in the burgeoning market for novels, see Nina Baym, *Novels, Readers, and Reviewers: Responses to Fiction in Antebellum America* (Ithaca, NY: Cornell University Press, 1984). See also a cluster of essays on publishing norms and the literary marketplace (authored by David Cody, Lesley Ginsberg, Laura Laffrado, Kristie Hamilton, Leland Person, and Magnus Ullén) in *Nathaniel Hawthorne in Context*, ed. Monika M. Elbert (Cambridge: Cambridge University Press, 2018).

75. Michael T. Gilmore, *American Romanticism and the Marketplace* (Chicago: University of Chicago Press, 1985), 74; Walter Benn Michaels, *The Gold Standard and the Logic of Naturalism: American Literature at the Turn of the Century* (Berkeley: University of California Press, 1988).

76. Betjemann, *Talking Shop*, 97, 103.

77. Nathaniel Hawthorne, *The Centenary Edition of the Works of Nathaniel Hawthorne*, vol. 4, *The Marble Faun*, ed. William Charvat (Columbus: Ohio State University Press, 1962), 6.

78. Even in the nineteenth century, after the center of the European art world had shifted from Rome to Paris, prestigious prizes like the Prix de Rome kept the old Renaissance sojourns in the Eternal City alive as an ideal for every art education.

79. Hawthorne, *Centenary Edition*, 4:138, 77, 41.

80. Hawthorne, *Centenary Edition*, 4:16. As Deanna Fernie writes, in sculpture's eternal repose lies the "objectifying power" of unrevealed pasts and unknown thoughts. Deanna Fernie, *Hawthorne, Sculpture, and the Question of American Art* (Burlington, VT: Ashgate, 2011), 216.

81. Hawthorne, *Centenary Edition*, 4:7, 6. John Dolis, while repeatedly using the word "gazing," writes that, for Hawthorne, because "the eye delights in the tangible, that around which it can playfully 'feel' in order to investigate the various aspects of an object, its operation mirrors the intentional unity of the perceptual object itself, the opaque appropriation of the object as a whole. . . . [Hawthorne's sketches], like sculpture, invite completion by virtue of [their] opaque suggestivity." John Dolis, "Hawthorne's Tactile Gaze and the Phenomenon of Depth," *Modern Language Quarterly* 44, no. 3 (1983): 277. See also Clayton Zuba, "Hawthorne's Empire: Sculpture and the Indigenous in *The Marble Faun*," *Studies in American Fiction* 43, no. 2 (Fall 2016): 161–82, on Hawthorne's use of sculpture as a narrative principle that exposes the self-destructiveness of orders built on racial difference.

82. Jonathan Auerbach, "Executing the Model: Painting, Sculpture, and Romance-Writing in Hawthorne's *The Marble Faun*," *ELH* 47, no. 1 (Spring 1980): 111.

83. Hawthorne, *Centenary Edition*, 4:29.

84. The subject of Donatello and the faun has often left the orbit of art qua art and led elsewhere, with scholars sometimes seeing the faun as racial or ethnic fetish (to which aesthetics serves as a means of control). See Evan Carton, *The Marble Faun: Hawthorne's*

Transformations (New York: Twayne, 1992); Eric Cheyfitz, "The Irresistibleness of Great Literature: Reconstructing Hawthorne's Politics," *American Literary History* 6 (1994): 539–58; Nancy Bentley, *The Ethnography of Manners: Hawthorne, James, Wharton* (Cambridge: Cambridge University Press, 1995); and, a departure from these readings, Arthur Riss in "The Art of Discrimination," *ELH* 71, no. 1 (Spring 2004): 251–87.

85. Hawthorne, *Centenary Edition*, 4:467, 44, 349.

86. Hawthorne, *Centenary Edition*, 4:107, 111.

87. Hawthorne, *Centenary Edition*, 4:341, 55, 59.

88. Susan Stewart, "Exogamous Relations: Travel Writing, the Incest Prohibition, and Hawthorne's *Transformation*," in *Culture/Contexture*, ed. E. Valentine Daniel and Jeffrey M. Peck (Berkeley: University of California Press, 1996), 142.

89. Hawthorne, *Centenary Edition*, 4:423–24 (emphasis mine).

90. Nathaniel Hawthorne, *The Centenary Edition of the Works of Nathaniel Hawthorne*, vol. 8, *The American Notebooks*, ed. William Charvat (Columbus: Ohio State University Press, 1962), 492–93, 498.

91. Hawthorne, *Centenary Edition*, 4:204–5.

92. Hawthorne, *Centenary Edition*, 4:65.

93. Dan Clinton, "Holographic Hawthorne," *J19* 3, no. 2 (Fall 2015): 414; Nathaniel Hawthorne, *The Marble Faun; or, The Romance of Monte Beni* (New York: Penguin, 1990), 59, 115, quoted in Clinton, "Holographic Hawthorne," 414.

94. Nathaniel Hawthorne, *The Centenary Edition of the Works of Nathaniel Hawthorne*, vol. 15, *The Letters, 1813–1843*, ed. Thomas Woodson, L. Neal Smith, and Norman Holmes Pearson (Columbus: Ohio State University Press, 1989), 384.

95. Immanuel Kant, *Critique of the Power of Judgment*, trans. Paul Guyer and Eric Matthews (Cambridge: Cambridge University Press, 2000), 108.

96. Hawthorne, *Centenary Edition*, 4:21.

97. See Tom Gunning, "Hand and Eye: Excavating a New Technology of the Image in the Victorian Era," *Victorian Studies* 54, no. 3 (2012): 495–516; and Wanda Strauven, "The Observer's Dilemma: To Touch or Not to Touch," in *Media Archaeology: Approaches, Applications, and Implications*, ed. Erkki Huhtamo and Jussi Parikka (Berkeley: University of California Press, 2011), 148–63, on the implications of these devices on the media concept of the observer.

98. Hawthorne, *Centenary Edition*, 4:190.

99. See Clinton, "Holographic Hawthorne," on lack of narrator omniscience in *The Marble Faun*, an effect hypothesized to parallel Hawthorne's view that "shared images anchor fancy in the senses, inviting narration, while inner states lacking an optical correlative are available only to conjecture" (415).

100. Hawthorne, *Centenary Edition*, 4:171.

101. Crary, *Techniques of the Observer*, 24.

102. Hermann von Helmholtz, *Treatise on Physiological Optics* (1925), 3 vols., ed. James P. C. Southall (New York: Dover, 1962), 3:537.

103. James, *Hawthorne*, 99.

104. Hawthorne, *Centenary Edition*, 4:171, 199, 459.

Chapter 2

1. Harriet Beecher Stowe, *Uncle Tom's Cabin* (Oxford: Oxford University Press, 1998), 10.

2. Frances Ellen Watkins Harper, *A Brighter Coming Day: A Frances Ellen Watkins*

Harper Reader, ed. Frances Smith Foster (New York: City University of New York, 1990), 64–65.

3. Saidiya Hartman, *Scenes of Subjection: Terror, Slavery, and Self-Making in Nineteenth-Century America* (Oxford: Oxford University Press, 1997).

4. Harper, *Brighter Coming Day*, 57. Philip Fisher argues that one of the primary elements of sentimental literature in America is family separation (especially mother and child), which he associates with Stowe but is clearly in regular effect in Harper's poetry, as we see here. See Philip Fisher, *Hard Facts: Setting and Form in the American Novel* (Oxford: Oxford University Press, 1985).

5. Hazel Carby, *Reconstructing Womanhood: The Emergence of the Afro-American Woman Novelist* (Oxford: Oxford University Press, 1987), 94, 63.

6. Carla L. Peterson, *"Doers of the Word": African-American Women Speakers and Writers in the North (1830–1880)* (Oxford: Oxford University Press, 1995), 125, 22.

7. By invoking lyric poetry in this chapter, I am offering a provocation to the new lyric studies—see my discussion on Virginia Jackson's and Yopie Prins's work later in this chapter—which questions the generic universality of the lyric and the lyric voice. I depart slightly from their critique of twentieth-century critical assumptions about lyric (and its corresponding marginalizations) by treating the possibility of lyricization, *including* historical obstacles to Black women like Harper being accepted as lyric poets in the picture of that process, as a horizon of liberation.

8. All these studies, including Luciano's and Hendler's discussed later in this chapter, are indebted to the work of Peterson, Frances Smith Foster, Joan Sherman, Melba Boyd, Maryemma Graham, and others who contributed to what Meredith McGill calls the "vital first wave of recovery of Harper's life and writing." Meredith McGill, "Frances Ellen Watkins Harper and the Circuits of Abolitionist Poetry," in *Early African American Print Culture*, ed. Lara Langer Cohen and Jordan Alexander Stein (Philadelphia: University of Pennsylvania Press, 2012), 62. On the trouble with forms, genres, or modes that are irreducibly or recognizably Black, and the work marginalized and misread because it supposedly was not, see Evie Shockley's *Renegade Poetics: Black Aesthetics and Formal Innovation in African American Poetry* (Iowa City: University of Iowa Press, 2011), a study primarily of twentieth-century African American poetics.

9. See George Yancy's *Black Bodies, White Gazes: Black Aesthetics and Formal Innovation in African American Poetry* (Iowa City: University of Iowa Press, 2011) for a philosophical synthesis of gaze theory along the axis of Fanonian critical race theory.

10. bell hooks, "The Oppositional Gaze: Black Female Spectators," in *Movies and Mass Culture*, ed. John Belton (New Brunswick, NJ: Rutgers University Press, 1996), 247, 248.

11. On my reading, Harper anticipates (and dialogues across the wake of slavery's afterlives with) Christina Sharpe's idea of "wake work." Sharpe writes "that to be *in* the wake is to occupy and to be occupied by the continuous and changing present of slavery's as yet unresolved unfolding." It is almost as if Harper's glancing lyrics anticipate a changed present that would absolve marked subjects from wake work, even while acknowledging that her fugitive poetic address *is* a kind of work done precisely in the wake and as part of a continuing process of challenging anti-Blackness in its least tractable forms. Christina Sharpe, *In the Wake: On Blackness and Being* (Durham, NC: Duke University Press, 2016), 13–14.

12. Gregory Laski, *Untimely Democracy: The Politics of Progress after Slavery* (Oxford: Oxford University Press, 2018), 27.

13. On sentimental writing's mixed narrative and lyric modes, see Mary Louise Kete,

Sentimental Collaborations: Mourning and Middle-Class Identity in Nineteenth-Century America (Durham, NC: Duke University Press, 2000). For a study on unfeeling as affective refusal of nineteenth-century sentimentalist politics, including in Harper, see Xine Yao, *Disaffected: The Cultural Politics of Unfeeling in Nineteenth-Century America* (Durham, NC: Duke University Press, 2021).

14. For a thorough examination of the construction of African Americans in painting and other visual art genres, in both hegemonic and counterhegemonic forms, see Michael D. Harris, *Colored Pictures: Race and Visual Representation* (Chapel Hill: University of North Carolina Press, 2003).

15. Eyre Crowe, "Sketches in the Free and Slave States of America," *Illustrated London News*, September 27, 1856.

16. Maurie D. McInnis, *Slaves Waiting for Sale: Abolitionist Art and the American Slave Trade* (Chicago: University of Chicago Press, 2011), 82.

17. For an account of Uncle Tom's evolution in the American imagination, see Adena Spingarn, *Uncle Tom: From Martyr to Traitor* (Stanford, CA: Stanford University Press, 2018).

18. McInnis, *Slaves Waiting for Sale*, 189 (emphasis mine).

19. Jo-Ann Morgan, *Uncle Tom's Cabin as Visual Culture* (Columbia: University of Missouri Press, 2007), 29, 41.

20. For a nuanced account of the marked body in nineteenth-century American culture that broadly relates literal and figurative marks, see Jennifer Putzi, *Identifying Marks: Race, Gender, and the Marked Body in Nineteenth-Century America* (Athens: University of Georgia Press, 2006).

21. "Exhibition of the Royal Academy," *Art Journal* 21 (June 1861), 165, quoted in McInnis, *Slaves Waiting for Sale*, 210.

22. McInnis, *Slaves Waiting for Sale*, 210.

23. Martha J. Cutter, *The Illustrated Slave: Empathy, Graphic Narrative, and the Visual Culture of the Transatlantic Abolition Movement, 1800–1852* (Athens: University of Georgia Press, 2017), 10.

24. Adam Smith, *The Theory of Moral Sentiments*, ed. Knut Haakonssen (Cambridge: Cambridge University Press, 2002), 11.

25. In *American Elegy: The Poetry of Mourning from the Puritans to Whitman* (Minneapolis: University of Minnesota Press, 2007), Max Cavitch considers the African American elegy as a struggle "to preserve traces of the severed affiliations from which [African Americans] *suffer disproportionately*" (18, emphasis mine).

26. Stowe, *Uncle Tom's Cabin*, 452, 290.

27. Jane Tompkins, *Sensational Designs: The Cultural Work of American Fiction, 1790–1860* (Oxford: Oxford University Press, 1985), 131.

28. Cutter, *Illustrated Slave*, 187.

29. Christopher Castiglia, *Interior States: Institutional Consciousness and the Inner Life of Democracy in the Antebellum United States* (Durham, NC: Duke University Press, 2008), 101, 3.

30. Glenn Hendler, *Public Sentiments: Structures of Feeling in Nineteenth-Century American Literature* (Chapel Hill: University of North Carolina Press, 2001), 6.

31. Stowe, *Uncle Tom's Cabin*, 89–90, 93.

32. Hendler, *Public Sentiments*, 7, 8.

33. Hartman, *Scenes of Subjection*, 19.

34. Similarly, in the context of nineteenth-century visual culture, one might ask whether or not the ubiquitous image of the Black body in pain always gathers participants in the wounding through newfound ease of (visual) access. For versions of this consideration, see Cassandra Jackson, *Violence, Visual Culture, and the Black Male Body* (New York: Routledge, 2010); and David Marriott, *On Black Men* (New York: Columbia University Press, 2000).

35. Castiglia, *Interior States*, 135.

36. Michel Foucault, *The Birth of the Clinic: An Archaeology of Medical Perception*, trans. Alan Sheridan (London: Tavistock, 1973), 15.

37. W. E. B. Du Bois, *The Souls of Black Folk* (New York: Library of America, 1990), 7–8.

38. Shawn Michelle Smith, *Photography on the Color Line: W. E. B. Du Bois, Race, and Visual Culture* (Durham, NC: Duke University Press, 2004), 32. For more on the mirror of racial difference, particularly via popular representations of racial difference that maintain fantasies of white dominance even after the successes of the Civil Rights Movement, see Eric Lott's *Black Mirror: The Cultural Contradictions of American Racism* (Cambridge, MA: Harvard University Press, 2017), his sequel to *Love and Theft: Blackface Minstrelsy and the American Working Class* (Oxford: Oxford University Press, 1993).

39. José Esteban Muñoz offers another psychoanalytically informed account of the self-reflexive structure Du Bois describes, which the former calls "disidentification" and which is defined by a (cultural) recognition of one's own failure to attain coherent, universalizable selfhood without submitting to the ideology of selfhood in the first place. See José Esteban Muñoz, *Disidentifications: Queers of Color and the Performance of Politics* (Minneapolis: University of Minnesota Press, 1999). In the context of racialized subjectivity, all the points of this discussion go at least as far back as Frantz Fanon's *Peau noire, masques blancs* (Paris: Éditions du Seuil, 1952).

40. Smith, *Photography on the Color Line*, 33 (italics in the original).

41. Monique-Adelle Callahan, *Between the Lines: Literary Transnationalism and African American Poetics* (Oxford: Oxford University Press, 2011), 87.

42. Jonathan Culler, "Apostrophe," *Diacritics* 7, no. 4 (Winter 1977): 67; Jonathan Culler, *The Pursuit of Signs: Semiotics, Literature, Deconstruction* (Ithaca, NY: Cornell University Press, 2002), 149.

43. Dana Luciano, *Arranging Grief: Sacred Time and the Body in Nineteenth-Century America* (New York: New York University Press, 2007), 188.

44. Yopie Prins, *Victorian Sappho* (Princeton, NJ: Princeton University Press, 1999), 19; Virginia Jackson, *Dickinson's Misery: A Theory of Lyric Reading* (Princeton, NJ: Princeton University Press, 2005), 70. I discuss Jackson's and Prins's critique of the New Critics' theories of the lyric, specifically W. K. Wimsatt's and M. C. Beardsley's, at more length in "Lyric Making: On Frostian Techne," *Robert Frost Review* 29 (2019): 60–73. I draw on some of that discussion in what follows.

45. Anthony Reed, *Freedom Time: The Poetics and Politics of Black Experimental Writing* (Baltimore: Johns Hopkins University Press, 2014), 98, 101.

46. G. Gabrielle Starr, *Lyric Generations: Poetry and the Novel in the Long Eighteenth Century* (Baltimore: Johns Hopkins University Press, 2004), 75.

47. Peterson, *"Doers of the Word,"* 122, quoting Grace Greenwood in William Still, *The Underground Railroad* (Philadelphia: Porter and Coates, 1872), 779, and William Wells Brown, *The Rising Son; or, The Antecedents and Advancement of the Colored Race* [1874] (New York: Negro Universities Press, 1970), 525.

48. See Carolyn Sorisio on the relationship between the body and the ideal, disembodied man she associates with American national ideology. Harper in particular, Sorisio claims following Peterson, redirects her public audience's attention away from the more abject, physical associations of Blackness to some inner point, "proposing self-discipline as a liberatory strategy." One can see how, if this is accurate, Harper might then be taken to be colonized by lyric associations. But I think her use of lyric is much more interesting than that, and her rhetorical interventions much more effective, if also more subtle, at imag(in)ing a future irreducible to further disciplining the Black body. Carolyn Sorisio, *Fleshing Out America: Race, Gender, and the Politics of the Body in American Literature, 1833–1879* (Athens: University of Georgia Press, 2002), 9.

49. On contemporary African American experimental lyric(ism) as a threshold where political urgency and individual sensibility meet, see Nikki Skillman, "Lyric Reading Revisited: Passion, Address, and Form in *Citizen*," *American Literary History* 31, no. 3 (Fall 2019): 419–57.

50. Elizabeth Barnes, *States of Sympathy: Seduction and Democracy in the American Novel* (New York: Columbia University Press, 1997), 97.

51. Frank M. Kirkland, "Modernity and Intellectual Life in Black," *Philosophical Forum* 24, no. 1–3 (1993): 159.

52. June Jordan, "The Difficult Miracle of Black Poetry in America or Something like a Sonnet for Phillis Wheatley," *Massachusetts Review* 27, no. 2 (Summer 1986): 261.

53. Luciano, *Arranging Grief*, 191.

54. On death and social death in nineteenth-century American culture, with a reading of Harper's *Iola Leroy* revealing corporeal death as parallel with births of political personhoods, see Russ Castronovo, *Necro Citizenship: Death, Eroticism, and the Public Sphere in the Nineteenth-Century United States* (Durham, NC: Duke University Press, 2001). For further analysis of the figurations of the social deaths of African Americans and other marginalized subjects in the twentieth century, see Sharon Patricia Holland, *Raising the Dead: Readings of Death and (Black) Subjectivity* (Durham, NC: Duke University Press, 2000).

55. Lott, *Love and Theft*, 153.

56. Lauren Berlant, "Poor Eliza," *American Literature* 70, no. 3 (September 1998): 655.

57. James Baldwin, "Everybody's Protest Novel," in *James Baldwin: Collected Essays*, ed. Toni Morrison, Library of America no. 98 (New York: Library of America, 1998), 12.

58. Harper, *Brighter Coming Day*, 60.

59. Maryemma Graham writes that "Harper's addition [to traditional sentimental ballad] of dramatic details, vivid imagery, and her effective understanding of Afro-American life, together with her political sensibility, transformed the common ballad into a distinctly Afro-American discourse." Sorisio argues that Harper's use of ballad form followed from an "awareness of the dynamics of spectatorship . . . [which] enabled her to create a method of representation that emphasized the importance of corporeal oppression without positioning the African American woman as a passive object available to anyone's vulgar gaze." Maryemma Graham, introduction to *Complete Poems of Frances E. W. Harper*, ed. Maryemma Graham (Oxford: Oxford University Press, 1988), lii; Sorisio, *Fleshing Out America*, 84.

60. Christopher Spaide, "Multiple Choice: Terrance Hayes's Response-Poems and the African American Lyric 'We,'" *Cambridge Quarterly* 48, no. 3 (September 2019): 235.

61. Harper, *Brighter Coming Day*, 60.

62. Several studies have expanded our sense of the relation between Blackness and the

distinctions man/animal, human/nonhuman, which I believe Harper does too in lines like these. While beyond the scope of this chapter, see Joshua Bennett, *Being Property Once Myself: Blackness and the End of Man* (Cambridge, MA: Harvard University Press, 2020); Colleen Glenney Boggs, *Animalia Americana: Animal Representations and Biopolitical Subjectivity* (New York: Columbia University Press, 2013); and Zakiyyah Iman Jackson, *Becoming Human: Matter and Meaning in an Antiblack World* (New York: New York University Press, 2020).

63. It is worth noting, especially given my eventual claim that lyric, for Harper, promises the impossible—to de-mark the marked body—the importance for other Black artists in maintaining or even embracing representations of the wounded body as a way of keeping slavery's systematic cruelty visible. See Kimberly Juanita Brown, *The Repeating Body: Slavery's Visual Resonance in the Contemporary* (Durham, NC: Duke University Press, 2015).

64. Psalms 17:8 (KJV), Job 8:9 (KJV), and Psalms 23:4 (KJV). For more on the tradition referenced, see John Hollander, *The Substance of Shadow: A Darkening Trope in Poetic History*, ed. Kenneth Gross (Chicago: University of Chicago Press, 2016).

65. For the interconnections between fugitivity and property law (including intellectual property law) in ante- and postbellum America, see Stephen M. Best, *The Fugitive's Properties: Law and the Poetics of Possession* (Chicago: University of Chicago Press, 2004).

66. Fred Moten, "The Case of Blackness," *Criticism* 50, no. 2 (Spring 2008): 179.

67. Moten elsewhere refers to Black life as "some kind of not-in-between suspension," which recasts fugitivity as rootlessness that persists beyond the spans of transitions between states. What I am calling Harper's two-sided construction could also be thought, as Moten prefers, in terms of entanglement, or blurring of self-possession and self-loss as achieved in (rather than suppressed by) lyric form. Fred Moten, *Black and Blur*, vol. 1 of *consent not to be a single being* (Durham, NC: Duke University Press, 2017), 10.

68. Hartman, *Scenes of Subjection*, 35.

69. Eleanor Jones Harvey, *The Civil War and American Art* (New Haven: Yale University Press, 2012), 188.

70. Caroline Levine, *Forms: Whole, Rhythm, Hierarchy, Network* (Princeton, NJ: Princeton University Press, 2015), 3.

71. For a more thorough discussion of various, heterogeneous forms of antebellum captivity—and corresponding forms of freedom and bondage illuminated by cultural texts, particularly slave narratives—see Keith Michael Green, *Bound to Respect: Antebellum Narratives of Black Imprisonment, Servitude, and Bondage, 1816–1861* (Tuscaloosa: University of Alabama Press, 2015).

72. Walt Whitman, *Complete Poetry and Collected Prose* (New York: Library of America, 1982), 306, 307. For an extended version of the following discussion, see Zachary Tavlin, "On the Road: Reevaluating an American Cultural Ideal," *ESQ* 64, no. 1 (2018): 1–30, where I consider Whitman and Douglass in the context of American interstate road system development.

73. Trish Loughran, *The Republic in Print: Print Culture in the Age of U.S. Nation Building, 1770–1870* (New York: Columbia University Press, 2007), 24.

74. Whitman, *Complete Poetry and Collected Prose*, 302, 306.

75. For more on the fugitive slaves' "spaces of freedom" beyond the binaries North/South, America/Canada, and even free/enslaved, with essays devoted to overlooked sites of both formal and semiformal freedom for fugitives, see Damian Alan Pargas, ed., *Fugitive Slaves and Spaces of Freedom in North America* (Gainesville: University Press of Florida, 2018).

76. Robert Abrams, *Landscape and Ideology in American Renaissance Literature: Topographies of Skepticism* (Cambridge: Cambridge University Press, 2004), 110.

77. Frederick Douglass, *My Bondage and My Freedom* (New York: Library of America, 1994), 310–11, 341–42, 311.

78. Michael A. Chaney, *Fugitive Vision: Slave Image and Black Identity in Antebellum Narrative* (Bloomington: Indiana University Press, 2008), 6.

79. Nathaniel Mackey, *Discrepant Engagement: Dissonance, Cross-Culturality, and Experimental Writing* (Tuscaloosa: University of Alabama Press, 1993), 269–70.

80. See Paul Jaussen on Mackey's "post-expectant futurity," an aesthetic that "articulates hope while abandoning concrete prescriptions for that awaited future of healing and reconnection." Paul Jaussen, *Writing in Real Time* (Oxford: Oxford University Press, 2017), 145.

81. Sharon Cameron, *Lyric Time: Dickinson and the Limits of the Genre* (Baltimore: Johns Hopkins University Press, 1979), 71.

82. Harper, *Brighter Coming Day*, 62.

83. McGill, "Circuits of Abolitionist Poetry," 56.

84. McGill, "Circuits of Abolitionist Poetry," 66. Laura L. Mielke, in *Provocative Eloquence: Theater, Violence, and Antislavery Speech in the Antebellum United States* (Ann Arbor: University of Michigan Press, 2019), makes parallel claims about antebellum theater, discussing plays like Harriet Beecher Stowe's *The Christian Slave* (1855), J. T. Trowbridge's *Neighbor Jackwood* (1857), William Wells Brown's *The Escape; or, A Leap for Freedom* (1858), and Dion Boucicault's *The Octoroon* (1859) in terms of antislavery discourse and the portability of dramatic forms of persuasion in nominally untheatrical contexts.

85. Amiri Baraka, *Blues People: Negro Music in White America* (New York: Harper, 2002), 153 (italics in the original).

86. Harper, *Brighter Coming Day*, 61.

87. For more on the potentials of abstraction in African American literature and culture, see Phillip Brian Harper, *Abstractionist Aesthetics: Artistic Form and Social Critique in African American Culture* (New York: New York University Press, 2015).

88. Cameron, *Lyric Time*, 206.

89. McGill, "Circuits of Abolitionist Poetry," 74.

90. Harper, *Brighter Coming Day*, 62.

Chapter 3

1. Emily Dickinson, *Selected Letters*, ed. Thomas H. Johnson (Cambridge, MA: Belknap Press of Harvard University Press, 1986), 175.

2. Marta L. Werner, "'For Flash and Click and Suddenness –': Emily Dickinson and the Photography Effect," in *A Companion to Emily Dickinson*, ed. Marta Nell Smith and Mary Loeffelholz (Malden, MA: Blackwell, 2008), 482. To the extent that theories of the gaze have been applied in Dickinson criticism, they tend to promote a distinction between the poet's look and the way the poet is looked at, as Werner does in her reading of this episode. There is much in her poetry, not to mention in the peculiar experience of looking closely at her daguerreotyped image, to support such an approach. According to Cynthia Hogue, "Dickinson perceived the dynamics of the [male] gaze," and managed to resist its mastery by splitting her self in her poetry, a defensive strategy that "places and displaces" the male seer in turn, that alternatively "locates him in and dislocates him from the position of knowledge about her." Lisa Harper enlists Laura Mulvey to argue that Dickinson's "poetics of veiling" is a "defensive strategy against the psychosexual and social consequences

of the male gaze" that also affords the poet "the space in which to pursue alternative configurations of gender and desire and to explore the female body." Cynthia Hogue, "'I Did'nt Be — Myself': Emily Dickinson's Semiotics of Presence," *Emily Dickinson Journal* 1, no. 2 (1992): 30–31, 38; Lisa Harper, "'The Eyes accost – and Sunder': Unveiling Emily Dickinson's Poetics," *Emily Dickinson Journal* 9, no. 1 (2000): 40. See also more general takes on Dickinson's fear of male sexuality in Clark Griffith, *The Long Shadow: Emily Dickinson's Tragic Poetry* (Princeton, NJ: Princeton University Press, 1964); John Cody, *After Great Pain: The Inner Life of Emily Dickinson* (Cambridge, MA: Harvard University Press, 1971); Joanne Feit Diehl, "'Come Slowly—Eden': An Exploration of Women Poets and Their Muse," *Signs* 3, no. 3 (1978): 572–87; Vivian R. Pollak, *Dickinson: The Anxiety of Gender* (Ithaca, NY: Cornell University Press, 1984); Joanne Dobson, *Dickinson and the Strategies of Reticence: The Woman Writer in Nineteenth-Century America* (Bloomington: Indiana University Press, 1989); and Mary Loeffelholz, *Dickinson and the Boundaries of Feminist Theory* (Urbana: University of Illinois Press, 1991).

3. Mary Elizabeth Kromer Bernhard, "Lost and Found: Emily Dickinson's Unknown Daguerreotypist," *New England Quarterly* 72, no. 4 (1999): 598. Bernhard's essay bases its claims on correspondence found at the Jones Library in Amherst and in contemporary issues of *The Hampshire and Franklin Express*, which ran North's advertisements.

4. The Emily Dickinson International Society's authentication process reminds one of the care taken in inspecting the status of a Honus Wagner baseball card. When Philip Gura purchased a possible second photograph of the poet on eBay in 2000, the society and Richard Jantz, director of the Forensic Anthropology Center at the University of Tennessee, examined the artifact. For a discussion on Dickinson photograph authentication via use of facial recognition technologies on her astigmatic eye, and the affective critical rhetoric of possessing Dickinson (visually, in relation to her materials), see Seth Perlow *The Poem Electric: Technology and the American Lyric* (Minneapolis: University of Minnesota Press, 2018).

5. Martin Wand and Richard B. Sewall, "'Eyes Be Blind, Heart Be Still': A New Perspective on Emily Dickinson's Eye Problem," *New England Quarterly* 52, no. 3 (1979): 403.

6. All Dickinson poems are referenced according to R. W. Franklin's numbers, as assigned in Emily Dickinson, *The Poems of Emily Dickinson: Variorum Edition*, ed. R. W. Franklin (Cambridge, MA: Belknap Press of Harvard University Press, 1998). I maintain manuscript lineation throughout.

7. I will return to Dickinson's birds later in the chapter, but see also Jefferey Simons, "Dickinson's Lyric Ornithology," *Emily Dickinson Journal* 28, no. 1 (2019): 1–22.

8. At the time this chapter was written, much of the energy in Dickinson criticism had turned in an ecocritical direction. Some highlights of this still-increasing body of work include Scott Knickerbocker, *Ecopoetics: The Language of Nature, the Nature of Language* (Amherst: University of Massachusetts Press, 2012); Christine Gerhardt, *A Place for Humility: Whitman, Dickinson, and the Natural World* (Iowa: University of Iowa Press, 2014); Juliana Chow, "'Because I see—New Englandly—': Seeing Species in the Nineteenth-Century and Emily Dickinson's Regional Specificity," *ESQ* 60, no. 3 (2014): 413–49; Cody Marrs, "Dickinson in the Anthropocene," *ESQ* 63, no. 2 (2017): 201–25; Mary Kuhn, "Dickinson and the Politics of Plant Sensibility," *ELH* 85, no. 1 (Spring 2018): 141–70; Gillian Kidd Osborne, "Dickinson and Historical Ecopoetics," in *The New Emily Dickinson Studies*, ed. Michelle Kohler (Cambridge: Cambridge University Press, 2019), 136–52; and Colleen Glenney Boggs, *Animalia Americana: Animal Representations and Biopolitical Subjectivity* (New York: Columbia University Press, 2013).

9. Dickinson, *Selected Letters*, 175.

10. Robert Taft, *Photography and the American Scene: A Social History, 1839–1889* (New York: Macmillan, 1942), 44.

11. Judith Farr, *The Passion of Emily Dickinson* (Cambridge, MA: Harvard University Press, 1992), 20.

12. Christa Vogelius, "'Paralyzed, with Gold - ': Dickinson's Poetics of Photography," *Emily Dickinson Journal* 18, no. 2 (2009): 27–28.

13. For an account of Dickinson's emphasis on the epistemic *narrowness* of photography's revelations, particularly with regard to Civil War photography, see Eliza Richards, "'Death's Surprise, Stamped Visible': Emily Dickinson, Oliver Wendell Holmes, and Civil War Photography," *Amerikastudien* 54, no. 1 (2009): 13–33; and Eliza Richards, *Battle Lines: Poetry and Mass Media in the US Civil War* (Philadelphia: University of Pennsylvania Press, 2018).

14. Werner, "'For Flash and Click and Suddenness –,'" 477.

15. A big topic, perhaps the biggest in Dickinson scholarship. In addition to Virginia Jackson's reconsideration of lyric (and lyric inwardness) in *Dickinson's Misery*, see Vivian R. Pollak, *Our Emily Dickinsons: American Women Poets and the Intimacies of Difference* (Philadelphia: University of Pennsylvania Press, 2016), for an account of Dickinson's impact on women poets who reconsidered the values of poetic connection and sociality instead of privacy and inwardness.

16. Diana Fuss, *The Sense of an Interior: Four Writers and the Rooms That Shaped Them* (New York: Routledge, 2004), 9, 14.

17. James J. Gibson, *The Perception of the Visual World* (Boston: Houghton Mifflin, 1950), 126.

18. Michelle Kohler, *Miles of Stare: Transcendentalism and the Problem of Literary Vision in Nineteenth-Century America* (Tuscaloosa: University of Alabama Press, 2014), 108.

19. Kohler, *Miles of Stare*, 109.

20. Edward Casey, *The World at a Glance* (Bloomington: Indiana University Press, 2007), 302.

21. Various implications and subtleties of this general principle are demonstrated in studies like Peiyuan He and Eileen Kowler, "The Role of Location Probability in the Programming of Saccades: Implications for 'Center-of-Gravity' Tendencies," *Vision Research* 29, no. 9 (1989): 1165–81.

22. Emile Javal, Helmholtz's French translator, would formalize many of his insights and designate the eye's jerks as "saccades" in 1878.

23. Hermann von Helmholtz, "Concerning the Perceptions in General," in *Helmholtz on Perception: Its Physiology and Development*, ed. R. M. Warren and R. P. Warren (New York: Wiley, 1968), 174.

24. Hermann von Helmholtz, "The Facts of Perception," in Warren and Warren, *Helmholtz on Perception*, 223.

25. Marta L. Werner, *Emily Dickinson's Open Folios: Scenes of Reading, Surfaces of Writing* (Ann Arbor: University of Michigan Press, 1995), 36, 12.

26. Sharon Cameron, *Choosing Not Choosing: Dickinson's Fascicles* (Chicago: University of Chicago Press, 1992), 6.

27. Alexandra Socarides, *Dickinson Unbound: Paper, Process, Poetics* (New York: Oxford University Press, 2012), 26. Like Cameron's and Socarides's studies, Paul Crumbley and Eleanor Elson Heginbotham's *Dickinson's Fascicles: A Spectrum of Possibilities* (Columbus:

Ohio State University Press, 2014)—a collection with essays by Cameron, Socarides, Domhnall Mitchell, Martha Nell Smith, Paula Bernat Bennett, and several others—also takes the fascicles as nonnarrative, nonlinear networks.

28. In further consideration of Dickinson's poetics of progress through an encroaching void, Anne-Lise François reads "After great pain a formal feeling comes" (F372) in a way that links its syntactic rhythm to a temporal experience of dissolution proper to poiesis in the midst of environmental collapse. As the syntactic units of the poem's last line lengthen across the iambic pentameter's stresses, "each stage, like the fingers of an unfolding hand, or like the confidence that grows in the act of finding one's way, is one, then two, syllables longer than the last, in an accretion that signifies the release by which the hour of lead expands to include its own dissolution." Anne-Lise François, "Ungiving Time: Reading Lyric by the Light of the Anthropocene," in *Anthropocene Reading: Literary History in Geologic Times*, ed. Tobias Menely and Jesse Oak Taylor (State College: Pennsylvania State University Press, 2017), 242–43.

29. See Helen Vendler, *Poets Thinking: Pope, Whitman, Dickinson, Yeats* (Cambridge, MA: Harvard University Press, 2004), on Dickinson's early technique at filling up a sequence without gaps, and the variety of structural modifications her poems undergo as she alters her approach to seriality over time.

30. Branka Arsić, "Thing-Poems: On Marta Werner's and Jen Bervin's *The Gorgeous Nothings: Emily Dickinson's Envelope Poems*," *J19* 3, no. 2 (2015): 238.

31. Cristanne Miller provides another, well-informed account of the divide(s) in Dickinson's practice, centered on 1865 as a break between careful preservation versus de-archived poetry, and more versus less responsiveness to public concerns. See Cristanne Miller, *Reading in Time* (Amherst: University of Massachusetts Press, 2012).

32. See Anthony Tuck, "Singing the Rug: Patterned Textiles and the Origins of Indo-European Metrical Poetry," *American Journal of Archaeology* 110, no. 4 (2006): 539–50.

33. Socarides, *Dickinson Unbound*, 84.

34. Jerome McGann argues that "while Dickinson wanted readers, and while she was even ambitious of fame as a poet, she rejected the traditional (early capitalist) institution for achieving those ends . . . not because of some large cultural or political sense of the limits of the 'auction' of publishing" but "because she came to see how restrictive and conventional that medium had become." McGann ultimately traces Dickinson's verse forms to her "epistolary habits and conventions," specifically the letter format that "encouraged her to seek an imaginative communion between the forms of prose and poetry." Jerome McGann, "Emily Dickinson's Visible Language," *Emily Dickinson Journal* 2, no. 2 (1993): 43, 50.

35. Socarides, *Dickinson Unbound*, 85.

36. McGann, "Emily Dickinson's Visible Language," 49.

37. Johann Wolfgang von Goethe, *Faust: A Tragedy*, trans. Bayard Taylor (Boston: Houghton Mifflin, 1906), 88.

38. Dickinson's unstitching practice put her at odds with feminine expectations in Amherst. An 1850 letter to Jane Humphrey sarcastically notes, "The Sewing Society has commenced again - and held its first meeting last week - now all the poor will be helped - the cold warmed - the warm cooled - the hungry fed - the thirsty attended to - the ragged clothed - and this suffering - tumbled down world will be helped to it's feet again - which will be quite pleasant to all. I don't attend - notwithstanding my hard approbation - which must puzzle the public exceedingly. I am already set down as one of those brands almost consumed - and my hardheartedness gets me many prayers." Dickinson, *Selected Letters*, 84.

39. Casey, *World at a Glance*, 149.

40. Dickinson, *Poems of Emily Dickinson*, xi.

41. Socarides, *Dickinson Unbound*, 109–10.

42. Jed Deppman, *Trying to Think with Emily Dickinson* (Amherst: University of Massachusetts Press, 2008), 94.

43. R. P. Blackmur and Forest Pyle both write of Dickinson's contextual evacuation following her poems' first lines (what they call her "disintegration of effect" and "radical aesthetic," respectively). Natalie Adler considers Dickinson's signature downward lyrical movement "a peculiar poetics of letting go," where "instead of coming to a conclusion, she shows her mastery by refusing to hold on." R. P. Blackmur, "Emily Dickinson: Notes on Prejudice and Fact," *Southern Review* 3, no. 2 (1937): 323–47; Forest Pyle, *Art's Undoing: In the Wake of a Radical Aestheticism* (New York: Fordham University Press, 2014); Natalie Adler, "Dickinson's Mastery," *Emily Dickinson Journal* 25, no. 2 (2016): 4, 21.

44. William James, *The Principles of Psychology* (New York: Dover, 1950), 1:107, 122.

45. Deppman, *Trying to Think with Emily Dickinson*, 97.

46. Luke 3:5 (KJV).

47. For more on Dickinson's anthropomorphisms (and analogical anthropomorphism in evolutionary science), see Aaron Shackelford, "Dickinson's Animals and Anthropomorphism," *Emily Dickinson Journal* 19, no. 2 (2010): 47–66.

48. Elisa New, *The Line's Eye: Poetic Experience, American Sight* (Cambridge, MA: Harvard University Press, 1998), 166.

49. New, *Line's Eye*, 167.

50. According to Barbara Novak, "Luminist space is achieved through a series of planes, parallel to the surface, which are never violated but proceed back in orderly, measured steps, like the lulls between the columns of the classical temple. There is little flow or sweep, but rather a containment of each part within its own spatial unit that arrests the moment in Emerson's 'concentrated eternity.'" Barbara Novak, *American Painting of the Nineteenth Century: Realism, Idealism, and the American Experience* (New York: Praeger Publishers, 1969), 105.

51. Henri Bergson, *Time and Free Will: An Essay on the Immediate Data of Consciousness*, trans. Frank Pogson (New York: Harper, 1960), 226.

52. Nelson Goodman, *Languages of Art: An Approach to a Theory of Symbols* (Indianapolis: Hackett, 1976), 136.

53. The tick has become Uexküll's most cited example due to the simplicity of its case: "Out of the vast world which surrounds the tick, three stimuli shine forth from the dark like beacons, and serve as guides to lead her unerringly to her goal." The tick's world is circumscribed by a limited number of cues, constitutive of its *Umwelt*, including the sun (which draws the sightless tick onto stems or leaves), a passing mammal (sensed through its body heat, on which the dangling tick falls), and the relation between the mammal's hair and skin (its hairless spots providing a site for bloodsucking and subsequent reproductive release). Jakob von Uexküll, "A Stroll through the Worlds of Animals and Men," in *Instinctive Behavior: The Development of a Modern Concept*, ed. and trans. Claire H. Schiller (New York: International Universities Press, 1957), 12.

54. Jakob von Uexküll, *Theoretical Biology*, trans. D. L. Mackinnon (New York: Harcourt, Brace, 1926), 42.

55. Martin Heidegger, *The Fundamental Concepts of Metaphysics: World, Finitude, Solitude*, trans. William McNeill and Nicholas Walker (Bloomington: Indiana University Press, 2008), 255.

56. Conceiving the sliding scope of attention in this way challenges Heidegger's distinction between comportment and behavior, which refers to a being's level of absorption in its surroundings, and its openness or closedness to being as such. For Heidegger, "the specific manner of being which belongs to man is quite different [from animals] and involves not behaviour but *comporting oneself toward*," while behavior "is only possible on the basis of the animal's *absorption* in itself" its "*captivation*." Heidegger, *Fundamental Concepts of Metaphysics*, 237–39. For a generalist study of poetry and attention, see Lucy Alford, *Forms of Poetic Attention* (New York: Columbia University Press, 2020). For historically situated studies of the poetics of attention, see Lily Gurton-Wachter, *Watchwords: Romanticism and the Poetics of Attention* (Stanford, CA: Stanford University Press, 2016); and Andrew Epstein, *Attention Equals Life: The Pursuit of the Everyday in Contemporary Poetry and Culture* (New York: Oxford University Press, 2016). On the related topic of distraction, see Paul North, *The Problem of Distraction* (Stanford, CA: Stanford University Press, 2011); and Natalie M. Phillips, *Distraction: Problems of Attention in Eighteenth-Century Literature* (Baltimore: Johns Hopkins University Press, 2016).

57. John McDowell, "What Myth?," *Inquiry* 50, no. 4 (2007): 348–49, 346.

58. Maurice Merleau-Ponty, *The Structure of Behavior*, trans. Alden Fisher (Boston, MA: Beacon Press, 1963), 175 (italics in the original).

59. Merleau-Ponty, *Structure of Behavior*, 86.

60. Maurice Merleau-Ponty, *Phenomenology of Perception*, trans. Colin Smith (London: Routledge Classics, 2002), 320–21.

61. Maurice Merleau-Ponty, *The Visible and the Invisible*, trans. Alphonso Lingis (Evanston, IL: Northwestern University Press, 1968), 152.

62. Gary Tomlinson, *A Million Years of Music: The Emergence of Human Modernity* (New York: Zone Books, 2015), 73.

63. Casey, *World at a Glance*, 309.

64. Theo Davis, *Ornamental Aesthetics: The Poetry of Attending in Thoreau, Dickinson, and Whitman* (Oxford: Oxford University Press, 2016), 117.

65. James Elkins's analysis of subsemiotic elements in painting and drawing—"marks, traces, *traits*, contours, *orli*, and *splendores*"—is designed to make interpreting visual art difficult, especially compared to semiotic theories of art history that either dispense with marks as meaningless or purely technical or assimilate them to linguistic models. James Elkins, "Marks, Traces, *Traits*, Contours, *Orli*, and *Splendores*: Nonsemiotic Elements in Pictures," *Critical Inquiry* 21, no. 4 (1995): 822. Dickinson's inscrutable late scrap poems put readers and poetic theorists in a similar position, forcing us to chart a narrow path between reading her expressively linguistic marks apart from the specificities of the object-page and turning the objects themselves into legible signs.

66. Colleen Glenney Boggs, "Emily Dickinson's Posthuman Worlds: Biopoetics and Environmental Subjectivity," in *The New Emily Dickinson Studies*, ed. Michelle Kohler (Cambridge: Cambridge University Press, 2019), 121–22.

67. Goodman, *Languages of Art*, 230.

68. By referencing the "protomodernism" of Dickinson's more experimental poetry, I am going against the grain of scholarship claiming that Dickinson's poetry is actually quite conventional in its nineteenth-century context. By doing so only to move elsewhere, on to a sense of her poetry's animality, I aim to leave this concern to others. In addition to Jackson's aforementioned work on genre, see Paula Bernat Bennett, "Emily Dickinson and Her Peers," in *A Companion to American Literature and Culture*, ed. Paul Lauter (Malden,

MA: Blackwell, 2010), 284–315; Sarah Wadsworth, "'Lifted Moments': Emily Dickinson, Hymn Revision, and the Revival Music Meme-Plex," *Emily Dickinson Journal* 23, no. 1 (2014): 46–74; Mary Loeffelholz's case for the memorability and memorizability of Dickinson's poetry in traditional forms in *The Value of Emily Dickinson* (New York: Cambridge University Press, 2016); and Alexandra Socarides's account of the conventions of nineteenth-century women's poetry in which Dickinson's work is embedded in *In Plain Sight* (Oxford: Oxford University Press, 2020). Edited by Eliza Richards, *Emily Dickinson in Context* (New York: Cambridge University Press, 2013) contains essays on Dickinson's many literary sources as well as sociohistorical contexts. Sandra Runzo studies a range of popular culture forms that she argues Dickinson engaged with on the levels of narrative and trope in *Theatricals of Day: Emily Dickinson and Nineteenth-Century American Popular Culture* (Amherst: University of Massachusetts Press, 2019). See also the essays in Michelle Kohler, ed., *The New Emily Dickinson Studies* (Cambridge: Cambridge University Press, 2019), especially Michael C. Cohen's "Generic Dickinson." While not focused particularly on Dickinson's poetry, Cohen's *The Social Lives of Poems in Nineteenth-Century America* (Philadelphia: University of Pennsylvania Press, 2015) discusses the intimate relationships between poetry and popular song across the period.

69. Lorraine Daston and Peter Galison, *Objectivity* (Cambridge, MA: MIT Press, 2007). For more on how Dickinson's poetry intersects with early environmentalism, particularly on ecologies of "place," see Christine Gerhardt's "'Often seen - but seldom felt': Emily Dickinson's Reluctant Ecology of Place," *Emily Dickinson Journal* 15, no. 1 (2006): 56–78.

70. Louis Agassiz, "Methods of Study in Natural History," *Atlantic Monthly* 9 no. 51 (1862): 457.

71. Some of the nineteenth-century's most influential clinical photographic studies include G. B. Duchenne de Boulogne's catalogues of facial muscular phenomena, Hugh Diamond's portraits of the committed at various stages of onset and cure in the Surrey County Lunatic Asylum, Jean-Martin Charcot's arrays of hysterical gestures, and Francis Galton's composite portraits used to synthesize classes of criminal physiognomies.

72. Marta L. Werner, "'Most Arrows': Autonomy and Intertextuality in Emily Dickinson's Late Fragments," *Text* 10 (1997): 42.

73. Thomas Wentworth Higginson even calls her handwriting "so peculiar that it seemed as if the writer might have taken her first lessons by studying the famous fossil bird-tracks in the museum of that college town [the Amherst Museum]." Thomas Wentworth Higginson, "Emily Dickinson's Handwriting," *Atlantic Monthly* 68 (October 1891): 444. For more on this moment, see Boggs, "Emily Dickinson's Posthuman Worlds," 131.

74. Melanie Hubbard, "Dickinson's Advertising Flyers: Theorizing Materiality and the Work of Reading," *Emily Dickinson Journal* 7, no. 1 (1998): 28.

75. Fuss, *Sense of an Interior*, 45, 49. The quotation from Todd's daughter is from Millicent Todd Bingham, *Ancestor's Brocades: The Literary Debut of Emily Dickinson* (New York: Harper & Brothers, 1945), 12.

76. Werner, "'Most Arrows,'" 46–47.

77. For a reading of weakness and other related concepts in terms of Dickinson's "disability poetics," including with reference to this particular envelope poem, see Clare Mullaney, "'Not to Discover Weakness Is the Artifice of Strength': Emily Dickinson, Constraint, and a Disability Poetics," *J19* 7, no. 1 (2019): 49–81.

78. Andy Clark and David Chalmers, "The Extended Mind," *Analysis* 58, no. 1 (1998): 12.

79. Louise Barrett discusses extended cognition in relation to animal minds and various evolutionary developments. These include "offloading" internal cognitive mechanisms to the environment or niche (much as, in her own domain, Dickinson offloads form onto made objects): "If there is information freely available in the environment, why would natural selection go to the trouble of building in internal mechanisms that do exactly the same job? . . . This isn't quite the same as saying that no internal activity takes place. Instead, it's an argument for giving the external environment as much attention as the inside of an animal's head when we are investigating their cognitive capacities." Louise Barrett, *Beyond the Brain: How Body and Environment Shape Animal and Human Minds* (Princeton, NJ: Princeton University Press, 2011), 110–11.

80. Socarides, *Dickinson Unbound*, 157–59.

81. Walter Benjamin, *Arcades Project*, trans. Howard Eiland and Kevin McLaughlin (Cambridge, MA: Harvard University Press, 1999), 216.

82. If, as Susan Stewart claims, we "cannot speak of the small, or miniature, work independent of the social values expressed toward private space—particularly, of the ways the domestic and the interior imply the social formation of an interior subject," Dickinson reveals that the miniature need not be "perfect and uncontaminated." Susan Stewart, *On Longing: Narratives of the Miniature, the Gigantic, the Souvenir, the Collection* (Durham, NC: Duke University Press, 1993), 95, 68. The further in one goes, the more the domestic space comes to seem an outside whose materials can indeed be contaminated and drift across the irregular borders established by the scrap torn out of its bourgeois context.

83. Jonathan Edwards, *A Jonathan Edwards Reader*, ed. John E. Smith, Harry S. Stout, and Kenneth P. Minkema (New Haven, CT: Yale University Press, 1995), 2.

84. New, *Line's Eye*, 23.

85. Edwards, *Jonathan Edwards Reader*, 6.

86. Gilles Deleuze references Muybridge's animal sequences at the beginning of his work on the cinematic "movement-image," referencing the "remarkable occasions" captured (like the moment when all the horse's hooves are in the air) as "privileged instants," but specifically as "singular points which belong to movement, not as the moments of actualization of a transcendent form." Gilles Deleuze, *Cinema 1: The Movement-Image*, trans. Hugh Tomlinson and Barbara Habberjam (London: Athlone, 1986), 5–6. But put together trigonometrically, in sequence, one does begin to think in terms of transcendent forms, even if there is nothing transcendent about the instants captured.

87. Werner, *Emily Dickinson's Open Folios*, 23.

88. Following Alix Beeston, one might argue that Dickinson's poetic distribution radicalizes rather than negates photographic logic, if "the irrepressible movement of photography toward multiplicity and sequentiality might well be understood as its elemental property." Alix Beeston, *In and Out of Sight: Modernist Writing and the Photographic Unseen* (New York: Oxford University Press, 2018), 14. Beeston's analysis tracks modernist photographic circulation in archives, collages, and sequential media like slideshows and montage.

89. Jonathan Crary, *Suspensions of Perception: Attention, Spectacle, and Modern Culture* (Cambridge, MA: MIT Press, 1999), 140.

90. Jen Bervin, "Studies in Scale," in *Emily Dickinson: The Gorgeous Nothings*, ed. Marta L. Werner and Jen Bervin (New York: New Directions, 2013), 9–10.

91. Marta L. Werner, "Itineraries of Escape: Emily Dickinson's Envelope Poems," in *Emily Dickinson, The Gorgeous Nothings*, ed. Marta Werner and Jen Bervin (New York: New Directions, 2013), 213.

92. Arsić, "Thing-Poems," 241–42.

Chapter 4

1. Colm Tóibín, "Henry James: Shadow and Substance," in *Henry James and American Painting*, ed. Colm Tóibín, Marc Simpson, and Declan Kiely (University Park: Pennsylvania State University Press and Morgan Library & Museum, 2017), 7, 35.

2. But for a biography that reinvigorates the perhaps otherwise tired American-international theme, see Martha Banta, *Henry James: An Alien's "History" of America* (Rome: Sapienza Università Editrice, 2016).

3. Henry James, *The American: A Norton Critical Edition*, ed. James W. Tuttleton (New York: W. W. Norton, 1978), 18, 18–19, 17.

4. For a focus on the relationship between James's late style and some of the characteristics I associate with the glance, but with an emphasis on their corrosive queerness, see Kevin Ohi, *Henry James and the Queerness of Style* (Minneapolis: University of Minnesota Press, 2011).

5. Henry James, *The Art of the Novel: Critical Prefaces*, ed. R. P. Blackmur (New York: Charles Scribner's Sons, 1962), 59, 154 (italics in the original).

6. Viola Hopkins Winner, *Henry James and the Visual Arts* (Charlottesville: University Press of Virginia, 1970), 1.

7. As Carolyn Porter argues, this is a complicated maneuver that initially relies on the realization that one is both seer and actor, capable of both immersion in and distance from a constructed visual field. She takes *The Sacred Fount* (1901) as a linchpin in James's corpus, with its unusual first-person narration introducing a visual problematic at the core of literary perspective. His recommitment to third-person consciousness enabled him "to invest a participating agent in the drama with the contemplative stance of the visionary seer without thereby running the risks entailed by according the seer power to speak directly to the reader. It allowed him, in short, to acknowledge the seer as a participant without sacrificing his crucial value as seer." Carolyn Porter, *Seeing and Being: The Plight of the Participant Observer in Emerson, James, Adams, and Faulkner* (Middletown, CT: Wesleyan University Press, 1981), 125.

8. Winner, *Henry James*, 1.

9. Maryanne Wolf, *Proust and the Squid: The Story and Science of the Reading Brain* (New York: Harper Collins, 2007), 83.

10. Ben Morgan, "Embodied Cognition and the Project of the Bildungsroman: *Wilhelm Meister's Apprenticeship* and *Daniel Deronda*," *Poetics Today* 38, no. 2 (2017): 346, 359.

11. Henry James, "The Art of Fiction," in *The Art of Fiction and Other Essays*, ed. Morris Roberts (New York: Oxford University Press, 1948), 14.

12. James, "Art of Fiction," 11.

13. Leo Bersani, *A Future for Astyanax: Characters and Desire in Literature* (New York: Little, Brown, 1976), 133; Colin Meissner, *Henry James and the Language of Experience* (Cambridge: Cambridge University Press, 1999), 33.

14. Daniel Hannah, *Henry James, Impressionism, and the Public* (Farnham: Ashgate, 2013), x, xii.

15. For indispensable work on Impressionism and its wider literary and cultural legacies, see Jesse Matz's *Literary Impressionism and Modernist Aesthetics* (Cambridge: Cambridge University Press, 2001) and *Lasting Impressions* (New York: Columbia University Press, 2016). On James and Paris, specifically the short but important period between 1875

and 1876 when he lived there and immersed himself in its literary and art cultures, see Peter Brooks, *Henry James Goes to Paris* (Princeton, NJ: Princeton University Press, 2007).

16. T. J. Clark, *The Painting of Modern Life: Paris in the Art of Manet and His Followers* (New York: A. A. Knopf, 1985), 48.

17. John House, *Impressionism: Paint and Politics* (New Haven: Yale University Press, 2004), 103.

18. Scholarship on James and the Impressionists keeps coming. For the most recent at the time of this writing, see John Scholar, *Henry James and the Art of Impressions* (New York: Oxford University Press, 2020).

19. As John Sweeney notes in his introduction to *The Painter's Eye*, James's art criticism tailed off considerably after publication of *The Portrait of a Lady*. "The gap is regrettable," Sweeney writes, "because it was between 1882 and 1897 that his sense of artistic experiment was sharpened and developed by his own exercises." Henry James, *The Painter's Eye: Notes and Essays on the Pictorial Arts*, ed. John L. Sweeney (Madison: University of Wisconsin Press, 1989), 25.

20. Astonishingly, in an essay on Sargent, James says "There is no greater work of art than a great portrait." Henry James, "John S. Sargent," in *Painter's Eye*, 227. For an account of James's regard for (and jealousy of the art of) portraiture, see Ruth Bernard Yeazell, "Henry James's Portrait-Envy," *New Literary History* 48, no. 2 (2017): 309–35.

21. Henry James, *The Portrait of a Lady: An Authoritative Text*, ed. Robert D. Bamberg (New York: W. W. Norton, 1975), 25, 309–10, 63.

22. For a more reception-oriented take on James's women and his fictional negotiations of femininity and nascent feminisms, see Kathryn Wichelns, *Henry James's Feminist Afterlives: Annie Fields, Emily Dickinson, Marguerite Duras* (Cham, Switzerland: Palgrave Macmillan, 2018).

23. James, *Portrait of a Lady*, 54, 61.

24. Sarah Blackwood argues that, for James, portraiture unsettles rather than merely captures a subject's elusive inner identity. See Blackwood's *The Portrait's Subject: Inventing Inner Life in the Nineteenth-Century United States* (Chapel Hill: University of North Carolina Press, 2019) for more on how portrait-like description and narration of Isabel shows her thinking and feeling both as a body and, as the novel develops, apart from her body.

25. Henry James, *Portrait of a Lady*, 8.

26. Hussey refers to Isabel in this vein as James's objet d'art, possessed by the male (inner) eye from the very beginning, even before crossing the threshold at Gardencourt. His analysis focuses on specific "moments" when Isabel, despite James's "exacting novelistic architecture" and social realism, "hovers, inextinguishable" (in James's words), like the "stray figure that pre-exists in possibility before the plot." Miciah Hussey, "Eyeing the Beholder: Henry James's Immaterial Portrait of a Lady," *Henry James Review* 37, no. 2 (2016): 182.

27. James, *Portrait of a Lady*, 7–8 (italics in the original).

28. Catherine M. Soussloff, *The Subject in Art: Portraiture and the Birth of the Modern* (Durham, NC: Duke University Press, 2006), 5, 8.

29. James, *Portrait of a Lady*, 8.

30. On the autobiography as performance of narrative self-portraiture, with a look at James's incomplete memoir, see Jerome Boyd Maunsell, *Portraits from Life: Modernist Novelists and Autobiography* (Oxford: Oxford University Press, 2018).

31. Soussloff, *Subject in Art*, 29.

32. James, *Portrait of a Lady*, 175 (italics in the original).

33. Jonathan L. Freedman, *Professions of Taste: Henry James, British Aestheticism, and Commodity Culture* (Stanford: Stanford University Press, 1990), 153, 201 (italics in the original).

34. Aestheticism, if Freedman is right, is a disease that threatens to take over the novel proper when Rosier identifies Isabel as a portrait: "At this moment, it appears that all the novel's characters and even its author are somehow implicated in one form or another of Gilbert's malevolent aestheticism." Freedman, *Professions of Taste*, 158. For more on James and nineteenth-century aestheticism, in this case John Ruskin's, see Tomoko Eguchi, *Ethical Aestheticism in the Early Works of Henry James* (Newcastle-upon-Tyne: Cambridge Scholars, 2016).

35. Bill Brown, *A Sense of Things: The Object Matter of American Literature* (Chicago: University of Chicago Press, 2003), 137, 141.

36. Edith Wharton follows James, in her masterpiece *The House of Mirth* (New York: Charles Scribner's Sons, 1905), by keeping her Archeresque heroine Lily Bart largely undescribed from the standpoint of objective narration, though also produces her as an unfolding visual product of her Gilded Age society spectators. For a thorough investigation into Bart's character as a product of naturalistic, masculinist visuality—but also into her often-denied status as viewing subject—see Laura Saltz, "'The Vision-Building Faculty': Naturalistic Vision in *The House of Mirth*." *Modern Fiction Studies* 57, no. 1 (2011): 17–46.

37. James, *Portrait of a Lady*, 41, 39.

38. Henry James, *The Notebooks of Henry James*, ed. F. O. Matthiessen and Kenneth B. Murdock (New York: Oxford University Press, 1961), 15.

39. James, *Portrait of a Lady*, 297.

40. James, *Portrait of a Lady*, 14.

41. James, *Portrait of a Lady*, 342 (italics in the original).

42. James, *Portrait of a Lady*, 342–43.

43. Edward Casey, *The World at a Glance* (Bloomington: Indiana University Press, 2007), 312.

44. For more on the significance of minute observed details or momentary "microexpressions," specifically in James's late fiction, see Rivky Mondal, "Henry James and the Device of the Observer: A Study on Microexpressions," *Henry James Review* 41, no. 1 (2020): 15–23.

45. James, *Portrait of a Lady*, 356, 355.

46. Henry James, *Henry James: Essays on Art and Drama*, ed. Peter Rawlings (Aldershot: Scolar Press, 1996), 164.

47. Jules-Antoine Castagnary, in *Le Siècle*, June 28, 1879, quoted in George Heard Hamilton, *Manet and His Critics* (New York: Norton, 1969), 215.

48. Michael Fried, *Manet's Modernism, or The Face of Painting in the 1860s* (Chicago: University of Chicago Press, 1996), 314.

49. Jonathan Crary, *Suspensions of Perception: Attention, Spectacle, and Modern Culture* (Cambridge, MA: MIT Press, 1999), 90–91 (italics in the original).

50. James, *Portrait of a Lady*, 354.

51. Crary, *Suspensions of Perception*, 93.

52. We look away, according to Terada, "when we want to create distance between ourselves and the given world, and this distance reads as a failure to endorse the given world. . . . The discourse of mere phenomenality stops short of objection: it only registers a wish to be relieved for a moment of the coercion to accept whatever one does not dispute." Rei

Terada, *Looking Away: Phenomenality and Dissatisfaction, Kant to Adorno* (Cambridge, MA: Harvard University Press, 2009), 3.

53. Erving Goffman, *Relations in Public: Microstudies of the Public Order* (New York: Harper & Row, 1971), 5.

54. Fried, *Manet's Modernism*, 405.

55. William James, *The Principles of Psychology* (New York: Dover, 1950), 1:444.

56. See Ross Posnock, *The Trial of Curiosity: Henry James, William James, and the Challenge of Modernity* (New York: Oxford University Press, 1991), which remains one of the best intellectual histories of the James brothers and accounts of their respective psychological and ideological theories of self.

57. James, *Portrait of a Lady*, 14.

58. Dorrit Cohn, *Transparent Minds: Narrative Modes for Presenting Consciousness in Fiction* (Princeton, NJ: Princeton University Press, 1978), 130.

59. Terada, *Looking Away*, 113.

60. James, *Portrait of a Lady*, 7–8.

61. James, *Portrait of a Lady*, 343, 464, 456.

62. Kate Stanley's study of surprise in American literature is useful in thinking through Jamesian moments like Isabel's vision, especially because Stanley devalues the assumption that surprise necessarily means disabling shock or rupture. Her reading of Lambert Strether's climactic realization in *The Ambassadors* shows how James blurs temporal modes to make perceptual revelation something already anticipated yet only recognized after the event. This strikes me as applicable to *The Portrait of a Lady* as well, and what I am calling its colliding modalities. See Kate Stanley, *Practices of Surprise in American Literature after Emerson* (Cambridge: Cambridge University Press, 2018).

63. See Peter Stowell, *Literary Impression, James and Chekhov* (Athens: University of Georgia Press, 1980), which connects literary Impressionism as a style to Lambert Strether's moral-perceptual development in *The Ambassadors*. Zachary Seager argues, in a reading of the novel's famous climax that departs from Impressionism as a contextual and interpretive heuristic, that James contrasts the novel's "art of duration" with Impressionist painting's "art of the instant." Zachary Seager, "Painting, Fiction, and 'the *Real Lapse of Time*' in *The Ambassadors*," *Henry James Review* 41, no. 2 (2020): 137.

64. Linda Nochlin, "Impressionist Portraits and the Construction of Modern Identity," in *Renoir's Portraits: Impressions of an Age*, ed. Colin B. Bailey (New Haven: Yale University Press, 1997), 55.

65. Crary, *Suspensions of Perception*, 113.

66. Casey, *World at a Glance*, 329.

67. James, *Portrait of a Lady*, 362, 17, 18.

68. Laurence Bedwell Holland, *The Expense of Vision: Essays on the Craft of Henry James* (Princeton, NJ: Princeton University Press, 1964), 46.

69. James, *Portrait of a Lady*, 17, 25, 26.

70. Holland, *Expense of Vision*, 48 (italics in the original).

71. James, *Portrait of a Lady*, 28, 465, 471, 485, 430, 430–31. The art and ruins of Rome are, in Adeline Tintner's evocative phrase, just one corner of James's "museum world," to which Tintner is our guide in *The Museum World of Henry James* (Ann Arbor, MI: UMI Research Press, 1986).

72. James, *Portrait of a Lady*, 7, 5 (italics in the original), 490.

73. James, *Portrait of a Lady*, 7.

74. Porter, *Seeing and Being*, 125.

75. Carol Shloss's *In Visible Light: Photography and the American Writer, 1840–1940* (New York: Oxford University Press, 1987) follows Porter on this theme in Hawthorne, James, and beyond, with specific focus on the observational ethics of photographic realism.

76. Sharon Cameron, *Thinking in Henry James* (Chicago: University of Chicago Press, 1989), 77 (italics in the original). According to Christine Britzolakis, in her reading of *What Maisie Knew*, James's "untethering of consciousness from the subjectivity of an individual, and its repositioning within a relational field, is a necessary byproduct of the new social, spatial and visual conditions of the metropolis." Christine Britzolakis, "Technologies of Vision in Henry James's *What Maisie Knew*," *Novel* 34, no. 3 (2001): 369.

77. Daniel T. O'Hara looks at James's "The Story of a Masterpiece" (1868) and "The Liar" (1888), two stories about an artist betraying the "real" character of another in a portrait, to argue that James "seductively dangles" his art "between realism and vision," ironically mediating while never accepting the optical-realistic or visionary-allegorical aesthetics alternatively expected of him. Daniel T. O'Hara, *Visions of Global America and the Future of Critical Reading* (Columbus: Ohio State University Press, 2009), 118.

78. Leon Edel, *Henry James: The Treacherous Years: 1895–1901* (Philadelphia: Lippincott, 1969), 343, quoted in Ralph F. Bogardus, *Pictures and Texts: Henry James, A. L. Coburn, and New Ways of Seeing in Literary Culture* (Ann Arbor: UMI Research Press, 1984), 132.

79. James, "The Real Thing," 195 (italics in the original), 192, 197, 198. For more on James's career-long negotiations (and antagonisms) with illustrators, publishers, and editors over the interplay of word and image in print, see Amy Tucker, *The Illustration of the Master* (Stanford, CA: Stanford University Press, 2010).

80. Alexandra K. Wettlaufer, *In the Mind's Eye: The Visual Impulse in Diderot, Baudelaire and Ruskin* (Amsterdam: Rodopi, 2003), 111.

81. Jennifer A. Greenhill, "Illustrating the Shadow of Doubt: Henry James, Blindness, and 'The Real Thing,'" *Word & Image Interactions* 6 (2009): 262.

82. Brown, *Sense of Things*, 141.

83. Alan Spiegel calls the Flaubertian visual detail "adventitious" to relate the way it "usually takes the form of an accident, the causes of which are not readily apparent; an accident that is seemingly without a narrative function and cannot be easily related to any pattern of artistic inevitability." Alan Spiegel, *Fiction and the Camera Eye: Visual Consciousness in Film and the Modern Novel* (Charlottesville: University Press of Virginia, 1976), 90. It is precisely the lack of narrative function that Roland Barthes argues produces the realist novel's "reality effect," where the concept signified by the adventitious detail is nothing other than realism itself. See Barthes, "The Reality Effect," in *The Rustle of Language*, trans. Richard Howard (Berkeley: University of California Press, 1989), 141–48. At times, including in "The Real Thing," James disparages these sorts of details as aesthetic obstacles. For an account of the development of novelistic realism that maintains "veridictory" truth or truthfulness beyond the relative meaninglessness of reality effects, see Ilya Kliger, *The Narrative Shape of Truth: Veridiction in Modern European Literature* (University Park: Pennsylvania State University Press, 2011). For an account of shifting descriptive techniques—from object-visualization to relationality—in the modernist novel (including James), see Dora Zhang, *Strange Likeness: Description and the Modernist Novel* (Chicago: Chicago University Press, 2020).

84. Henry James, *What Maisie Knew* (New York: Penguin, 1985), 24.

85. Spiegel, *Fiction and the Camera Eye*, 55–56, 58.

86. For more on the visual epistemology of the snapshot in *Maisie*, see Angela Berkley, "Snapshot Seeing, Kodak Fiends, Child Photographers, and Henry James's *What Maisie Knew*," *Modern Fiction Studies* 61, no. 3 (2015): 375–403.

87. James, *What Maisie Knew*, 166.

88. On "the motions of a mind that is trying to solve a mystery," see Spiegel, *Fiction and the Camera Eye*, 59. On the "medial child" in James, a concept that explains how children mediate experiences in fiction and also mediate relationships to books and other media, see Patricia Crain, *Reading Children: Literacy, Property, and the Dilemmas of Childhood in Nineteenth-Century America* (Philadelphia: University of Pennsylvania Press, 2016).

89. Sheila Teahan, "*What Maisie Knew* and the Improper Third Person," in *"The Turn of the Screw" and "What Maisie Knew,"* ed. Neil Cornwell and Maggie Malone (New York: St. Martin's, 1998), 221.

90. James, *Art of the Novel*, 144.

91. James, *The Notebooks*, 149. "It is not a mere coincidence," writes Boosung Kim, "that only six days after James expressed his writerly ambition for a new literary method to 'show' to his readers what takes place before a child through the child's eyes the Lumière brothers, with their newly invented Cinématographe, showed projected moving images to the public." Boosung Kim, "Shock and Astonishment: The Rise of Cinema Spectatorship and *What Maisie Knew*," *Henry James Review* 40, no. 1 (2019): 1–2. See Kim, "Shock and Astonishment," for more on the connection between *What Maisie Knew* and the contemporaneous emergence of cinema and its modes of spectatorship.

92. James, *What Maisie Knew*, 27 (italics in the original).

93. For more on James and the phenomenologists, see Paul B. Armstrong, *The Phenomenology of Henry James* (Chapel Hill: University of North Carolina Press, 1983).

94. James, *What Maisie Knew*, 39.

95. Britzolakis, "Technologies of Vision," 375–76.

96. Karl Marx and Friedrich Engels, "The German Ideology," in *The Marx-Engels Reader*, 2nd ed., ed. Robert C. Tucker (New York: W. W. Norton, 1978), 154.

97. James, *What Maisie Knew*, 101.

98. Andrew H. Miller, *Novels behind Glass: Commodity Culture and Victorian Narrative* (Cambridge: Cambridge University Press, 1995), 6.

99. Britzolakis, "Technologies of Vision," 370.

100. The following consideration of portability is drawn from Zachary Tavlin and Bob Hodges, "Portable Vision, Form, and Objects in Henry James," in *Portable Prose: The Novel and the Everyday*, eds. Cogle et al. (Lanham, MD: Lexington Books, 2019). In that chapter we extend our analysis of portability and diagrammatic seeing to other modes of Jamesian writing. For a longer discussion of Victorian-era cultural portability, see John Plotz, *Portable Property: Victorian Culture on the Move* (Princeton, NJ: Princeton University Press, 2009).

101. For an account of Jamesian style in the wake of the *Guy Domville* fiasco, see Kurnick's reading of James's subsequent fictions, formal and generic experiments that bring a "phantom theater" into the house of the novel. Kurnick refers to theater and performance as a "desired but unachieved referent" in James's fiction. David Kurnick, *Empty Houses: Theatrical Failure and the Novel* (Princeton, NJ: Princeton University Press, 2012), 112, 119.

102. James, *Essays on Art and Drama*, 524–25. For more on James's artistic predicament in the face of mass vernacular photography, see Peter Rawlings, "A Kodak Refraction of Henry James's 'The Real Thing,'" *Journal of American Studies* 32, no. 3 (1998): 447–62.

103. James to Rhoda Broughton, January 1, 1900, quoted in Leon Edel, *Henry James: A Life* (New York: Harper & Row, 1985), 501.

104. Henry James, *Henry James: A Life in Letters*, ed. Philip Horne (New York: Viking, 1999), 405–6.

105. Michael Anesko, *Generous Mistakes: Incidents of Error in Henry James* (Oxford: Oxford University Press, 2017), 10.

106. For accounts of Jamesian transatlanticism focused more on his place in larger modernist literary networks, see Anne Fernihough, *Freewomen and Supermen: Edwardian Radicals and Literary Modernism* (Oxford: Oxford University Press, 2013); Robert Burden, *Travel, Modernism, and Modernity* (Farnham: Ashgate, 2015); and Megan Quigley, *Modernist Fiction and Vagueness* (New York: Cambridge University Press, 2015).

107. Jordan Brower, "'Written with the Movies in Mind': Twentieth-Century American Literature and Transmedial Possibility," *Modern Language Quarterly* 78, no. 2 (2017): 258.

108. For more on what the "Kodak era" might mean, see Nancy Martha West, *Kodak and the Lens of Nostalgia* (Charlottesville: University Press of Virginia, 2000), which argues for an expansive account of kodaking as a marketing logic that offered new memory forms for domestic life and American culture.

109. James, letter to editor, *Century Magazine*, quoted in Leon Edel, *Henry James: The Middle Years, 1882–1895* (New York: Avon, 1962), 156–57.

110. Edel, *Henry James: A Life*, 465.

111. James, *Essays on Art and Drama*, 164, 164–65.

112. Henry James, *The Painter's Eye: Notes and Essays on the Pictorial Arts*, ed. John L. Sweeney (Madison: University of Wisconsin Press, 1989), 217.

113. Winner, *Henry James and the Visual Arts*, 50.

114. Joel Isaacson, "Constable, Duranty, Mallarmé, Impressionism, Plein Air, and Forgetting," *Art Bulletin* 76, no. 3 (1994): 432–33. Isaacson is quoting from Emile Blémont, "Les Impressionnistes," *Le Rappel*, April 9, 1876, in J. Letheve, *Impressionnistes et symbolistes devant la Presse* (Paris, 1959), 79; A. Descubes [Amedee Descubes-Desgueraines], "L'Exposition des Impressionnistes," *Gazette des lettres, des sciences et des arts*, I, April 20, 1877, 185; and "Les Peintres impressionnistes," Paris, 1878, in Théodore Duret, *Critique d'avant-garde*, Paris, 1885, 70, 73.

115. Wendy Graham, "Pictures for Texts," *Henry James Review* 24, no. 1 (2003): 15.

116. James, *Essays on Art and Drama*, 430.

117. Graham, "Pictures for Texts," 16.

118. Paul B. Armstrong, "Reading James's Prefaces and Reading James," in *Henry James's New York Edition: The Construction of Authorship*, ed. David McWhirter (Stanford: Stanford University Press, 1995), 131, 133.

119. James, *Art of the Novel*, 344–45, 332.

120. James, *Art of the Novel*, 345.

121. Henry James, *The Letters of Henry James*, ed. Leon Edel, vol. 4, *1895–1916* (Cambridge, MA: Harvard University Press, 1984), 428.

122. David McWhirter, "'The Whole Chain of Relation and Responsibility': Henry James and the New York Edition," in *Henry James's New York Edition: The Construction of Authorship*, ed. David McWhirter (Stanford: Stanford University Press, 1995), 8.

123. Anna Kornbluh, "The Realist Blueprint," *Henry James Review* 36, no. 3 (2015): 202.

124. John Bender and Michael Marrinan, *The Culture of Diagram* (Stanford: Stanford University Press, 2010), 23.

125. James, *Art of the Novel*, 101, 332.

126. Kendall Johnson, *Henry James and the Visual* (New York: Cambridge University Press, 2007), 5.

127. James, *Art of the Novel*, 333. For more on James's, Coburn's, and Joseph Pennell's attraction to London, see Douglas Tallack, "'One walked of course with one's eyes greatly open' (Henry James): London Sights in Alvin Langdon Coburn, Henry James, and Joseph Pennell," *Textual Practice* 24, no. 2 (2010): 197–222.

128. Kendall Johnson, "Visual Culture," in *Henry James in Context*, ed. David McWhirter (Cambridge: Cambridge University Press, 2010), 371.

129. Walter Benjamin, "The Work of Art in the Age of Mechanical Reproduction" [1935], in *Illuminations*, trans. Harry Zohn and ed. Hannah Arendt (New York: Schocken Books, 1969), 221, 223, 224.

130. Holland, *Expense of Vision*, x (italics in the original).

131. James, "Art of Fiction," 10.

132. Charles Scott Sherrington's influential work on the nervous system, just prior to James's late phase, described a seeing subject in constant motion amid the flow of urban life's intense velocities. "Part of Sherrington's task was to explain the human organism's capacity to integrate in a functional and practical way the overwhelmingly complex amount of sensory information in a given milieu." Jonathan Crary, *Techniques of the Observer: On Vision and Modernity in the Nineteenth Century* (Cambridge, MA: MIT Press, 1990), 348. Sherrington linked human vision—already dispersed among "137 million separate 'seeing' elements spread out in the sheet of the retina"—to motor behavior, with "wide tracts of musculature as a whole," with the entire body's movement through the world. Charles Scott Sherrington, *The Integrative Action of the Nervous System* (New York: Charles Scribner's Sons, 1906), 234.

133. For more on commodification in James, especially on the representational value he found in shops, shopping, and shopkeepers, see Miranda El-Rayess, *Henry James and the Culture of Consumption* (Cambridge: Cambridge University Press, 2014). See Patricia McKee, *Reading Constellations: Urban Modernity in Victorian Fiction* (Oxford: Oxford University Press, 2014), for a Benjaminian take on representations of urban experience in James, Dickens, and Hardy as collective antidote to capitalist development (even as the urban also exposes the damage wrought by that development).

134. Royal Cortissoz, *John La Farge: A Memoir and a Study* (New York: Houghton Mifflin, 1911), 117.

135. Bogardus, *Pictures and Texts*, 133 (italics in the original).

136. Henry James, *A Small Boy and Others* (New York: Charles Scribner's Sons, 1913), 308.

137. James, *Art of the Novel*, 59–60.

138. Bogardus, *Pictures and Texts*, 134.

139. Charles Baudelaire, *The Mirror of Art: Critical Studies*, trans. and ed. Jonathan Mayne (New York: Phaidon, 1955), 230.

140. Charles Baudelaire, *The Painter of Modern Life and Other Essays*, trans. and ed. Jonathan Mayne (New York: Da Capo, 1986), 16–17, 12.

141. Paul Virilio, *The Vision Machine* (London: British Film Institute, 1994), 21 (italics in the original).

142. Henry James, *The American Scene*, ed. Leon Edel (Bloomington: Indiana University Press, 1968), 116.

143. Thierry de Duve, *Pictorial Nominalism: On Marcel Duchamp's Passage from Painting to the Readymade*, trans. Dana Polan and Thierry de Duve (Minneapolis: University of Minnesota Press, 1991), 77.

144. Paul Cézanne, *Letters*, ed. John Rewald (London: Bruno Cassirer, 1941), 262.

145. Crary, *Suspensions of Perception*, 355.

Coda

Epigraph: Emily Dickinson, *The Poems of Emily Dickinson: Variorum Edition*, ed. R. W. Franklin (Cambridge, MA: Belknap Press of Harvard University Press, 1998); Willem de Kooning, "Content Is a Glimpse . . . ," in *Willem de Kooning*, ed. Thomas B. Hess (New York: Museum of Modern Art, 1969), 148; The Pixies, "Debaser," *Doolittle* (1989).

1. Dai Vaughan, "Let There Be Lumière," in *Early Cinema: Space Frame Narrative*, ed. Thomas Elsaesser (London: British Film Institute, 1990), 65, 66.

2. Noël Burch, *Life to Those Shadows*, trans. Ben Brewster (Berkeley: University of California Press, 1990), 18.

3. Lumière quoted in Georges Sadoul, *Louis Lumière* (Paris: Seghers, 1964), 107, cited in Burch, *Life to Those Shadows*, 19.

4. Lorraine Daston and Peter Galison, *Objectivity* (Cambridge: MIT Press, 2007), 17.

5. Christian Metz, "The Cinema: Language or Language System?" in *Film Language: A Semiotics of the Cinema*, trans. Michael Taylor (Chicago: University of Chicago Press, 1991), 49.

6. André Gaudreault, "Showing and Telling: Image and Word in Early Cinema," in *Early Cinema: Space Frame Narrative*, ed. Thomas Elsaesser (London: British Film Institute, 1990), 277.

7. Van C. Lee, "The Value of a Lecture," *Moving Picture World* 8 (1908): 93.

8. Susan McCabe, *Cinematic Modernism: Modernist Poetry and Film* (Cambridge: Cambridge University Press, 2005), 32. McCabe is quoting from Sergei Eisenstein, *Film Form: Essays in Film Theory*, ed. and trans. Jay Leyda (New York: Harcourt, Brace, 1949), 29.

9. Hugh Kenner, *The Pound Era* (Berkeley: University of California Press, 1973), 367.

10. Amy Lowell, *Tendencies in Modern American Poetry* (New York: Macmillan, 1920), 240, 239–40.

11. Ezra Pound, "A Retrospect," in *Literary Essays of Ezra Pound*, ed. T. S. Eliot (New York: New Directions, 1954), 3.

12. Ezra Pound, *Selected Poems* (New York: New Directions, 1957), 35.

13. Brian Reed, *Phenomenal Reading: Essays on Modern and Contemporary Poetics* (Tuscaloosa: University of Alabama Press, 2012), 66.

14. William Carlos Williams, *Spring and All* (New York: New Directions, 2011), 54.

15. Béla Balázs, *Early Film Theory*, ed. Erica Carter, trans. Rodney Livingstone (New York: Berghahn, 2010), 11 (italics in the original).

16. Williams, *Spring and All*, 3.

17. William Carlos Williams, *The Great American Novel*, in *Imaginations* (New York: New Directions, 1971), 159–60.

18. Williams, *Great American Novel*, 175.

19. William Carlos Williams, *Paterson* (New York: New Directions, 1995), 54.

20. Williams, *Spring and All*, 50, 12.

21. Williams, *Spring and All*, 30.

22. Bonnie Costello, *Planets on Tables: Poetry, Still Life, and the Turning World* (Ithaca, NY: Cornell University Press, 2008), 55.

23. Williams, *Spring and All*, 31.

24. McCabe, *Cinematic Modernism*, 127.

25. Williams, *Spring and All*, 47, 26, 48.

26. Williams, *Spring and All*, 75, 76–7.

27. J. Hillis Miller, *Poets of Reality: Six Twentieth-Century Writers* (Cambridge, MA: Harvard University Press, 1965), 308.

28. Linda Williams, *Figures of Desire: A Theory and Analysis of Surrealist Film* (Berkeley: University of California Press, 1981), 71.

29. Luis Buñuel, "Notes on the Making of *Un chien andalou*," in *Art in Cinema: A Symposium on the Avantgarde Film*, ed. Frank Stauffacher (New York: Arno Press, 1968), 30.

30. Georges Bataille, "The 'Lugubrious Game,'" in *Visions of Excess: Selected Writings, 1927–1939*, ed. Allan Stoekl (Minneapolis: University of Minnesota Press, 1985), 29.

31. Martin Jay, *Downcast Eyes: The Denigration of Vision in Twentieth-Century French Thought* (Berkeley: University of California Press, 1993), 259.

32. Buñuel, "Notes," 29.

33. Hugh Kenner to Mike Weaver, quoted in Mike Weaver, *William Carlos Williams: An American Background* (Cambridge: Cambridge University Press, 1971), 85–86.

34. T. Hugh Crawford, "Walking with William Carlos Williams," *William Carlos Williams Review* 34, no. 2 (2017): 107.

35. Williams, *Paterson*, 78.

36. Williams, *Paterson*, 3.

37. Robert Frank, "Robert Frank," *Camera Austria* 22 (1987): 19.

BIBLIOGRAPHY

Abrams, Robert. *Landscape and Ideology in American Renaissance Literature: Topographies of Skepticism*. Cambridge: Cambridge University Press, 2004.

Adler, Natalie. "Dickinson's Mastery." *Emily Dickinson Journal* 25, no. 2 (2016): 1–23.

Agassiz, Louis. "Methods of Study in Natural History." *Atlantic Monthly* 9, no. 51 (1862): 446–60.

Alford, Lucy. *Forms of Poetic Attention*. New York: Columbia University Press, 2020.

Allen, Thomas M. *A Republic in Time: Temporality and Social Imagination in Nineteenth-Century America*. Chapel Hill: University of North Carolina Press, 2008.

Alpers, Svetlana. *The Art of Describing: Dutch Art in the Seventeenth Century*. Chicago: University of Chicago Press, 1983.

Anesko, Michael. *Generous Mistakes: Incidents of Error in Henry James*. Oxford: Oxford University Press, 2017.

Arac, Jonathan. *The Emergence of American Literary Narrative, 1820–1860*. Cambridge, MA: Harvard University Press, 2005.

Armstrong, Nancy. *Desire and Domestic Fiction: A Political History of the Novel*. Oxford: Oxford University Press, 1990.

Armstrong, Paul B. *The Phenomenology of Henry James*. Chapel Hill: University of North Carolina Press, 1983.

———. "Reading James's Prefaces and Reading James." In *Henry James's New York Edition: The Construction of Authorship*, edited by David McWhirter, 125–37. Stanford, CA: Stanford University Press, 1995.

Arsić, Branka. *On Leaving: A Reading in Emerson*. Cambridge, MA: Harvard University Press, 2010.

———. "Thing-Poems: On Marta Werner's and Jen Bervin's *The Gorgeous Nothings: Emily Dickinson's Envelope Poems*." *J19* 3, no. 2 (Fall 2015): 236–47.

Auerbach, Erich. *Mimesis: The Representation of Reality in Western Literature*. Translated by Willard R. Trask. Princeton, NJ: Princeton University Press, 1953.

Auerbach, Jonathan. "Executing the Model: Painting, Sculpture, and Romance-Writing in Hawthorne's *The Marble Faun*." *ELH* 47, no. 1 (Spring 1980): 103–20.

Baker, Anne. "Word, Image, and National Geography: Panorama Pamphlets and Manifest Destiny." In *American Literary Geographies*, edited by Hsuan Hsu and Martin Brueckner, 89–108. Newark: University of Delaware Press, 2007.

Baker, Jennifer J. "Hawthorne's Picturesque at Home and Abroad." *Studies in Romanticism* 55, no. 3 (Fall 2016): 417–44.

Balázs, Béla. *Early Film Theory*. Edited by Erica Carter. Translated by Rodney Livingstone. New York: Berghahn, 2010.

Baldwin, James. "Everybody's Protest Novel." In *James Baldwin: Collected Essays*, edited by Toni Morrison, Library of America no. 98, 11–18. New York: Library of America, 1998.

Banta, Martha. *Henry James: An Alien's "History" of America*. Rome: Sapienza Università Editrice, 2016.

Baraka, Amiri. *Blues People: Negro Music in White America*. New York: Harper, 2002.

Barnes, Elizabeth. *States of Sympathy: Seduction and Democracy in the American Novel*. New York: Columbia University Press, 1997.

Barrett, Louise. *Beyond the Brain: How Body and Environment Shape Animal and Human Minds*. Princeton, NJ: Princeton University Press, 2011.

Barthes, Roland. *Camera Lucida: Reflections on Photography*. Translated by Richard Howard. New York: Farrar, Straus, and Giroux, 2010.

———. "The Reality Effect." In *The Rustle of Language*, translated by Richard Howard, 141–48. Berkeley: University of California Press, 1989.

Bataille, Georges. "The 'Lugubrious Game.'" In *Visions of Excess: Selected Writings, 1927–1939*, edited by Allan Stoekl, 24–30. Minneapolis: University of Minnesota Press, 1985.

———. *Story of the Eye*. San Francisco: City Lights, 1987.

Baudelaire, Charles. *The Mirror of Art: Critical Studies*. Translated by Jonathan Mayne. New York: Phaidon, 1955.

———. *The Painter of Modern Life and Other Essays*. Translated and edited by Jonathan Mayne. New York: Da Capo, 1986.

Baumgarten, Alexander Gottlieb. *Aesthetica*. Turnhout, Belgium: Brepols, 2010.

Baym, Nina. *Novels, Readers, and Reviewers: Responses to Fiction in Antebellum America*. Ithaca, NY: Cornell University Press, 1984.

Beeston, Alix. *In and Out of Sight: Modernist Writing and the Photographic Unseen*. New York: Oxford University Press, 2018.

Bellion, Wendy. *Citizen Spectator: Art, Illusion, and Visual Perception in Early National America*. Chapel Hill: University of North Carolina Press, 2011.

Bender, John, and Michael Marrinan. *The Culture of Diagram*. Stanford, CA: Stanford University Press, 2010.

Benjamin, Walter. *Arcades Project*. Translated by Howard Eiland and Kevin McLaughlin. Cambridge, MA: Harvard University Press, 1999.

———. "The Work of Art in the Age of Mechanical Reproduction." In *Illuminations*, translated by Harry Zohn and edited by Hannah Arendt, 217–51. New York: Schocken Books, 1969.

Bennett, Joshua. *Being Property Once Myself: Blackness and the End of Man*. Cambridge, MA: Harvard University Press, 2020.

Bennett, Paula Bernat. "Emily Dickinson and Her Peers." In *A Companion to American Literature and Culture*, edited by Paul Lauter, 284–315. Malden, MA: Blackwell, 2010.

Bentley, Nancy. *The Ethnography of Manners: Hawthorne, James, Wharton*. Cambridge: Cambridge University Press, 1995.

Bercovitch, Sacvan. *The American Jeremiad*. Madison: University of Wisconsin Press, 1978.

———. "The Image of America: From Hermeneutic to Symbolism." In *Early American*

Literature: A Collection of Critical Essays, edited by Michael T. Gilmore, 158–67. Englewood Cliffs, NJ: Prentice-Hall, 1980.

———. *The Puritan Origins of the American Self*. New Haven, CT: Yale University Press, 1975.

Berger, John. *Ways of Seeing*. London: Penguin, 1972.

Bergson, Henri. *Time and Free Will: An Essay on the Immediate Data of Consciousness*. Translated by Frank Pogson. New York: Harper, 1960.

Berkley, Angela. "Snapshot Seeing, Kodak Fiends, Child Photographers, and Henry James's *What Maisie Knew*." *Modern Fiction Studies* 61, no. 3 (2015): 375–403.

Berlant, Lauren. *The Anatomy of National Fantasy: Hawthorne, Utopia, and Everyday Life*. Chicago: University of Chicago Press, 1991.

———. "Poor Eliza." *American Literature* 70, no. 3 (September 1998): 635–68.

Bernhard, Mary Elizabeth Kromer. "Lost and Found: Emily Dickinson's Unknown Daguerreotypist." *New England Quarterly* 72, no. 4 (1999): 594–601.

Bersani, Leo. *A Future for Astyanax: Characters and Desire in Literature*. New York: Little, Brown, 1976.

Berthold, Dennis. "Charles Brockden Brown, *Edgar Huntly*, and the Origins of the American Picturesque." *William and Mary Quarterly* 41, no. 1 (January 1984): 62–84.

Bervin, Jen. "Studies in Scale." In *Emily Dickinson: The Gorgeous Nothings*, edited by Marta Werner and Jen Bervin, 8–14. New York: New Directions, 2013.

Best, Stephen M. *The Fugitive's Properties: Law and the Poetics of Possession*. Chicago: University of Chicago Press, 2004.

Best, Stephen, and Sharon Marcus. "Surface Reading: An Introduction." *Representations* 108, no. 1 (November 2009): 1–21.

Betjemann, Peter. *Talking Shop: The Language of Craft in an Age of Consumption*. Charlottesville: University of Virginia Press, 2011.

Blackmur, R. P. "Emily Dickinson: Notes on Prejudice and Fact." *Southern Review* 3, no. 2 (1937): 323–47.

Blackwood, Sarah. *The Portrait's Subject: Inventing Inner Life in the Nineteenth-Century United States*. Chapel Hill: University of North Carolina Press, 2019.

Blower, Brooke, and Mark Philip Bradley, eds. *The Familiar Made Strange: American Icons and Artifacts after the Transnational Turn*. Ithaca, NY: Cornell University Press, 2015.

Bogardus, Ralph F. *Pictures and Texts: Henry James, A. L. Coburn, and New Ways of Seeing in Literary Culture*. Ann Arbor: UMI Research Press, 1984.

Boggs, Colleen Glenney. *Animalia Americana: Animal Representations and Biopolitical Subjectivity*. New York: Columbia University Press, 2013.

———. "Emily Dickinson's Posthuman Worlds: Biopoetics and Environmental Subjectivity." In *The New Emily Dickinson Studies*, edited by Michelle Kohler, 118–35. Cambridge: Cambridge University Press, 2019.

Boime, Albert. *The Magisterial Gaze: Manifest Destiny and American Landscape Painting c. 1830–1865*. Washington, DC: Smithsonian, 1991.

Britzolakis, Christine. "Technologies of Vision in Henry James's *What Maisie Knew*." *Novel* 34, no. 3 (2001): 369–90.

Brooks, Peter. *Henry James Goes to Paris*. Princeton, NJ: Princeton University Press, 2007.

Brower, Jordan. "'Written with the Movies in Mind': Twentieth-Century American Literature and Transmedial Possibility." *Modern Language Quarterly* 78, no. 2 (2017): 243–73.

Brown, Bill. *A Sense of Things: The Object Matter of American Literature*. Chicago: University of Chicago Press, 2003.

Brown, Kimberly Juanita. *The Repeating Body: Slavery's Visual Resonance in the Contemporary*. Durham, NC: Duke University Press, 2015.

Brownlee, Peter John. *The Commerce of Vision: Optical Culture and Perception in Antebellum America*. Philadelphia: University of Pennsylvania Press, 2018.

Brückner, Martin. *The Social Life of Maps in America, 1750–1860*. Chapel Hill: University of North Carolina Press, 2017.

Bryson, Norman. *Vision and Painting: The Logic of the Gaze*. New Haven, CT: Yale University Press, 1983.

Buñuel, Luis. "Notes on the Making of *Un chien andalou*." In *Art in Cinema: A Symposium on the Avantgarde Film*, edited by Frank Stauffacher, 29–30. New York: Arno Press, 1968.

Burch, Noël. *Life to Those Shadows*. Translated by Ben Brewster. Berkeley: University of California Press, 1990.

Burden, Robert. *Travel, Modernism, and Modernity*. Farnham: Ashgate, 2015.

Burrows, Stuart. *A Familiar Strangeness: American Fiction and the Language of Photography, 1839–1945*. Athens: University of Georgia Press, 2010.

Callahan, Monique-Adelle. *Between the Lines: Literary Transnationalism and African American Poetics*. Oxford: Oxford University Press, 2011.

Cameron, Sharon. *Choosing Not Choosing: Dickinson's Fascicles*. Chicago: University of Chicago Press, 1992.

———. *Lyric Time: Dickinson and the Limits of the Genre*. Baltimore: Johns Hopkins University Press, 1979.

———. *Thinking in Henry James*. Chicago: University of Chicago Press, 1989.

Carby, Hazel. *Reconstructing Womanhood: The Emergence of the Afro-American Woman Novelist*. Oxford: Oxford University Press, 1987.

Carton, Evan. *The Marble Faun: Hawthorne's Transformations*. New York: Twayne, 1992.

Case, Kristen. *American Pragmatism and Poetic Practice*. New York: Camden House, 2011.

Casey, Edward. *The World at a Glance*. Bloomington: Indiana University Press, 2007.

Castiglia, Christopher. *Interior States: Institutional Consciousness and the Inner Life of Democracy in the Antebellum United States*. Durham, NC: Duke University Press, 2008.

Castronovo, Russ. *Necro Citizenship: Death, Eroticism, and the Public Sphere in the Nineteenth-Century United States*. Durham, NC: Duke University Press, 2001.

Cavell, Stanley. "What's the Use of Calling Emerson a Pragmatist?" In *The Revival of Pragmatism*, edited by Morris Dickstein, 72–80. Durham, NC: Duke University Press, 1998.

Cavitch, Max. *American Elegy: The Poetry of Mourning from the Puritans to Whitman*. Minneapolis: University of Minnesota Press, 2007.

Cennini, Cennino d'Andrea. *The Craftsman's Handbook*. Translated by Daniel V. Thompson Jr. New York: Dover, 1954.

Cézanne, Paul. *Letters*. Edited by John Rewald. London: Bruno Cassirer, 1941.

Chaney, Michael A. *Fugitive Vision: Slave Image and Black Identity in Antebellum Narrative*. Bloomington: Indiana University Press, 2008.

Cheyfitz, Eric. "The Irresistibleness of Great Literature: Reconstructing Hawthorne's Politics." *American Literary History* 6 (1994): 539–58.

Chow, Juliana. "'Because I see—New Englandly—': Seeing Species in the Nineteenth-Century and Emily Dickinson's Regional Specificity." *ESQ* 60, no. 3 (2014): 413–49.

Clark, Andy, and David Chalmers. "The Extended Mind." *Analysis* 58, no. 1 (1998): 7–19.

———. *Supersizing the Mind: Embodiment, Action, and Cognitive Extension*. Oxford: Oxford University Press, 2008.

Clark, T. J. *The Painting of Modern Life: Paris in the Art of Manet and His Followers*. New York: A. A. Knopf, 1985.

Clinton, Dan. "Holographic Hawthorne." *J19* 3, no. 2 (Fall 2015): 413–21.

Cody, John. *After Great Pain: The Inner Life of Emily Dickinson*. Cambridge, MA: Harvard University Press, 1971.

Cohen, Michael C. "Generic Dickinson." In *The New Emily Dickinson Studies*, edited by Michelle Kohler, 33–48. Cambridge: Cambridge University Press, 2019.

———. *The Social Lives of Poems in Nineteenth-Century America*. Philadelphia: University of Pennsylvania Press, 2015.

Cohn, Dorrit. *Transparent Minds: Narrative Modes for Presenting Consciousness in Fiction*. Princeton, NJ: Princeton University Press, 1978.

Cohn, Elisha. *Still Life: Suspended Development in the Victorian Novel*. New York: Oxford University Press, 2016.

Colacurcio, Michael. *The Province of Piety: Moral History in Hawthorne's Early Tales*. Durham, NC: Duke University Press, 1995.

Coleridge, Samuel Taylor. *Biographia Literaria, or Biographical Sketches of My Literary Life and Opinion*. Edited by James Engell and Walter Jackson Bate. London: Routledge & Kegan Paul, 1983.

———. *The Notebooks of Samuel Taylor Coleridge*. Edited by Kathleen Coburn. New York: Pantheon, 1973.

Collins, Christopher. *The Uses of Observation: A Study of Correspondential Vision in the Writings of Emerson, Thoreau, and Whitman*. The Hague: Mouton, 1971.

Cortissoz, Royal. *John La Farge: A Memoir and a Study*. New York: Houghton Mifflin, 1911.

Costello, Bonnie. *Planets on Tables: Poetry, Still Life, and the Turning World*. Ithaca, NY: Cornell University Press, 2008.

Crain, Patricia. *Reading Children: Literacy, Property, and the Dilemmas of Childhood in Nineteenth-Century America*. Philadelphia: University of Pennsylvania Press, 2016.

Crary, Jonathan. *Suspensions of Perception: Attention, Spectacle, and Modern Culture*. Cambridge, MA: MIT Press, 1999.

———. *Techniques of the Observer: On Vision and Modernity in the Nineteenth Century*. Cambridge, MA: MIT Press, 1990.

Crawford, T. Hugh. "Walking with William Carlos Williams." *William Carlos Williams Review* 34, no. 2 (2017): 93–109.

Crews, Frederick. *The Sins of the Fathers: Hawthorne's Psychological Themes*. Oxford: Oxford University Press, 1966.

Crowe, Eyre. "Sketches in the Free and Slave States of America." *Illustrated London News*, September 27, 1856.

Crumbley, Paul, and Eleanor Elson Heginbotham, eds. *Dickinson's Fascicles: A Spectrum of Possibilities*. Columbus: Ohio State University Press, 2014.

Culler, Jonathan. "Apostrophe." *Diacritics* 7, no. 4 (Winter 1977): 59–69.

———. *The Pursuit of Signs: Semiotics, Literature, Deconstruction*. Ithaca, NY: Cornell University Press, 2002.

Cutter, Martha J. *The Illustrated Slave: Empathy, Graphic Narrative, and the Visual Culture of the Transatlantic Abolition Movement, 1800–1852*. Athens: University of Georgia Press, 2017.

Daston, Lorraine. "The Coup d'Oeil: On a Mode of Understanding." *Critical Inquiry* 45, no. 2 (Winter 2019): 307–31.

Daston, Lorraine, and Peter Galison. *Objectivity*. Cambridge, MA: MIT Press, 2007.

Davis, Theo. *Ornamental Aesthetics: The Poetry of Attending in Thoreau, Dickinson, and Whitman*. Oxford: Oxford University Press, 2016.

Davis, Whitney. *Replications: Archaeology, Art History, Psychoanalysis*. University Park: Pennsylvania State University Press, 1996.

de Duve, Thierry. *Pictorial Nominalism: On Marcel Duchamp's Passage from Painting to the Readymade*. Translated by Dana Polan and Thierry de Duve. Minneapolis: University of Minnesota Press, 1991.

de Kooning, Willem. "Content Is a Glimpse . . ." In *Willem de Kooning*, edited by Thomas B. Hess, 146–50. New York: Museum of Modern Art, 1969.

Deleuze, Gilles. *Cinema 1: The Movement-Image*. Translated by Hugh Tomlinson and Barbara Habberjam. London: Athlone, 1986.

Deppman, Jed. *Trying to Think with Emily Dickinson*. Amherst: University of Massachusetts Press, 2008.

Derrida, Jacques. *Memoirs of the Blind: The Self-Portrait and Other Ruins*. Translated by Pascale-Anne Brault and Michael Naas. Chicago: University of Chicago Press, 1993.

———. *The Truth in Painting*. Translated by Geoff Bennington and Ian McLeod. Chicago: University of Chicago Press, 1987.

Descartes, René. *The Philosophical Writings*. Vol. 1. Translated by John Cottingham, Robert Stoothoff, and Dugald Murdoch. Cambridge: Cambridge University Press, 1985.

Dickinson, Emily. *The Poems of Emily Dickinson: Variorum Edition*. Edited by R. W. Franklin. Cambridge, MA: Belknap Press of Harvard University Press, 1998.

———. *Selected Letters*. Edited by Thomas H. Johnson. Cambridge, MA: Belknap Press of Harvard University Press, 1986.

Diehl, Joanne Feit. "'Come Slowly—Eden': An Exploration of Women Poets and Their Muse." *Signs* 3, no. 3 (1978): 572–87.

Dinius, Marcy J. *The Camera and the Press: American Visual and Print Culture in the Age of the Daguerreotype*. Philadelphia: University of Pennsylvania Press, 2012.

Dobranski, Stephen. *Milton's Visual Imagination: Imagery in Paradise Lost*. Cambridge: Cambridge University Press, 2015.

Dobson, Joanne. *Dickinson and the Strategies of Reticence: The Woman Writer in Nineteenth-Century America*. Bloomington: Indiana University Press, 1989.

Dolan, Frederick M. *Allegories of America: Narratives, Metaphysics, Politics*. Ithaca, NY: Cornell University Press, 1994.

Dolis, John. "Hawthorne's Tactile Gaze and the Phenomenon of Depth." *Modern Language Quarterly* 44, no. 3 (1983): 267–84.

Douglass, Frederick. *My Bondage and My Freedom*. New York: Library of America, 1994.

Du Bois, W. E. B. *The Souls of Black Folk*. New York: Library of America, 1990.

Edel, Leon. *Henry James: A Life*. New York: Harper & Row, 1985.

———. *Henry James: The Middle Years, 1882–1895*. New York: Avon, 1962.

Edgerton, Samuel Y. *The Mirror, the Window, and the Telescope: How Renaissance Linear Perspective Changed Our View of the Universe*. Ithaca, NY: Cornell University Press, 2009.

Edwards, Jonathan. *A Jonathan Edwards Reader*. Edited by John E. Smith, Harry S. Stout, and Kenneth P. Minkema. New Haven, CT: Yale University Press, 1995.

Eguchi, Tomoko. *Ethical Aestheticism in the Early Works of Henry James*. Newcastle-upon-Tyne: Cambridge Scholars, 2016.

Elbert, Monika M., ed. *Nathaniel Hawthorne in Context*. Cambridge: Cambridge University Press, 2018.

Elkins, James. "Marks, Traces, *Traits*, Contours, *Orli*, and *Splendores*: Nonsemiotic Elements in Pictures." *Critical Inquiry* 21, no. 4 (1995): 822–60.

———. *What Painting Is*. New York: Routledge, 1999.

El-Rayess, Miranda. *Henry James and the Culture of Consumption*. Cambridge: Cambridge University Press, 2014.

Emerson, Ralph Waldo. *Essays and Lectures*. Edited by Joel Porte. New York: Library of America, 1983.

Epstein, Andrew. *Attention Equals Life: The Pursuit of the Everyday in Contemporary Poetry and Culture*. New York: Oxford University Press, 2016.

"Exhibition of the Royal Academy." *Art Journal* 21 (June 1861): 164–65.

Fanon, Frantz. *Peau noire, masques blancs*. Paris: Éditions du Seuil, 1952.

Farr, Judith. *The Passion of Emily Dickinson*. Cambridge, MA: Harvard University Press, 1992.

Fernie, Deanna. *Hawthorne, Sculpture, and the Question of American Art*. Burlington, VT: Ashgate, 2011.

Fernihough, Anne. *Freewomen and Supermen: Edwardian Radicals and Literary Modernism*. Oxford: Oxford University Press, 2013.

Fisher, Philip. *Hard Facts: Setting and Form in the American Novel*. Oxford: Oxford University Press, 1985.

Foucault, Michel. *The Birth of the Clinic: An Archaeology of Medical Perception*. Translated by Alan Sheridan. London: Tavistock, 1973. Originally published in French in 1963.

———. *Discipline and Punish: The Birth of the Prison*. Translated by Alan Sheridan. New York: Pantheon Books, 1977. Originally published in French in 1975.

François, Anne-Lise. *Open Secrets: The Literature of Uncounted Experience*. Stanford, CA: Stanford University Press, 2008.

———. "Ungiving Time: Reading Lyric by the Light of the Anthropocene." In *Anthropocene Reading: Literary History in Geologic Times*, edited by Tobias Menely and Jesse Oak Taylor, 239–58. University Park: Pennsylvania State University Press, 2017.

Frank, Robert. *The Americans*. Göttingen: Steidl, 2008.

———. "Robert Frank." *Camera Austria* 22 (1987): 17–23.

Freedgood, Elaine. *Worlds Enough: The Invention of Realism in the Victorian Novel*. Princeton, NJ: Princeton University Press, 2019.

Freedman, Jonathan L. *Professions of Taste: Henry James, British Aestheticism, and Commodity Culture*. Stanford, CA: Stanford University Press, 1990.

Fresonke, Kris. *West of Emerson: The Design of Manifest Destiny*. Berkeley: University of California Press, 2003.

Fried, Michael. *Absorption and Theatricality: Painting and Beholder in the Age of Diderot*. Berkeley: University of California Press, 1980.

———. *Manet's Modernism, or The Face of Painting in the 1860s*. Chicago: University of Chicago Press, 1996.

Fuss, Diana. *The Sense of an Interior: Four Writers and the Rooms That Shaped Them*. New York: Routledge, 2004.

Gaudreault, André. "Showing and Telling: Image and Word in Early Cinema." In *Early Cinema: Space Frame Narrative*, edited by Thomas Elsaesser, 274–81. London: British Film Institute, 1990.

Gerhardt, Christine. "'Often seen - but seldom felt': Emily Dickinson's Reluctant Ecology of Place." *Emily Dickinson Journal* 15, no. 1 (2006): 56–78.

———. *A Place for Humility: Whitman, Dickinson, and the Natural World*. Iowa: University of Iowa Press, 2014.

Gibson, James J. *The Perception of the Visual World*. Boston: Houghton Mifflin, 1950.

Gilmore, Michael T. *American Romanticism and the Marketplace*. Chicago: University of Chicago Press, 1985.

———. *Surface and Depth: The Quest for Legibility in American Culture*. Oxford: Oxford University Press, 2003.

Goethe, Johann Wolfgang von. *Faust: A Tragedy*. Translated by Bayard Taylor. Boston: Houghton Mifflin, 1906.

———. *Theory of Colours*. Translated by Charles Eastlake. Cambridge, MA: MIT Press, 1970.

Goffman, Erving. *Relations in Public: Microstudies of the Public Order*. New York: Harper & Row, 1971.

Gombrich, E. H. *Art and Illusion: A Study in the Psychology of Pictorial Representation*. New York: Pantheon, 1961.

Goodman, Nelson. *Languages of Art: An Approach to a Theory of Symbols*. Indianapolis: Hackett, 1976.

Gorra, Michael. *Portrait of a Novel: Henry James and the Making of an American Masterpiece*. New York: Liveright, 2012.

Graham, Maryemma. Introduction to *Complete Poems of Frances E. W. Harper*. Edited by Maryemma Graham, xxxiii–lvii. Oxford: Oxford University Press, 1988.

Graham, Wendy. "Pictures for Texts." *Henry James Review* 24, no. 1 (2003): 1–26.

Green, Keith Michael. *Bound to Respect: Antebellum Narratives of Black Imprisonment, Servitude, and Bondage, 1816–1861*. Tuscaloosa: University of Alabama Press, 2015.

Greene, Jack P. *The Intellectual Construction of America: Exceptionalism and Identity from 1492 to 1800*. Chapel Hill: University of North Carolina Press, 1993.

Greenhill, Jennifer A. "Illustrating the Shadow of Doubt: Henry James, Blindness, and 'The Real Thing.'" *Word & Image Interactions* 6 (2009): 261–80.

Greven, David. *The Fragility of Manhood: Hawthorne, Freud, and the Politics of Gender*. Columbus: Ohio State University Press, 2012.

———. "Incest and Intertextuality: Female Desire and Milton's Legacy in *The House of the Seven Gables*." *ESQ* 62, no. 1 (2016): 39–76.

Griffith, Clark. *The Long Shadow: Emily Dickinson's Tragic Poetry*. Princeton, NJ: Princeton University Press, 1964.

Grosz, Elizabeth. *Volatile Bodies: Toward a Corporeal Feminism*. Bloomington: Indiana University Press, 1994.

Gunning, Tom. "Hand and Eye: Excavating a New Technology of the Image in the Victorian Era." *Victorian Studies* 54, no. 3 (2012): 495–516.

Gurton-Wachter, Lily. *Watchwords: Romanticism and the Poetics of Attention*. Stanford, CA: Stanford University Press, 2016.

Haines, Christian P. *A Desire Called America: Biopolitics, Utopia, and the Literary Commons*. New York: Fordham University Press, 2019.

Hall, David D. *The Puritans: A Transatlantic History*. Princeton, NJ: Princeton University Press, 2019.

Hamilton, George Heard. *Manet and His Critics*. New York: Norton, 1969.

Hannah, Daniel. *Henry James, Impressionism, and the Public*. Farnham: Ashgate, 2013.

Harper, Frances Ellen Watkins. *A Brighter Coming Day: A Frances Ellen Watkins Harper Reader*. Edited by Frances Smith Foster. New York: City University of New York, 1990.

Harper, Lisa. "'The Eyes accost – and Sunder': Unveiling Emily Dickinson's Poetics." *Emily Dickinson Journal* 9, no. 1 (2000): 21–48.

Harper, Phillip Brian. *Abstractionist Aesthetics: Artistic Form and Social Critique in African American Culture*. New York: New York University Press, 2015.

Harris, Michael D. *Colored Pictures: Race and Visual Representation*. Chapel Hill: University of North Carolina Press, 2003.

Hartman, Saidiya. *Scenes of Subjection: Terror, Slavery, and Self-Making in Nineteenth-Century America*. Oxford: Oxford University Press, 1997.

Harvey, Eleanor Jones. *The Civil War and American Art*. New Haven, CT: Yale University Press, 2012.

Hawthorne, Nathaniel. *The Business of Reflection: Hawthorne in His Notebooks*. Edited by Robert Milder and Randall Fuller. Columbus: Ohio State University Press, 2009.

———. *The Centenary Edition of the Works of Nathaniel Hawthorne*. Vol. 1, *The Scarlet Letter*, edited by William Charvat. Columbus: Ohio State University Press, 1962.

———. *The Centenary Edition of the Works of Nathaniel Hawthorne*. Vol. 2, *The House of the Seven Gables*, edited by William Charvat. Columbus: Ohio State University Press, 1965.

———. *The Centenary Edition of the Works of Nathaniel Hawthorne*. Vol. 4, *The Marble Faun*, edited by William Charvat. Columbus: Ohio State University Press, 1962.

———. *The Centenary Edition of the Works of Nathaniel Hawthorne*. Vol. 8, *The American Notebooks*, edited by William Charvat. Columbus: Ohio State University Press, 1962.

———. *The Centenary Edition of the Works of Nathaniel Hawthorne*. Vol. 9, *Twice-told Tales*, edited by William Charvat. Columbus: Ohio State University Press, 1974.

———. *The Centenary Edition of the Works of Nathaniel Hawthorne*. Vol. 14, *The French and Italian Notebooks*, edited by Thomas Woodson. Columbus: Ohio State University Press, 1980.

———. *The Centenary Edition of the Works of Nathaniel Hawthorne*. Vol. 15, *The Letters, 1813–1843*, edited by Thomas Woodson, L. Neal Smith, and Norman Holmes Pearson. Columbus: Ohio State University Press, 1989.

He, Peiyuan, and Eileen Kowler. "The Role of Location Probability in the Programming of Saccades: Implications for 'Center-of-Gravity' Tendencies." *Vision Research* 29, no. 9 (1989): 1165–81.

Hegel, G. W. F. *Hegel's Aesthetics: Lectures on Fine Art*. Translated by T. M. Knox. Oxford: Oxford University Press, 1975.

Heidegger, Martin. *The Fundamental Concepts of Metaphysics: World, Finitude, Solitude*. Translated by William McNeill and Nicholas Walker. Bloomington: Indiana University Press, 2008.

Helmholtz, Hermann von. "Concerning the Perceptions in General." In *Helmholtz on Perception: Its Physiology and Development,* edited by R. M. Warren and R. P. Warren, 171–203. New York: Wiley, 1968.

———. "The Facts of Perception." In *Helmholtz on Perception: Its Physiology and Development,* edited by R. M. Warren and R. P. Warren, 207–46. New York: Wiley, 1968.

———. *Treatise on Physiological Optics.* 1925. 3 vols. Edited by James P. C. Southall. New York: Dover, 1962.

Hendler, Glenn. *Public Sentiments: Structures of Feeling in Nineteenth-Century American Literature.* Chapel Hill: University of North Carolina Press, 2001.

Higginson, Thomas Wentworth. "Emily Dickinson's Handwriting." *Atlantic Monthly* 68 (October 1891): 444–56.

Hogue, Cynthia. "'I Did'nt Be — Myself': Emily Dickinson's Semiotics of Presence." *Emily Dickinson Journal* 1, no. 2 (1992): 30–53.

Holland, Laurence Bedwell. *The Expense of Vision: Essays on the Craft of Henry James.* Princeton, NJ: Princeton University Press, 1964.

Holland, Sharon Patricia. *Raising the Dead: Readings of Death and (Black) Subjectivity.* Durham, NC: Duke University Press, 2000.

Hollander, John. *The Substance of Shadow: A Darkening Trope in Poetic History.* Edited by Kenneth Gross. Chicago: University of Chicago Press, 2016.

hooks, bell. *Black Looks: Race and Representation.* Boston: South End, 1992.

———. "The Oppositional Gaze: Black Female Spectators." In *Movies and Mass Culture,* edited by John Belton, 247–64. New Brunswick, NJ: Rutgers University Press, 1996.

House, John. *Impressionism: Paint and Politics.* New Haven, CT: Yale University Press, 2004.

Hubbard, Melanie. "Dickinson's Advertising Flyers: Theorizing Materiality and the Work of Reading." *Emily Dickinson Journal* 7, no. 1 (1998): 27–54.

Husserl, Edmund. *On the Phenomenology of the Consciousness of Internal Time (1893–1917).* Translated by John Barnett Brough. Dordrecht: Springer Netherlands, 1991.

Hussey, Miciah. "Eyeing the Beholder: Henry James's Immaterial Portrait of a Lady." *Henry James Review* 37, no. 2 (2016): 174–90.

Ingold, Tim. "Five Questions of Skill." *Cultural Geographies* 25, no. 1 (2018): 159–63.

———. *The Perception of the Environment.* New York: Routledge, 2000.

Isaacson, Joel. "Constable, Duranty, Mallarmé, Impressionism, Plein Air, and Forgetting." *Art Bulletin* 76, no. 3 (1994): 427–50.

Jackson, Cassandra. *Violence, Visual Culture, and the Black Male Body.* New York: Routledge, 2010.

Jackson, Virginia. *Dickinson's Misery: A Theory of Lyric Reading.* Princeton, NJ: Princeton University Press, 2005.

Jackson, Zakiyyah Iman. *Becoming Human: Matter and Meaning in an Antiblack World.* New York: New York University Press, 2020.

Jacobson, David. *Emerson's Pragmatic Vision: The Dance of the Eye.* University Park: Pennsylvania State University Press, 1993.

James, Henry. *The Ambassadors: A Norton Critical Edition.* Edited by S. P. Rosenbaum. New York: W. W. Norton, 1994.

———. *The American: A Norton Critical Edition.* Edited by James W. Tuttleton. New York: W. W. Norton, 1978.

———. *The American Scene*. Edited by Leon Edel. Bloomington: Indiana University Press, 1968.

———. "The Art of Fiction." In *The Art of Fiction and Other Essays*, edited by Morris Roberts, 3–23. New York: Oxford University Press, 1948.

———. *The Art of the Novel: Critical Prefaces*. Edited by R. P. Blackmur. New York: Charles Scribner's Sons, 1962.

———. *Hawthorne*. Ithaca, NY: Cornell University Press, 1997.

———. *Henry James: A Life in Letters*. Edited by Philip Horne. New York: Viking, 1999.

———. *Henry James: Essays on Art and Drama*. Edited by Peter Rawlings. Aldershot: Scolar Press, 1996.

———. "John S. Sargent." In *The Painter's Eye: Notes and Essays on the Pictorial Arts*, edited by John L. Sweeney, 216–28. Madison: University of Wisconsin Press, 1989.

———. *The Letters of Henry James*. Edited by Leon Edel. Vol. 4, *1895–1916*. Cambridge, MA: Harvard University Press, 1984.

———. *The Notebooks of Henry James*. Edited by F. O. Matthiessen and Kenneth B. Murdock. New York: Oxford University Press, 1961.

———. *The Painter's Eye: Notes and Essays on the Pictorial Arts*. Edited by John L. Sweeney. Madison: University of Wisconsin Press, 1989.

———. *The Portrait of a Lady: An Authoritative Text*. Edited by Robert D. Bamberg. New York: W. W. Norton, 1975.

———. "The Real Thing." In *Tales of Henry James: A Norton Critical Edition*, edited by Christof Wegelin and Henry B. Wonham, 189–211. New York: W. W. Norton, 2003.

———. *A Small Boy and Others*. New York: Charles Scribner's Sons, 1913.

———. *What Maisie Knew*. New York: Penguin, 1985.

James, William. *The Principles of Psychology*. 2 vols. in 1. New York: Dover, 1950.

Jameson, Fredric. *The Antinomies of Realism*. London: Verso, 2013.

Jarenski, Shelly. *Immersive Words: Mass Media, Visuality, and American Literature, 1839–1893*. Tuscaloosa: University of Alabama Press, 2015.

Jaussen, Paul. *Writing in Real Time*. Oxford: Oxford University Press, 2017.

Jay, Martin. *Downcast Eyes: The Denigration of Vision in Twentieth-Century French Thought*. Berkeley: University of California Press, 1993.

Jehlen, Myra. *American Incarnation: The Individual, the Nation, and the Continent*. Cambridge, MA: Harvard University Press, 1986.

Johnson, Kendall. *Henry James and the Visual*. New York: Cambridge University Press, 2007.

———. "'Rising from the stain on a painter's palette': George Catlin's Picturesque and the Legibility of Seminole Removal." *Nineteenth-Century Prose* 29, no. 2 (Fall 2002): 69–93.

———. "Visual Culture." In *Henry James in Context*, edited by David McWhirter, 364–77. Cambridge: Cambridge University Press, 2010.

Johnson, Rochelle L. *Passions for Nature: Nineteenth-Century America's Aesthetics of Alienation*. Athens: University of Georgia Press, 2009.

Jordan, June. "The Difficult Miracle of Black Poetry in America or Something like a Sonnet for Phillis Wheatley." *Massachusetts Review* 27, no. 2 (1986): 252–62.

Kant, Immanuel. *Critique of the Power of Judgment*. Translated by Paul Guyer and Eric Matthews. Cambridge: Cambridge University Press, 2000.

Kaplan, Amy. *The Social Construction of American Realism*. Chicago: University of Chicago Press, 1988.

Kenner, Hugh. *The Pound Era*. Berkeley: University of California Press, 1973.

Kermode, Frank. "Hawthorne's Modernity." *Partisan Review* 41 (1974): 428–41.

Kete, Mary Louise. *Sentimental Collaborations: Mourning and Middle-Class Identity in Nineteenth-Century America*. Durham, NC: Duke University Press, 2000.

Kim, Boosung. "Shock and Astonishment: The Rise of Cinema Spectatorship and *What Maisie Knew*." *Henry James Review* 40, no. 1 (2019): 1–17.

Kirkland, Frank M. "Modernity and Intellectual Life in Black." *Philosophical Forum* 24, no. 1–3 (1993): 136–65.

Kliger, Ilya. *The Narrative Shape of Truth: Veridiction in Modern European Literature*. University Park: Pennsylvania State University Press, 2011.

Knickerbocker, Scott. *Ecopoetics: The Language of Nature, the Nature of Language*. Amherst: University of Massachusetts Press, 2012.

Kohler, Michelle. *Miles of Stare: Transcendentalism and the Problem of Literary Vision in Nineteenth-Century America*. Tuscaloosa: University of Alabama Press, 2014.

———. ed. *The New Emily Dickinson Studies*. Cambridge: Cambridge University Press, 2019.

Kolodny, Annette. *The Lay of the Land: Metaphor as Experience and History in American Life and Letters*. Chapel Hill: University of North Carolina Press, 1984.

Kornbluh, Anna. *The Order of Forms: Realism, Formalism, and Social Space*. Chicago: University of Chicago Press, 2019.

———. "The Realist Blueprint." *Henry James Review* 36, no. 3 (2015): 199–211.

Kramnick, Jonathan. *Paper Minds: Literature and the Ecology of Consciousness*. Chicago: University of Chicago Press, 2018.

Kuhn, Mary. "Dickinson and the Politics of Plant Sensibility." *ELH* 85, no. 1 (Spring 2018): 141–70.

Kunin, Aaron. *Character as Form*. London: Bloomsbury, 2019.

Kurnick, David. *Empty Houses: Theatrical Failure and the Novel*. Princeton, NJ: Princeton University Press, 2012.

Lacan, Jacques. "The Mirror Stage as Formative of the *I* Function, as Revealed in Psychoanalytic Experience." In *Écrits: A Selection*, translated by Bruce Fink, 3–9. New York: Norton, 2002.

Laski, Gregory. *Untimely Democracy: The Politics of Progress after Slavery*. Oxford: Oxford University Press, 2018.

Leader, Jennifer L. *Knowing, Seeing, Being: Jonathan Edwards, Emily Dickinson, Marianne Moore, and the American Typological Tradition*. Amherst: University of Massachusetts Press, 2016.

Lee, Van C. "The Value of a Lecture." *Moving Picture World* 8 (1908): 93–94.

Lessing, Gotthold Ephraim. *Laocoon: An Essay upon the Limits of Painting and Poetry*. Translated by Ellen Frothingham. New York: Noonday, 1957.

Levin, Harry. *The Power of Blackness: Hawthorne, Poe, Melville*. New York: Alfred A. Knopf, 1958.

Levine, Caroline. *Forms: Whole, Rhythm, Hierarchy, Network*. Princeton, NJ: Princeton University Press, 2015.

Levine, Robert S. *Dislocating Race and Nation: Episodes in Nineteenth-Century American Literary Nationalism*. Chapel Hill: University of North Carolina Press, 2008.

Locke, John. *An Essay Concerning Human Understanding*. 2 vols. New York: Dover, 1959.

Loeffelholz, Mary. *Dickinson and the Boundaries of Feminist Theory*. Urbana: University of Illinois Press, 1991.

———. *The Value of Emily Dickinson*. New York: Cambridge University Press, 2016.

Lott, Eric. *Black Mirror: The Cultural Contradictions of American Racism*. Cambridge, MA: Harvard University Press, 2017.

———. *Love and Theft: Blackface Minstrelsy and the American Working Class*. Oxford: Oxford University Press, 1993.

Loughran, Trish. *The Republic in Print: Print Culture in the Age of U.S. Nation Building, 1770–1870*. New York: Columbia University Press, 2007.

Love, Heather. "Close but Not Deep: Literary Ethics and the Descriptive Turn." *New Literary History* 41, no. 2 (Spring 2010): 371–91.

———. "Small Change: Realism, Immanence, and the Politics of the Micro." *Modern Language Quarterly* 77, no. 3 (September 2016): 419–45.

Lowell, Amy. *Tendencies in Modern American Poetry*. New York: Macmillan, 1920.

Luciano, Dana. *Arranging Grief: Sacred Time and the Body in Nineteenth-Century America*. New York: New York University Press, 2007.

Luck, Chad. *The Body of Property: Antebellum American Fiction and the Phenomenology of Possession*. New York: Fordham University Press, 2014.

Lukács, Georg. *History and Class Consciousness: Studies in Marxist Dialectics*. Translated by Rodney Livingstone. Cambridge, MA: MIT Press, 1971.

———. *The Ontology of Social Being*. Vol. 3, *Labour*, translated by David Fernbach. London: Merlin, 1980.

Lukasik, Christopher. *Discerning Characters: The Culture of Appearance in Early America*. Philadelphia: University of Pennsylvania Press, 2011.

Mackey, Nathaniel. *Discrepant Engagement: Dissonance, Cross-Culturality, and Experimental Writing*. Tuscaloosa: University of Alabama Press, 1993.

Magee, Michael. *Emancipating Pragmatism*. Tuscaloosa: University of Alabama Press, 2004.

"The Magnetic Daguerreotypes." *Photographic Art-Journal*, June 1852, 353–59.

Marriott, David. *On Black Men*. New York: Columbia University Press, 2000.

Marrs, Cody. "Dickinson in the Anthropocene." *ESQ* 63, no. 2 (2017): 201–25.

Marx, Karl, and Friedrich Engels. "The German Ideology." In *The Marx-Engels Reader*, 2nd ed., edited by Robert C. Tucker, 146–200. New York: W. W. Norton, 1978.

Matz, Jesse. *Lasting Impressions*. New York: Columbia University Press, 2016.

———. *Literary Impressionism and Modernist Aesthetics*. Cambridge: Cambridge University Press, 2001.

Maunsell, Jerome Boyd. *Portraits from Life: Modernist Novelists and Autobiography*. Oxford: Oxford University Press, 2018.

McCabe, Susan. *Cinematic Modernism: Modernist Poetry and Film*. Cambridge: Cambridge University Press, 2005.

McCauley, Alex, and Zachary Tavlin. "The Art of Extraction and Preservation: Hawthorne's 'Dirty Nature.'" *Nathaniel Hawthorne Review* 43, no. 2 (Fall 2017): 19–34.

McDowell, John. "What Myth?" *Inquiry* 50, no. 4 (2007): 338–51.

McGann, Jerome. "Emily Dickinson's Visible Language." *Emily Dickinson Journal* 2, no. 2 (1993): 40–57.

McGill, Meredith. "Frances Ellen Watkins Harper and the Circuits of Abolitionist Poetry." In *Early African American Print Culture*, edited by Lara Langer Cohen and Jordan Alexander Stein, 53–74. Philadelphia: University of Pennsylvania Press, 2012.

McGowan, Todd. *The Real Gaze: Film Theory after Lacan*. Albany: State University of New York Press, 2007.

McInnis, Maurie D. *Slaves Waiting for Sale: Abolitionist Art and the American Slave Trade*. Chicago: University of Chicago Press, 2011.

McKee, Patricia. *Reading Constellations: Urban Modernity in Victorian Fiction*. Oxford: Oxford University Press, 2014.

McKeon, Michael. *The Secret History of Domesticity: Public, Private, and the Division of Knowledge*. Baltimore: Johns Hopkins University Press, 2005.

McWhirter, David. "'The Whole Chain of Relation and Responsibility': Henry James and the New York Edition." In *Henry James's New York Edition: The Construction of Authorship*, edited by David McWhirter, 1–22. Stanford, CA: Stanford University Press, 1995.

Meissner, Colin. *Henry James and the Language of Experience*. Cambridge: Cambridge University Press, 1999.

Merleau-Ponty, Maurice. "Eye and Mind." Translated by Carlton Dallery. In *The Primacy of Perception*, edited by James M. Edie, 159–90. Evanston, IL: Northwestern University Press, 1964.

———. *Phenomenology of Perception*. Translated by Colin Smith. London: Routledge Classics, 2002.

———. *The Structure of Behavior*. Translated by Alden Fisher. Boston, MA: Beacon Press, 1963.

———. *The Visible and the Invisible*. Translated by Alphonso Lingis. Evanston, IL: Northwestern University Press, 1968.

Metz, Christian. "The Cinema: Language or Language System?" In *Film Language: A Semiotics of the Cinema*, translated by Michael Taylor, 31–91. Chicago: University of Chicago Press, 1991.

———. *The Imaginary Signifier: Psychoanalysis and the Cinema*. Translated by Celia Britton, Annwyl Williams, Ben Brewster, and Alfred Guzzetti. Bloomington: Indiana University Press, 1982.

Michaels, Walter Benn. *The Gold Standard and the Logic of Naturalism: American Literature at the Turn of the Century*. Berkeley: University of California Press, 1988.

Mielke, Laura L. *Provocative Eloquence: Theater, Violence, and Antislavery Speech in the Antebellum United States*. Ann Arbor: University of Michigan Press, 2019.

Miller, Andrew H. *Novels behind Glass: Commodity Culture and Victorian Narrative*. Cambridge: Cambridge University Press, 1995.

Miller, Angela. *The Empire of the Eye: Landscape Representation and American Cultural Politics, 1825–1875*. Ithaca, NY: Cornell University Press, 1993.

Miller, Cristanne. "Controversy in the Study of Emily Dickinson." *Literary Imagination: The Review of the Association of Literary Scholars and Critics* 6, no. 1 (2004): 39–50.

———. *Reading in Time*. Amherst: University of Massachusetts Press, 2012.

Miller, David. *Dark Eden: The Swamp in Nineteenth-Century American Culture*. Cambridge: Cambridge University Press, 2010.

Miller, J. Hillis. *Poets of Reality: Six Twentieth-Century Writers*. Cambridge, MA: Harvard University Press, 1965.

Miller, Perry. *Nature's Nation*. Cambridge, MA: Harvard University Press, 1967.

Mitchell, W. J. T. *Iconology: Image, Text, Ideology*. Chicago: University of Chicago Press, 1986.

Mondal, Rivky. "Henry James and the Device of the Observer: A Study on Microexpressions." *Henry James Review* 41, no. 1 (2020): 15–23.

Moretti, Franco. *The Way of the World: The Bildungsroman in European Culture*. London: Verso, 1987.

Morgan, Ben. "Embodied Cognition and the Project of the Bildungsroman: *Wilhelm Meister's Apprenticeship* and *Daniel Deronda*." *Poetics Today* 38, no. 2 (2017): 341–62.

Morgan, Jo-Ann. *Uncle Tom's Cabin as Visual Culture*. Columbia: University of Missouri Press, 2007.

Moten, Fred. *Black and Blur*. Vol. 1 of *consent not to be a single being*. Durham, NC: Duke University Press, 2017.

———. "The Case of Blackness." *Criticism* 50, no. 2 (Spring 2008): 177–218.

Mullaney, Clare. "'Not to Discover Weakness Is the Artifice of Strength': Emily Dickinson, Constraint, and a Disability Poetics." *J19* 7, no. 1 (2019): 49–81.

Mulvey, Laura. "Visual Pleasure and Narrative Cinema." *Screen* 16, no. 3 (October 1975): 6–18.

Muñoz, José Esteban. *Disidentifications: Queers of Color and the Performance of Politics*. Minneapolis: University of Minnesota Press, 1999.

Nemerov, Alexander. *The Body of Raphaelle Peale: Still Life and Selfhood, 1812–1824*. Berkeley: University of California Press, 2001.

Nersessian, Anahid. *Utopia, Limited: Romanticism and Adjustment*. Cambridge, MA: Harvard University Press, 2015.

New, Elisa. *The Line's Eye: Poetic Experience, American Sight*. Cambridge, MA: Harvard University Press, 1998.

Ngai, Sianne. *Ugly Feelings*. Cambridge, MA: Harvard University Press, 2005.

Nietzsche, Friedrich. *Thus Spoke Zarathustra*. In *The Portable Nietzsche*, edited by Walter Kaufmann, 103–439. New York: Viking Penguin, 1976.

Nochlin, Linda. "Impressionist Portraits and the Construction of Modern Identity." In *Renoir's Portraits: Impressions of an Age*, edited by Colin B. Bailey, 53–76. New Haven, CT: Yale University Press, 1997.

Noë, Alva. *Action in Perception*. Cambridge, MA: MIT Press, 2004.

———. *Varieties of Presence*. Cambridge, MA: Harvard University Press, 2012.

North, Michael. *What Is the Present?* Princeton, NJ: Princeton University Press, 2018.

North, Paul. *The Problem of Distraction*. Stanford, CA: Stanford University Press, 2011.

Novak, Barbara. *American Painting of the Nineteenth Century: Realism, Idealism, and the American Experience*. New York: Praeger, 1969.

O'Hara, Daniel T. *Visions of Global America and the Future of Critical Reading*. Columbus: Ohio State University Press, 2009.

Ohi, Kevin. *Henry James and the Queerness of Style*. Minneapolis: University of Minnesota Press, 2011.

Osborne, Gillian Kidd. "Dickinson and Historical Ecopoetics." In *The New Emily Dickinson Studies*, edited by Michelle Kohler, 136–52. Cambridge: Cambridge University Press, 2019.

Panofsky, Erwin. *Perspective as Symbolic Form*. Translated by Christopher S. Wood. New York: Zone, 1991.

Pargas, Damian Alan, ed. *Fugitive Slaves and Spaces of Freedom in North America*. Gainesville: University Press of Florida, 2018.

Pease, Donald. *Visionary Compacts: American Renaissance Writings in Cultural Context.* Madison: University of Wisconsin Press, 1987.

Perlow, Seth. *The Poem Electric: Technology and the American Lyric.* Minneapolis: University of Minnesota Press, 2018.

Peterson, Carla L. *"Doers of the Word": African-American Women Speakers and Writers in the North (1830–1880).* Oxford: Oxford University Press, 1995.

Phillips, Natalie M. *Distraction: Problems of Attention in Eighteenth-Century Literature.* Baltimore: Johns Hopkins University Press, 2016.

Plotz, John. *Portable Property: Victorian Culture on the Move.* Princeton, NJ: Princeton University Press, 2009.

Pollak, Vivian R. *Dickinson: The Anxiety of Gender.* Ithaca, NY: Cornell University Press, 1984.

———. *Our Emily Dickinsons: American Women Poets and the Intimacies of Difference.* Philadelphia: University of Pennsylvania Press, 2016.

Porter, Carolyn. *Seeing and Being: The Plight of the Participant Observer in Emerson, James, Adams, and Faulkner.* Middletown, CT: Wesleyan University Press, 1981.

Posnock, Ross. *The Trial of Curiosity: Henry James, William James, and the Challenge of Modernity.* New York: Oxford University Press, 1991.

Pound, Ezra. "A Retrospect." In *Literary Essays of Ezra Pound,* edited by T. S. Eliot, 3–14. New York: New Directions, 1954.

———. *Selected Poems.* New York: New Directions, 1957.

Prins, Yopie. *Victorian Sappho.* Princeton, NJ: Princeton University Press, 1999.

Putzi, Jennifer. *Identifying Marks: Race, Gender, and the Marked Body in Nineteenth-Century America.* Athens: University of Georgia Press, 2006.

Pyle, Forest. *Art's Undoing: In the Wake of a Radical Aestheticism.* New York: Fordham University Press, 2014.

Quigley, Megan. *Modernist Fiction and Vagueness.* New York: Cambridge University Press, 2015.

Rancière, Jacques. *Aisthesis: Scenes from the Aesthetic Regime of Art.* Translated by Zakir Paul. London: Verso, 2013.

———. *The Politics of Aesthetics: The Distribution of the Sensible.* Edited by Gabriel Rockhill. London: Bloomsbury, 2013.

Rawlings, Peter. "A Kodak Refraction of Henry James's 'The Real Thing.'" *Journal of American Studies* 32, no. 3 (1998): 447–62.

Reed, Anthony. *Freedom Time: The Poetics and Politics of Black Experimental Writing.* Baltimore: Johns Hopkins University Press, 2014.

Reed, Brian. *Phenomenal Reading: Essays on Modern and Contemporary Poetics.* Tuscaloosa: University of Alabama Press, 2012.

Richards, Eliza. *Battle Lines: Poetry and Mass Media in the US Civil War.* Philadelphia: University of Pennsylvania Press, 2018.

———. "'Death's Surprise, Stamped Visible': Emily Dickinson, Oliver Wendell Holmes, and Civil War Photography." *Amerikastudien* 54, no. 1 (2009): 13–33.

———, ed. *Emily Dickinson in Context.* New York: Cambridge University Press, 2013.

Riss, Arthur. "The Art of Discrimination." *ELH* 71, no. 1 (Spring 2004): 251–87.

Rorty, Richard. *Philosophy and the Mirror of Nature.* Princeton, NJ: Princeton University Press, 1979.

Runzo, Sandra. *Theatricals of Day: Emily Dickinson and Nineteenth-Century American Popular Culture*. Amherst: University of Massachusetts Press, 2019.

Saltz, Laura. "'The Vision-Building Faculty': Naturalistic Vision in *The House of Mirth*." *Modern Fiction Studies* 57, no. 1 (2011): 17–46.

Sartre, Jean-Paul. *Being and Nothingness: An Essay on Phenomenological Ontology*. Translated by Hazel E. Barnes. New York: Philosophical Library, 1943.

Scholar, John. *Henry James and the Art of Impressions*. New York: Oxford University Press, 2020.

Schufreider, Gregory. "Iconoclastic Images." *Yearbook of Comparative Literature* 56 (2010): 24–63.

Seager, Zachary. "Painting, Fiction, and 'the *Real Lapse of Time*' in *The Ambassadors*." *Henry James Review* 41, no. 2 (2020): 135–51.

Seltzer, Mark. "The Official World." *Critical Inquiry* 37, no. 4 (Summer 2011): 724–53.

Sennett, Richard. *The Craftsman*. New Haven, CT: Yale University Press, 2008.

Shackelford, Aaron. "Dickinson's Animals and Anthropomorphism." *Emily Dickinson Journal* 19, no. 2 (2010): 47–66.

Sharpe, Christina. *In the Wake: On Blackness and Being*. Durham, NC: Duke University Press, 2016.

Sherrington, Charles Scott. *The Integrative Action of the Nervous System*. New York: Charles Scribner's Sons, 1906.

Shloss, Carol. *In Visible Light: Photography and the American Writer, 1840–1940*. New York: Oxford University Press, 1987.

Shockley, Evie. *Renegade Poetics: Black Aesthetics and Formal Innovation in African American Poetry*. Iowa City: University of Iowa Press, 2011.

Shumway, David R. *Creating American Civilization: A Genealogy of American Literature as an Academic Discipline*. Minneapolis: University of Minnesota Press, 1994.

Simons, Jefferey. "Dickinson's Lyric Ornithology." *Emily Dickinson Journal* 28, no. 1 (2019): 1–22.

Skillman, Nikki. "Lyric Reading Revisited: Passion, Address, and Form in *Citizen*." *American Literary History* 31, no. 3 (Fall 2019): 419–57.

Slotkin, Richard. *Regeneration through Violence: The Mythology of the American Frontier, 1600–1860*. Middletown, CT: Wesleyan University Press, 1973.

Smith, Adam. *The Theory of Moral Sentiments*. Edited by Knut Haakonssen. Cambridge: Cambridge University Press, 2002.

Smith, Andy. "Sensitive Emulsions: Hawthorne's Proto-Photography." *Nathaniel Hawthorne Review* 35, no. 1 (2009): 46–69.

Smith, Shawn Michelle. *American Archives: Gender, Race, and Class in Visual Culture*. Princeton, NJ: Princeton University Press, 1999.

———. *Photography on the Color Line: W. E. B. Du Bois, Race, and Visual Culture*. Durham, NC: Duke University Press, 2004.

Smithson, Robert. "A Sedimentation of the Mind: Earth Projects." In *Robert Smithson: Collected Writings*, edited by Jack Flam, 100–113. Berkeley: University of California Press, 1996.

Socarides, Alexandra. *Dickinson Unbound: Paper, Process, Poetics*. New York: Oxford University Press, 2012.

———. *In Plain Sight*. Oxford: Oxford University Press, 2020.

Sorisio, Carolyn. *Fleshing Out America: Race, Gender, and the Politics of the Body in American Literature, 1833–1879.* Athens: University of Georgia Press, 2002.

Soussloff, Catherine M. *The Subject in Art: Portraiture and the Birth of the Modern.* Durham, NC: Duke University Press, 2006.

Spaide, Christopher. "Multiple Choice: Terrance Hayes's Response-Poems and the African American Lyric 'We.'" *Cambridge Quarterly* 48, no. 3 (September 2019): 231–57.

Spiegel, Alan. *Fiction and the Camera Eye: Visual Consciousness in Film and the Modern Novel.* Charlottesville: University Press of Virginia, 1976.

Spingarn, Adena. *Uncle Tom: From Martyr to Traitor.* Stanford, CA: Stanford University Press, 2018.

Stanley, Kate. *Practices of Surprise in American Literature after Emerson.* Cambridge: Cambridge University Press, 2018.

Starr, G. Gabrielle. *Lyric Generations: Poetry and the Novel in the Long Eighteenth Century.* Baltimore: Johns Hopkins University Press, 2004.

Staten, Henry. "The Origin of the Work of Art in Material Practice." *New Literary History* 43, no. 1 (Winter 2012): 43–64.

Stewart, Susan. "Exogamous Relations: Travel Writing, the Incest Prohibition, and Hawthorne's *Transformation.*" In *Culture/Contexture*, edited by E. Valentine Daniel and Jeffrey M. Peck, 132–55. Berkeley: University of California Press, 1996.

———. *On Longing: Narratives of the Miniature, the Gigantic, the Souvenir, the Collection.* Durham, NC: Duke University Press, 1993.

Stoichita, Victor I. *A Short History of the Shadow.* London: Reaktion, 1997.

Stowe, Harriet Beecher. *Uncle Tom's Cabin.* Oxford: Oxford University Press, 1998.

Stowell, Peter. *Literary Impression, James and Chekhov.* Athens: University of Georgia Press, 1980.

Strauven, Wanda. "The Observer's Dilemma: To Touch or Not to Touch." In *Media Archaeology: Approaches, Applications, and Implications*, edited by Erkki Huhtamo and Jussi Parikka, 148–63. Berkeley: University of California Press, 2011.

Sweeney, John L. Introduction to *The Painter's Eye: Notes and Essays on the Pictorial Arts*, by Henry James, edited by John L. Sweeney, 9–31. Madison: University of Wisconsin Press, 1989.

Taft, Robert. *Photography and the American Scene: A Social History, 1839–1889.* New York: Macmillan, 1942.

Tallack, Douglas. "'One walked of course with one's eyes greatly open' (Henry James): London Sights in Alvin Langdon Coburn, Henry James, and Joseph Pennell." *Textual Practice* 24, no. 2 (2010): 197–222.

Tavlin, Zachary. "Lyric Making: On Frostian Techne." *Robert Frost Review* 29 (2019): 60–73.

———. "On the Road: Reevaluating an American Cultural Ideal." *ESQ* 64, no. 1 (2018): 1–30.

Tavlin, Zachary, and Bob Hodges. "Portable Vision, Form, and Objects in Henry James." In *Portable Prose: The Novel and the Everyday*, edited by Jarrad Cogle, N. Cyril Fischer, Lydia Saleh Rofail, and Vannessa Smith, 1–23. Lanham, MD: Lexington Books, 2019.

Tawil, Ezra. *Literature, American Style: The Originality of Imitation in the Early Republic.* Philadelphia: University of Pennsylvania Press, 2018.

Teahan, Sheila. "*What Maisie Knew* and the Improper Third Person." In "*The Turn of the*

Screw" and "What Maisie Knew," edited by Neil Cornwell and Maggie Malone, 220–36. New York: St. Martin's, 1998.

Terada, Rei. *Looking Away: Phenomenality and Dissatisfaction, Kant to Adorno*. Cambridge, MA: Harvard University Press, 2009.

Tintner, Adeline. *The Museum World of Henry James*. Ann Arbor, MI: UMI Research Press, 1986.

Tóibín, Colm. "Henry James: Shadow and Substance." In *Henry James and American Painting*, edited by Colm Tóibín, Marc Simpson, and Declan Kiely, 1–47. University Park: Pennsylvania State University Press and Morgan Library & Museum, 2017.

Tomlinson, Gary. *A Million Years of Music: The Emergence of Human Modernity*. New York: Zone Books, 2015.

Tompkins, Jane. *Sensational Designs: The Cultural Work of American Fiction, 1790–1860*. Oxford: Oxford University Press, 1985.

Trachtenberg, Alan. "Seeing and Believing: Hawthorne's Reflections on the Daguerreotype in *The House of the Seven Gables*." *American Literary History* 9, no. 3 (October 1997): 460–81.

Tuck, Anthony. "Singing the Rug: Patterned Textiles and the Origins of Indo-European Metrical Poetry." *American Journal of Archaeology* 110, no. 4 (2006): 539–50.

Tucker, Amy. *The Illustration of the Master*. Stanford, CA: Stanford University Press, 2010.

Uexküll, Jakob von. "A Stroll through the Worlds of Animals and Men." In *Instinctive Behavior: The Development of a Modern Concept*, edited and translated by Claire H. Schiller, 5–80. New York: International Universities Press, 1957.

———. *Theoretical Biology*. Translated by D. L. MacKinnon. New York: Harcourt, Brace, 1926.

Vaughan, Dai. "Let There Be Lumière." In *Early Cinema: Space Frame Narrative*, edited by Thomas Elsaesser, 63–67. London: British Film Institute, 1990.

Vendler, Helen. *Poets Thinking: Pope, Whitman, Dickinson, Yeats*. Cambridge, MA: Harvard University Press, 2004.

Virilio, Paul. *The Vision Machine*. London: British Film Institute, 1994.

Vogelius, Christa. "'Paralyzed, with Gold - ': Dickinson's Poetics of Photography." *Emily Dickinson Journal* 18, no. 2 (2009): 21–37.

Wadsworth, Sarah. "'Lifted Moments': Emily Dickinson, Hymn Revision, and the Revival Music Meme-Plex." *Emily Dickinson Journal* 23, no. 1 (2014): 46–74.

Waggoner, Hyatt H. *American Visionary Poetry*. Baton Rouge: Louisiana University Press, 1982.

Wald, Priscilla. *Constituting Americans: Cultural Anxiety and Narrative Form*. Durham, NC: Duke University Press, 1995.

Wand, Martin, and Richard B. Sewall. "'Eyes Be Blind, Heart Be Still': A New Perspective On Emily Dickinson's Eye Problem." *New England Quarterly* 52, no. 3 (1979): 400–406.

Weaver, Mike. *William Carlos Williams: An American Background*. Cambridge: Cambridge University Press, 1971.

Weinstein, Cindy. *Time, Tense, and American Literature: When Is Now?* Cambridge: Cambridge University Press, 2015.

Werner, Marta L., ed. *Emily Dickinson's Open Folios: Scenes of Reading, Surfaces of Writing*. Ann Arbor: University of Michigan Press, 1995.

———. "'For Flash and Click and Suddenness –': Emily Dickinson and the Photography-Effect." In *A Companion to Emily Dickinson*, edited by Marta Nell Smith and Mary Loeffelholz, 471–89. Malden, MA: Blackwell, 2008.

———. "Itineraries of Escape: Emily Dickinson's Envelope Poems." In *Emily Dickinson: The Gorgeous Nothings*, edited by Marta Werner and Jen Bervin, 199–223. New York: New Directions, 2013.

———. "'Most Arrows': Autonomy and Intertextuality in Emily Dickinson's Late Fragments." *Text* 10 (1997): 41–72.

West, Nancy Martha. *Kodak and the Lens of Nostalgia*. Charlottesville: University Press of Virginia, 2000.

Wettlaufer, Alexandra K. *In the Mind's Eye: The Visual Impulse in Diderot, Baudelaire and Ruskin*. Amsterdam: Rodopi, 2003.

Wharton, Edith. *The House of Mirth*. New York: Charles Scribner's Sons, 1905.

Whitman, Walt. *Complete Poetry and Collected Prose*. New York: Library of America, 1982.

Wichelns, Kathryn. *Henry James's Feminist Afterlives: Annie Fields, Emily Dickinson, Marguerite Duras*. Cham, Switzerland: Palgrave Macmillan, 2018.

Williams, Linda. *Figures of Desire: A Theory and Analysis of Surrealist Film*. Berkeley: University of California Press, 1981.

Williams, Susan. "'The Aspiring Purpose of an Ambitious Demagogue': Portraiture and *The House of the Seven Gables*." *Nineteenth-Century Literature* 49, no. 2 (1994): 221–44.

———. *Confounding Images: Photography and Portraiture in Antebellum American Fiction*. Philadelphia: University of Pennsylvania Press, 1997.

Williams, William Carlos. *The Great American Novel*. In *Imaginations*, 158–227. New York: New Directions, 1971.

———. *Paterson*. New York: New Directions, 1995.

———. *Spring and All*. New York: New Directions, 2011.

Winner, Viola Hopkins. *Henry James and the Visual Arts*. Charlottesville: University Press of Virginia, 1970.

Wolf, Bryan Jay. *Romantic Re-Vision: Culture and Consciousness in Nineteenth-Century American Painting and Literature*. Chicago: University of Chicago Press, 1982.

Wolf, Maryanne. *Proust and the Squid: The Story and Science of the Reading Brain*. New York: Harper Collins, 2007.

Woloch, Alex. *The One vs. the Many: Minor Characters and the Space of the Protagonist in the Novel*. Princeton, NJ: Princeton University Press, 2003.

Woodbury, Charles J. *Talks with Ralph Waldo Emerson*. New York: Baker & Taylor, 1890.

Yancy, George. *Black Bodies, White Gazes: The Continuing Significance of Race in America*. Lanham, MD: Rowman, 2017.

Yao, Xine. *Disaffected: The Cultural Politics of Unfeeling in Nineteenth-Century America*. Durham, NC: Duke University Press, 2021.

Yeazell, Ruth Bernard. "Henry James's Portrait-Envy." *New Literary History* 48, no. 2 (2017): 309–35.

Young, Kevin. *The Grey Album: On the Blackness of Blackness*. Minneapolis: Greywolf Press, 2012.

Zhang, Dora. *Strange Likeness: Description and the Modernist Novel*. Chicago: Chicago University Press, 2020.

Zuba, Clayton. "Hawthorne's Empire: Sculpture and the Indigenous in *The Marble Faun*." *Studies in American Fiction* 43, no. 2 (Fall 2016): 161–82.

INDEX